ORANGE

TEACHER'S RESOURCE BOOK

Phoenix Edition

LANGUAGE FOR DAILY USE

Curriculum and Instruction
Dr. Dorothy S. Strickland

Professor of Education
Department of Curriculum and Teaching
Teachers College, Columbia University

Harcourt Brace Jovanovich, Publishers
New York   Chicago   San Francisco   Atlanta   Dallas   and   London

HBJ

TO THE TEACHER

This Teacher's Resource Book, when used with the pupil's textbook and the Teacher's Edition, provides a complete elementary English program and classroom management system.

A Teacher's Resource Book is not automatically included with each shipment of a classroom set of textbooks. However, a Teacher's Resource Book will be forwarded when requested by a teacher, an administrator, or a representative of Harcourt Brace Jovanovich, Inc.

ACKNOWLEDGMENTS

For permission to reprint copyrighted material, grateful acknowledgment is given to the following sources:

The Bobbs-Merrill Co., Inc.: "The Tutor" from *Folly for the Wise.* Copyright 1904 by Carolyn Wells, 1931 by Carolyn Wells Houghton.

Marchette Chute: "Snowflakes" from *Around and About* by Marchette Chute. Copyright 1957 (Dutton).

Thomas Y. Crowell, Publishers: Text of "A basketball player...," "Down South it's so hot...," and "Old Jen had a burro...," from *Tiny Tall Tales* by Ennis Rees. An Abelard-Schuman book. Copyright © 1967 by Ennis Rees.

Dodd, Mead & Company, Inc.: From "Gorillas" by Kay McDearmon. Copyright © 1979 by Katherine M. McDearmon.

Doubleday & Company, Inc.: "I'd Like to Be a Lighthouse" by Rachel Field from the book *Taxis and Toadstools* by Rachel Field. Copyright 1926 by Doubleday & Company, Inc.

E. P. Dutton, Inc.: "Dribble" adapted from *Tales of a Fourth Grade Nothing* by Judy Blume. Text copyright © 1972 by Judy Blume.

Farrar, Straus & Giroux, Inc.: "Sun" from *Small Poems* by Valerie Worth. Copyright © 1972 by Valerie Worth.

Harcourt Brace Jovanovich, Inc.: Pronunciation key and entries reprinted and reproduced from *THe HBJ School Dictionary,* copyright © 1977 by Harcourt Brace Jovanovich, Inc.

Harper & Row, Publishers, Inc.: Text of "First Snow" from *A Pocketful of Poems* by Marie Louise Allen. Text copyright © 1957 by Marie Louise Allen Howarth. Text of "Cynthia in the Snow" from *Bronzeville Boys and Girls* by Gwendolyn Brooks. Copyright © 1956 by Gwendolyn Brooks Blakely.

Holiday House, Inc.: Excerpt from *Ol' Paul the Mighty Logger* by Glen Rounds. Copyright 1936, 1949 by Holiday House, Inc.

J. B. Lippincott, Publishers: Text of "Summer Song" from *The Man Who Sang the Sillies* by John Ciardi. Copyright © 1961 by John Ciardi.

Eve Merriam: "Schenectady" from *Catch a Little Rhyme* by Eve Merriam. Copyright © 1966 by Even Merriam.

Scholastic Inc.: "I Heard a Bird Sing" by Oliver Herford in *Poems Children Will Sit Still For* compiled by Beatrice Schenk de Regniers.

Viking Penguin Inc.: "Giraffes" from *The Raucous Auk* by Mary Ann Hoberman, illustrated by Joseph Low. Text copyright © 1973 by Mary Ann Hoberman, *Stormalong* selection adapted from *American Tall Tales* by Adrien Stoutenberg. Copyright © 1966 by Adrien Stoutenberg.

ART CREDITS

Workbook: Len Ebert: 31, 61, 76, 106, 107; Ethel Gold: 8, 15, 33, 48, 55, 64, 80, 97, 111, 121; Leigh Grant: 12, 34, 50, 62, 66, 95, 113; Merryl Henderson: 21, 22, 44, 51, 63, 79, 96, 105, 110; Sal Murdocca: 1, 3, 5, 11, 17, 24, 35, 42, 56, 58, 59, 68, 74, 82, 85, 94, 96, 99, 101, 102, 112, 119, 120; Jan Pyk: 4, 16, 37, 41, 53, 75, 90; Jerry Smath: 2, 7, 14, 20, 25, 39, 49, 54, 70, 87, 116.

Cover Photograph: Bruce Roberts

Printed in the United States of America
ISBN 0-15-317024-7

CONTENTS

WORKBOOK

EXTRA PRACTICE MASTERS

TESTS

TEACHING AIDS

Teaching Aid 1: Student Response Cards
Teaching Aid 2: Student Response Cards
Teaching Aid 3: Student Response Cards
Teaching Aid 4: Student Response Cards
Teaching Aid 5: Student Response Cards
Teaching Aid 6: Student Response Cards
Teaching Aid 7: Student Response Cards
Teaching Aid 8: Composition Evaluation Form
Teaching Aid 9: Enrichment Master for Unit 1
Teaching Aid 10: Enrichment Master for Unit 2
Teaching Aid 11: Enrichment Master for Unit 3
Teaching Aid 12: Enrichment Master for Unit 4
Teaching Aid 13: Enrichment Master for Unit 5
Teaching Aid 14: Enrichment Master for Unit 6
Teaching Aid 15: Enrichment Master for Unit 7
Teaching Aid 16: Enrichment Master for Unit 8
Teaching Aid 17: Parent Letter for Unit 1
Teaching Aid 18: Parent Letter for Unit 2
Teaching Aid 19: Parent Letter for Unit 3
Teaching Aid 20: Parent Letter for Unit 4
Teaching Aid 21: Parent Letter for Unit 5
Teaching Aid 22: Parent Letter for Unit 6
Teaching Aid 23: Parent Letter for Unit 7
Teaching Aid 24: Parent Letter for Unit 8
Teaching Aid 25: Spanish Parent Letter for Unit 1
Teaching Aid 26: Spanish Parent Letter for Unit 2
Teaching Aid 27: Spanish Parent Letter for Unit 3
Teaching Aid 28: Spanish Parent Letter for Unit 4
Teaching Aid 29: Spanish Parent Letter for Unit 5
Teaching Aid 30: Spanish Parent Letter for Unit 6
Teaching Aid 31: Spanish Parent Letter for Unit 7
Teaching Aid 32: Spanish Parent Letter for Unit 8
Teaching Aid 33: Individual Record Form
Teaching Aid 34: Class Record Form
Teaching Aid 35: Class Record Form
Teaching Aid 36: Test Answer Form
Teaching Aid 37: Test Answer Form

WORKBOOK

The workbook pages that accompany this level of *Language for Daily Use, Phoenix Edition* appear on the following pages. They provide students with additional practice on all major concepts and skills taught and developed in the program. Reference is made in the appropriate lesson plan each time a workbook page can be assigned. Each workbook page also appears in reduced form at the bottom of the lesson plan it accompanies. The answer key for the Workbook follows these pages in this Teacher's Resource Book.

(The Workbook for this level is also available as a separate consumable book and as spirit duplicating masters. There is a teacher's annotated edition of the Workbook.)

Name _____

Sentences pages 2–3

(● A **sentence** is a group of words that states a
complete thought. *EXAMPLE:* Insects are fun to watch.)

Remember that every sentence begins with a capital letter.
Every sentence ends with a punctuation mark.

A. Underline each group of words that is a sentence.

1. Do you know how insects protect themselves?
2. Hard outer shells.
3. Protected by their color.
4. A walking stick looks like a tiny tree branch.
5. A bee or a wasp.
6. Sting you to protect themselves.
7. A monarch butterfly tastes awful.
8. Some insects fly to escape danger.
9. Can jump away from their enemies.
10. Insects' small size also helps protect them.

B. For each group of words in Practice A that is not a sentence, add words to
make a sentence. Write the new sentences.

11. _____

12. _____

13. _____

14. _____

15. _____

Name _____

Declarative and Interrogative Sentences
pages 4–5

- **A declarative sentence** makes a statement. It ends with a period. *EXAMPLE:* The animal is a lion.

- An **interrogative sentence** asks a question. It ends with a question mark.
EXAMPLE: How many lions do you see?

A. On a separate piece of paper draw an imaginary animal. It can be a silly or a scary one. Then use a declarative sentence to answer each question.

1. What kind of animal did you draw?

   _____

2. Where does this animal live?

   _____

3. Is it a silly or a scary animal?

   _____

B. Make up interrogative sentences to ask about each statement. Then draw the animal on a separate piece of paper.

4. _____

   It has four legs.

5. _____

   It has three eyes in its head.

6. _____

   It wears a hat with daisies on it.

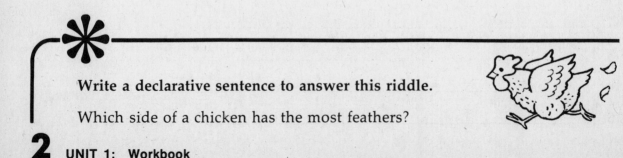

Write a declarative sentence to answer this riddle.

Which side of a chicken has the most feathers?

2 UNIT 1: Workbook

Name _____

Imperative and Exclamatory Sentences pages 6–7

- ● An **imperative sentence** gives a command or makes a request. It ends with a period.
  EXAMPLE: Please bring me the newspaper.

- ● An **exclamatory sentence** shows strong feeling or surprise. It ends with an exclamation point.
  EXAMPLE: What an exciting day this has been!

A. Add correct punctuation marks to each sentence. Then write *imperative* or *exclamatory* to tell the kind of sentence each is.

_____ 1. What a smart dog I have

_____ 2. Bring me that stick

_____ 3. Watch what Chester can do

_____ 4. Throw the stick for Chester to fetch

_____ 5. Wow, that is a great trick

B. Write five commands that you might give your dog.

6. _____

7. _____

8. _____

9. _____

10. _____

C. Write four exclamatory sentences you might say about your pet.

11. _____

12. _____

13. _____

14. _____

Name _____

Questions and Answers pages 8–9

 Always answer a question in a complete sentence. Begin
the sentence by borrowing some of the words from the
question. Then complete the statement.

EXAMPLE: Who is Mickey Mouse?
 Mickey Mouse is a cartoon character.

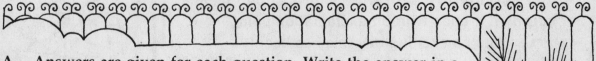

**A.   Answers are given for each question. Write the answer in a
complete sentence. Remember to use words from the question
in your answer.**

1.   Who is Ling-Ling? (a giant panda)

_____

2.   Where is she? (in the Washington Zoo)

_____

3.   What is she doing? (eating bamboo shoots)

_____

4.   How much does Ling-Ling weigh? (almost 300 pounds)

_____

5.   Who is with Ling-Ling? (her keeper)

_____

**B.   Answer each question in a complete sentence. Use words
from the question in your answer.**

6.   Who are these creatures?

_____

7.   How many monkeys are there?

_____

8.   Where are the animals?

_____

Complete Subjects and Predicates

- The **complete subject** is all the words in the subject of the sentence.

- The **complete predicate** is all the words that tell something about the subject.

- Subjects and predicates go together to make sentences.

(Complete Subject)   (Complete Predicate)

EXAMPLE: The seven lumberjacks   chopped wood.

A. Draw one line under the complete subject of each sentence. Draw two lines under the complete predicate.

1. Our class went on a nature hike.
2. The clear stream trickled over the rocks.
3. Several small insects crawled over a log.
4. The galloping horses raced across the field.
5. Cheerful birds chirped a sweet song.
6. Three rabbits hopped across the meadow.

B. Add a complete subject or a complete predicate to each group of words. Write the new sentences.

7. a blue mist
8. whistled a cheerful tune
9. blew branches of the trees
10. an angry bluejay
11. bloomed brightly
12. leaped across the brook

_____

_____

_____

_____

_____

_____

The Card Catalog pages 16–17

A card catalog is a set of cards for every book in the library. There are three kinds of cards. A title card shows the title of the book first. An author card lists the author's last name first. A subject card gives the subject of the book first.

Title Card	Author Card	Subject Card
553 Oil and Gas N Nixon, Hershell H. Oil and Gas Harcourt Brace Jovanovich c. 1977 60 pp. illus.	**796.9 Burchard, S.H.** B Dorothy Hamill Harcourt Brace Jovanovich c. 1978 66 pp. illus.	**746.4 Needlecraft** M Meyer, Carolyn Stitch by Stitch Harcourt Brace Jovanovich c. 1970 93 pp. ilus.

A. Answer the questions using the cards from a card catalog.

1. List the author of each book.

   a. _____

   b. _____

   c. _____

2. List the title of each book.

   a. _____

   b. _____

   c. _____

3. List the subject of each book.

   a. _____

   b. _____

   c. _____

B. Write the letter of the alphabet you would use to find each book in a card catalog.

_____ **4.** a book by Beatrix Potter

_____ **5.** a book about whales

_____ **6.** the book *Black Beauty*

_____ **7.** a book about geology

_____ **8.** the book *Crickets*

_____ **9.** a book by Beverly Cleary

_____ **10.** the book *Little House on the Prairie*

Name _____

Combining Sentences pages 18–19

Two short sentences about the same topic can often be combined. Use the words *and, but,* or *or* to connect the sentences. Place a comma before the connecting word.

EXAMPLES: Peter wanted to play. We had to study.
          Peter wanted to play **, but** we had to study.

Combine each set of sentences using the word in parentheses ( ). Remember to use commas.

1. It was lunchtime. Children filled the school cafeteria. (and)

   _____

   _____

2. Walter opened his lunch bag. He took out a peanut butter sandwich. (and)

   _____

   _____

3. Greta brought fried chicken to eat. She forgot to bring napkins. (but)

   _____

   _____

4. Brenda ate a hot dog. She munched a cookie for dessert. (and)

   _____

   _____

5. Fred and Brian bought hot lunches. They carried them to a table. (and)

   _____

   _____

6. The students could buy hot lunches. They could buy sandwiches. (or)

   _____

   _____

7. Brian chewed on a carrot. He didn't like it very much. (but)

   _____

   _____

8. The boys and girls finished their lunches. They cleared the tables. (and)

_____

_____

9. They played outside in the yard. They went to the gym. (or)

_____

_____

10. The bell rang. It was time for class again. (and)

_____

_____

11. Samuel went to class. He did not feel well. (but)

_____

_____

12. Karen took Samuel's hand. She took him to the nurse. (and)

_____

_____

13. Samuel could lie down in the nurse's office. He could call his mom. (or)

_____

_____

14. Soon Samuel felt better. He returned to class. (and)

_____

_____

Editing Sentences page 22

Always edit sentences after you write them. You may find mistakes or ideas you want to change. Use editing marks to show the changes.

Editing Marks
≡ capitalize
⊙ make a period
∧ add something
⋋ add a comma
⏝ add quotation marks
⤸ take something away
◯ spell correctly
¶ indent the paragraph
/ make a lower case letter
tr⌢ transpose

A. Edit these sentences. Use editing marks to correct the mistakes. Then copy the sentences correctly.

1. some new neighbors moved into the house next door

   _____

2. their last name is Mahnster

   _____

3. their best friends are Mr. and Mrs. Ghoolie

   _____

4. lately I've heard strange noises at night

   _____

5. sometimes I play with their son, Harry Mahnster

   _____

6. he has four pet spiders and a black cat

   _____

7. you should see their house on Halloween

   _____

8. harry's mother, Ima Mahnster, doesn't need a costume

   _____

9. watching their home movies is always exciting

   _____

10. once they invited me over for bat stew

   _____

B. On a separate piece of paper write five more sentences about the Mahnster family. Then edit your sentences.

Writing Sentences page 23
Mechanics Practice

- Begin a sentence with a capital letter.

- Use a period to end a declarative or imperative sentence.

- Use a question mark to end an interrogative sentence.

- Use an exclamation point to end an exclamatory sentence.

EXAMPLES: Today is warm and sunny. (Declarative)
Please take me to the beach. (Imperative)
Can Todd and Martha come too? (Interrogative)
How cold the water is! (Exclamatory)

Write the sentences correctly. Use capital letters and punctuation marks where they are needed.

1. a little sand crab skittered along the sand _____

_____

2. how angry it looked _____

_____

3. four sea gulls soared overhead _____

_____

4. do you know what they were looking for _____

_____

5. how hungry the little babies are _____

_____

6. do you know why the sea animals are hiding _____

_____

Name _____

Rhythm and Rhyme in Poetry pages 24–26

When lines of poetry have the same last sounds, the lines
rhyme. Many poems have lines that end with rhyming words.
Poems also have a beat, like the beat of a song. This beat is
the **rhythm** of the poem.

A. Clap softly to the beat as you read this poem.

Summer Song

By the sand between my toes,
By the waves behind my ears,
By the sunburn on my nose,
By the little salty tears
That make rainbows in the sun
When I squeeze my eyes and run,
By the way the seagulls screech,
Guess where I am? At the . . . . !
By the way the children shout
Guess what happened? School is . . . . !
By the way I sing this song
Guess if summer lasts too long:
You must answer Right or . . . . . . !

JOHN CIARDI

B. Write words the poet might have used in his poem.

1. At the _____   2. School is _____   3. Right or _____

C. Here are some more beach words. Write a word that
rhymes with each. Then write a poem of your own using the
pairs of rhyming words. Write your poem on a separate piece
of paper.

4. sand

_____

5. beach

_____

6. wave

_____

7. shell

_____

Name _____

Sound in Poetry   pages 27–29

Poets have special ways of using sound. Words like
tinkle, snap, crash, and *buzz* are sound words. They sound
like what they mean. Poets may also repeat the same beginning
sound. This is called **alliteration.**

Read this poem.

Cynthia in the Snow

IT SHUSHES.
It hushes
The loudness in the road.
It flitter-twitters,
And laughs away from me.
It laughs a lovely whiteness,
And whitely whirs away,
To be
Some otherwhere,
Still white as milk or shirts.
So beautiful it hurts.

GWENDOLYN BROOKS

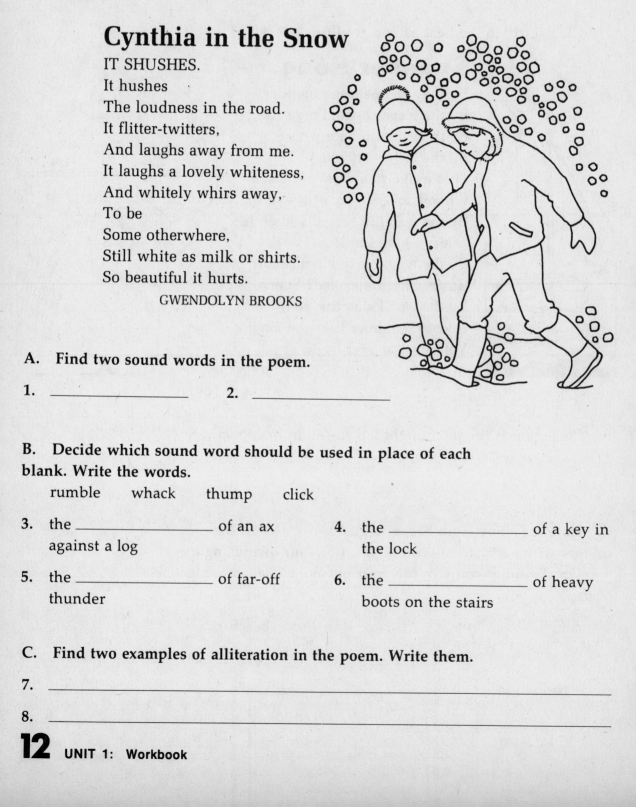

A. Find two sound words in the poem.

1. _____   2. _____

**B. Decide which sound word should be used in place of each
blank. Write the words.**

    rumble   whack   thump   click

3. the _____ of an ax
   against a log

4. the _____ of a key in
   the lock

5. the _____ of far-off
   thunder

6. the _____ of heavy
   boots on the stairs

C. Find two examples of alliteration in the poem. Write them.

7. _____

8. _____

Name _____

Unit Review

A. Underline the complete sentence in each group.

1. Our classroom is very large.
   Up on the third floor.
2. Thirty students' seats in rows.
   Thirty students are in the class.
3. Our plants grow on the windowsill.
   Our plants for five weeks.

B. Add a period, a question mark, or an exclamation point at the end of each sentence.

4. Meet my dog
5. Do you think he's cute
6. I got him when he was a puppy
7. How frisky the puppy is
8. Please bring me the puppy's leash
9. My puppy and I will go for a walk

C. Answers are given for each question. Write the answer in a complete sentence. Remember to use words from the question in your answer.

10. Who was George Washington? (our first President)

   _____

11. What did Betsy Ross do? (made America's first flag)

   _____

12. What is Paul Revere famous for? (his warning that British troops were coming)

   _____

D. Draw one line under the complete subject in each sentence. Draw two lines under the complete predicate.

13. The warm rain falls on fields and trees.
14. Max and I got dressed to go out.
15. We wear boots, rain hats, and raincoats.

Name _____

Unit Review

E. Next to each book title write if it is *fiction, nonfiction, biography,* or *reference.*

_____ 16. <u>Amelia Earhart: Her Life</u>

_____ 17. <u>All About Cats</u>

_____ 18. <u>Atlas of the World</u>

_____ 19. <u>Tubby the Tuba</u>

_____ 20. <u>First Picture Dictionary</u>

F. Combine the two sentences. Use the word in parentheses ( ).

21. Marcie raced off. I raced after her. (and)

   _____

22. She had a good lead. I was gaining on her. (but)

   _____

23. Would Marcie win the race? Would I win? (or)

   _____

G. Write a sentence about each topic. Then edit your sentences. Be sure each one begins with a capital letter and ends with a punctuation mark.

24. Sneakers: _____

25. Sleep: _____

26. Friends: _____

27. Careers: _____

H. Read the poem.
28. How many beats are in each line?

   _____

I Heard a Bird Sing

I heard a bird sing
In the dark of December
A magical thing
And sweet to remember:

OLIVER HERFORD

Name _____

Nouns pages 36–37

> ● A **noun** is a word that names a person, place, or thing.
> *EXAMPLE:* The <u>grocer</u> sold <u>vegetables</u> at the <u>market</u>.

A. Underline the nouns in each sentence.

1. Bananas are my favorite kind of fruit.
2. We enjoyed grapefruit every day in Florida.
3. Sam made a salad with potatoes, onions, and celery.
4. There are many different kinds of apples.
5. Did you know that a tomato is really a fruit?

B. Use the pictures to answer the questions.

6. Write four nouns that name persons in the pictures.

_____   _____

_____   _____

7. Write four nouns that name places in the pictures.

_____   _____

_____   _____

8. Write four nouns that name things in the pictures.

_____

_____

Copyright © 1983 by Harcourt Brace Jovanovich, Inc.
All rights reserved.

UNIT 2: Workbook **15**

Plural Nouns That End with s and es

- **To form the plural of most nouns, add s.**
  EXAMPLE: dog—dogs
- **To form the plural of nouns ending in s, x, ch, or sh, add es.** *EXAMPLE:* bench—benches
- **To form the plural of nouns ending with a consonant and y, change the y to i and add es.** *EXAMPLE:* pony—ponies

A.   Help the store manager complete her order. Read the sentences. Fill in each blank with the plural form of the word in parentheses (   ).

1. We need to order more lunch _____. (box)

2. We must have some dolls that are _____. (princess)

3. Be sure to add _____ to the list. (wrench)

4. Almost all of the _____ have been bought. (leash)

5. Our supply of _____ is almost gone. (crayon)

6. Add ten _____ to the order. (dish)

7. Stock more dolls that are _____ on the shelves. (baby)

8. We need more boats that are _____. (ferry)

9. Get 25 school _____. (notebook)

10. Order some cartons of _____. (bandage)

B.   Use the plural form of each noun in a sentence.

11. fox _____

12. bush _____

13. city _____

14. desk _____

15. berry _____

Nouns with Special Plural Forms

pages 40–41

Some nouns have special plural forms that must be remembered.

EXAMPLES: woman–women   sheep–sheep

A. Read each clue. Fill in the puzzle with the plural form of the underlined word.

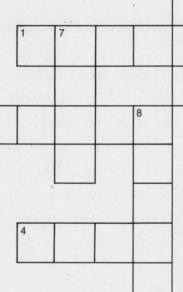

Across

1. more than one <u>moose</u>
2. more than one pair of <u>trousers</u>
3. more than one <u>man</u>
4. more than one <u>mouse</u>

Down

5. more than one <u>foot</u>
6. more than one <u>woman</u>
7. more than one <u>ox</u>
8. more than one <u>sheep</u>
9. more than one <u>deer</u>

B. Choose five plural nouns from the crossword puzzle. Use each one in a sentence.

10. _____

11. _____

12. _____

13. _____

14. _____

Name _____

Common and Proper Nouns pages 42–43

> ● A **common noun** names any person, place, or thing. It is a general word that begins with a small letter. *EXAMPLE:* river
>
> ● A **proper noun** names a particular person, place, or thing. A proper noun begins with a capital letter. *EXAMPLE:* Ohio River

A. Read the sentences. Underline the common nouns. Circle the proper nouns.

1. Marcy Russo and her family went on a trip across the United States.
2. They began in the state of Maine and ended in the state of California.
3. They crossed the Mississippi River and many other small rivers.
4. Marcy Russo liked crossing the Mojave Desert.
5. John Russo was most excited about going over the Rocky Mountains.
6. As they crossed the country, the Russos went through towns and cities.
7. On the Fourth of July they watched fireworks in Denver, Colorado.
8. The Russos enjoyed their vacation.

Marcy Russo has drawn a map of part of her trip. Look at the map key she has made. It lists the features she will show on her map. They are common nouns.

Now look at the map. Make up proper nouns for each symbol Marcy has drawn on the map. Write each name next to the correct symbol.

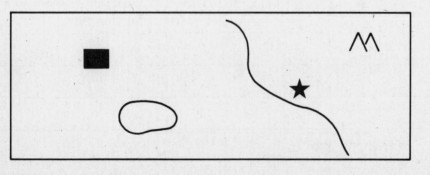

Map Key
mountains ⋀⋀
river ⌇
lake ◯
city ★
tourist ▪
  attraction

Name _____

Writing Names and Titles pages 44–45

> ● **All names and titles of people begin with a capital letter.**
> *EXAMPLES:* Miss Jones   Governor Madison   Martha Shuman
>
> ● **An abbreviation for a title or an initial begins with a capital letter and ends with a period.**
> *EXAMPLES:* Dr. R. A. White   Mrs. Sara J. King   Sen. Crane

A. Write the names and titles correctly.

1. sen. robin horn

   _____

2. gov. esther a jones

   _____

3. Mr harold papas

   _____

4. miss A. A Reed

   _____

5. mrs. Rosa Sanchez

   _____

6. gov. kevin G. goodwin

   _____

7. dr Frank j. purcell

   _____

8. Mr les Roy

   _____

9. ms mary i. Proto

   _____

10. Mrs Ruth roth

    _____

B. Rewrite these titles and names on the lines. Use abbreviations for the titles. Write initials for the first and middle names.

11. governor marie anthony tobian   _____

12. mister henry lester tolman   _____

13. senator anna maria bianco   _____

14. doctor dan melvin starr   _____

15. miss pearl mary owens   _____

16. doctor paula maria gomez   _____

Writing Names of Places   pages 46–47

● **Begin all important words in the names of streets, cities, states, and countries with a capital letter. These words are proper nouns. Use a period after an abbreviation.**
EXAMPLES: United States of America   Winston St.   Leaman Rd.

A. Write each sentence correctly. Use information from the map. On the map print the names of the places talked about in the sentences.

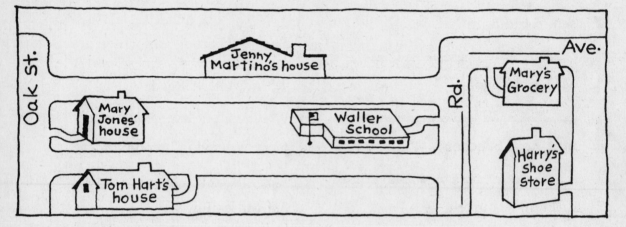

1. Tom Hart lives on cherry St.

   _____

2. You can shop at Harry's Shoe Store on main st.

   _____

3. Jenny Martino lives on clinton ave.

   _____

4. Littletown, idaho, is in the united states of america.

   _____

B. Make up names for these places. Label them on the map.

5. The name for the avenue where Mary's Grocery is found:

   _____

6. The name for the road where the Waller School is located:

   _____

20 UNIT 2: **Workbook**

Name _____

Possessive Nouns pages 48–51

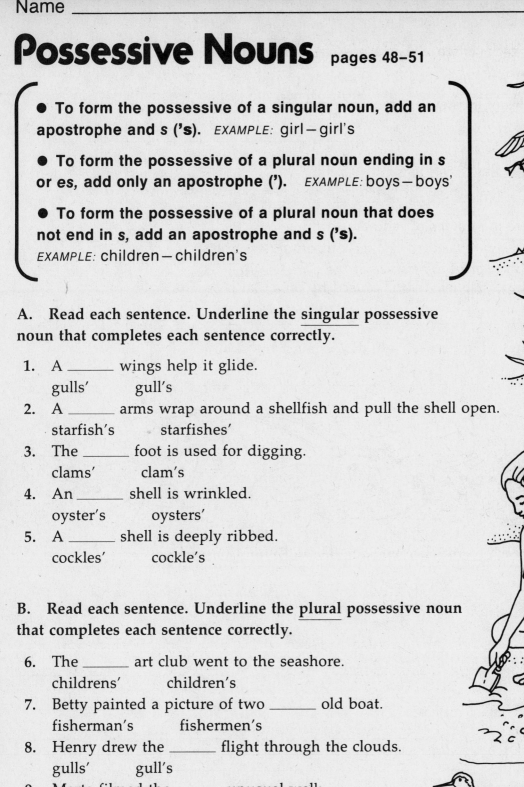

- **To form the possessive of a singular noun, add an apostrophe and s ('s).** *EXAMPLE:* girl—girl's

- **To form the possessive of a plural noun ending in s or es, add only an apostrophe (').** *EXAMPLE:* boys—boys'

- **To form the possessive of a plural noun that does not end in s, add an apostrophe and s ('s).** *EXAMPLE:* children—children's

A. Read each sentence. Underline the <u>singular</u> possessive noun that completes each sentence correctly.

1. A _____ wings help it glide.
   gulls'   gull's
2. A _____ arms wrap around a shellfish and pull the shell open.
   starfish's   starfishes'
3. The _____ foot is used for digging.
   clams'   clam's
4. An _____ shell is wrinkled.
   oyster's   oysters'
5. A _____ shell is deeply ribbed.
   cockles'   cockle's

B. Read each sentence. Underline the <u>plural</u> possessive noun that completes each sentence correctly.

6. The _____ art club went to the seashore.
   childrens'   children's
7. Betty painted a picture of two _____ old boat.
   fisherman's   fishermen's
8. Henry drew the _____ flight through the clouds.
   gulls'   gull's
9. Marta filmed the _____ unusual walk.
   sand crab's   sand crabs'
10. Juan photographed the _____ catch.
    divers'   diver's

Name _____

C.   Rewrite each sentence. Use a possessive noun for the underlined words.

11.   The claws of lobsters are tools to get food.

_____

12.   The home of the sponge is in wet places.

_____

13.   Shells are the homes of sand crabs.

_____

14.   The sting of the jellyfish is caused by cells that blow up.

_____

15.   The wings of the geese were dark against the sky.

_____

D.   Next to each word write the singular and plural possessive forms.

	Singular Possessive	*Plural Possessive*
16. boat	_____	_____
17. fish	_____	_____
18. lifeguard	_____	_____
19. swimmer	_____	_____
20. captain	_____	_____
21. box	_____	_____
22. clam	_____	_____
23. gull	_____	_____
24. shark	_____	_____
25. tooth	_____	_____

Finding the Main Idea pages 54–55

The main idea is the one most important thing a passage states about a topic. All the sentences in the passage tell you something about the main idea.

Read each passage and the sentences that follow. Underline the sentence that best states the main idea of each passage.

1.   Shoes have improved over the years. Long ago shoes had the same shape. Shoemakers did not make a left and a right shoe. People often complained about aching feet and toes. In 1818 someone began making left and right shoes. After that feet got better treatment.

  a. In 1818 someone made a left and a right shoe.
  b. Long ago both shoes had the same shape.
  c. Shoes are better now than they were in the past.

2.   Musical instruments have a long history. The first musical instrument was probably a drum. Then flutes and other instruments you blow into were probably made. Finally people made instruments with strings, such as a guitar.

  a. People have been making musical instruments for a long time.
  b. Guitars have strings.
  c. Long ago people made drums.

3.   Scientists believe that people in the Stone Age bowled. Ancient Egyptians bowled too. The first bowling balls were round stones. Later people used wooden balls. The game of bowling is older than baseball, soccer, or football.

  a. Ancient Egyptians liked to bowl.
  b. The first bowling balls were round stones.
  c. Bowling is one of the world's oldest games.

4.   Sailors of the past made many objects by tying cord or rope into fancy knots. This hobby helped them to pass long hours at sea. They made such things as covers for sea chests and bell ropes. Knotting of this kind is called macramé.

  a. Sailors had many hobbies.
  b. Sailors spent many long hours at sea.
  c. Sailors often made objects by tying rope into knots.

Name _____

Facts and Opinions pages 58–59

    A **statement of fact** tells about something that can be checked or proved to be true or false. A **statement of opinion** tells what a person thinks or believes. It is not based on what is certain. Someone else may disagree, or have a different opinion.

A. Write *fact* or *opinion* next to each statement.

1. Bicycles are fun to ride. _____

2. There are several parts your bicycle must have. _____

3. Every bicycle should have a headlight. _____

4. A front basket is a nice thing to have. _____

5. Your bicycle should have a bell or horn. _____

6. Bicycle riders must obey all traffic rules. _____

7. Red is the best color for a bicycle. _____

B. Write one fact and one opinion about each of the following topics.

8. PETS

    fact: _____

    _____

    opinion: _____

    _____

9. SPORTS

    fact: _____

    _____

    opinion: _____

    _____

10. HOMEWORK

    fact: _____

    opinion: _____

    _____

Book Reports pages 60–61

Remember to do these things when you write a book report. Write the title of the book. Tell the author's name. Write a summary of the book. Include the main idea and some interesting details. Tell your opinion of the book.

A. Rewrite the book titles correctly.

1. hortense the hippo _____

2. the disappearing dog catcher _____

3. the book of baby animals _____

4. the tale of the mountain goat _____

5. a rabbit named red _____

B. Use the information about a book called *Misunderstood Animals,* by Sara L. Fernandez. Copy the information into a book report.

I enjoyed this book because it told many interesting facts about animals.

This book is about animals such as the wolf, the bat, and the octopus. The book says that these animals have frightened people for centuries. It explains why people have been afraid of them. The book says that many of these animals are actually helpful.

BOOK REPORT

TITLE _____

AUTHOR _____

SUMMARY _____

_____

_____

_____

OPINION _____

_____

Editing Book Reports

page 62

When you edit a book report, remember to capitalize the first word, the last word, and all important words in a book title. Use editing marks to correct mistakes in your book report.

A. Edit the book report. Use editing marks to correct the mistakes. Add words to show which part is an opinion.

BOOK REPORT

TITLE   baney's lake

AUTHOR   nan hayden agle

SUMMARY   Eleven-year-old baney trimble buys some land from miss luke. baney discovers that a lake and a dam will soon be built on the land. He tries to save his land by going to court and talking to judge grimes. baney loses his case, but the story has a happy end anyhow.

OPINION   Baney's Lake was interesting because you didn't know if baney would be able to keep his land.

B. Recopy the book report. Make all the corrections and additions you showed above with editing marks.

_____

_____

_____

_____

_____

_____

_____

_____

_____

_____

Writing Names page 63

Mechanics Practice

- **Begin each part of the name of a person with a capital letter.**

- **Begin titles of people such as *Ms., Mrs., Mr.,* and *Dr.* with a capital letter.**

- **Always capitalize the word *I*.**
- **Begin the names of pets with a capital letter.**
- **Use a period after an initial.**
- **Use a period after an abbreviation of a title.**

EXAMPLES: Mr. Frank Colin and I visited Mrs. R. Whitney.
We brought our dog Rags.

A. Write these names of people and pets correctly.

1. dr.anna bianco _____

2. prince charles _____

3. spot _____

4. ms.chung lee _____

5. mr.a l lewis _____

6. bruce t wilks _____

B. Show where capital letters and periods are needed in these sentences. Write the sentences correctly on a separate piece of paper.

7. This morning i was running with my dog

8. i didn't see the groundhog hole, but buttons did

9. Dad took me to see dr.antonio madrid

10. dr.madrid told me i had sprained my ankle

11. His partner, dr.marta roja, will wrap my ankle

12. She asked me how buttons was doing

Name _____

A Biography pages 66–69

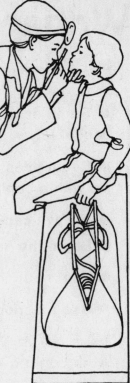

A book about the life of a famous person is called a **biography**. A biography is the story of a real person's life. It includes many details about the person's life.

Read this story about the first woman doctor in America.

Elizabeth Blackwell wanted to be a doctor, but in her time women were not allowed to go to medical school. A man named Dr. Elder knew Elizabeth would make a fine doctor. He tried to help her. He let her study his medical books at night. He helped her write letters to medical schools. For two years he and Elizabeth searched for a school that would accept her.

At last Geneva Medical College in New York accepted her. She graduated first in her class. Now she was Dr. Blackwell. But no American hospital would let her be a doctor in training. Elizabeth refused to give up. She traveled all the way to Europe, where she could work in a hospital. Elizabeth Blackwell paved the way for other women who wanted to be doctors.

1. What is the name of this kind of story? _____

2. Is this a true story? _____

3. Who is the main character? _____

4. Why is she famous? _____

_____

5. Who helped the main character become a doctor? _____

_____

6. What did he do to help? _____

_____

7. Underline five details in the story that tell about the main character.

_____

8. What did Elizabeth do that shows you how badly she wanted to be a

doctor? _____

_____

_____

Name _____

Unit Review

A. Underline the nouns in each sentence.

1. Mack was very bored.
2. His older brother had gone to the store.
3. What was this boy going to do?
4. Maybe he would call his friend Bonnie on the telephone.

B. Write the plural form of each noun.

5. dragon _____   6. beach _____

7. bus _____   8. boy _____

9. sheep _____   10. woman _____

11. box _____   12. mouse _____

C. Circle each common noun. Underline each proper noun.

13. Maryvale Street is the street where we live.

14. It is in the town of Sacramento.

15. On a holiday such as Labor Day we have fun.

D. Rewrite each name. Use capital letters and periods where they are needed.

16. king ferdinand _____

17. dr les green _____

18. mrs g l lopez _____

19. london, england _____

20. stevens blvd _____

21. heathcote rd _____

E. Write the possessive form of the word in parentheses (   ) in each sentence.

22. The team used _____ bats for the game. (Leslie)

23. The _____ shirts were green. (players)

24. On the first day, two _____ masks broke. (catchers)

Unit Review

F. Read the paragraph. Then answer the questions.

Marty takes good care of his dog, Spin. He brushes and
feeds it every day. He takes Spin out for exercise. Once a year
he takes Spin to the veterinarian for a checkup.

25. What is the main idea of the paragraph? _____

_____

26. Underline two detail sentences from the paragraph.

G. Read what a coach says about her baseball team. Write *fact*
or *opinion* next to each statement.

27. We have six new players this year.   _____

28. Our first practice is April 16.   _____

29. You've never seen a pitcher like ours.   _____

H. Make a check next to each sentence that is true about
writing a book report.

30. _____ Tell your opinion of the book.

31. _____ Tell the title and author of the book.

32. _____ Give only the facts about the book.

33. _____ Don't tell the whole story.

I. Read this part of a biography. Then answer the questions.

Elizabeth's head drooped down low as she dragged her feet
along the sidewalk. Why had it happened to the pup? Her eyes
filled with tears. If only she had closed the gate. Now it was too
late. She'd have to explain to Martha what had happened. She
gulped hard, took a deep breath and straightened her shoulders.
She could do it.

34. Who is the main character? _____

35. Write two words that describe this character.

_____

30 UNIT 2: Workbook

Name _____

Action Verbs pages 78–79

(• An **action verb** is a word that shows action.
An action verb is often the key word in the predicate.
It tells what the subject does.
EXAMPLE: Marsha packed her suitcase.)

A.   Draw two lines under each action verb. Some sentences have more than one.

1.   This summer we visited a ranch.
2.   Before lunch we chopped wood for the fireplace.
3.   Everyone cooked and cleaned in the kitchen.
4.   Every day we rode horses in the meadow.
5.   The horses jumped and galloped.
6.   We always brush and groom the horses after a ride.
7.   I learned a lot about horses.
8.   We returned to the stables late in the afternoon.
9.   At night we sat around the campfire.
10.   We enjoyed every minute of our time at the ranch.

B.   Write five sentences about an activity you enjoy. Use action verbs from this list, or use your own action verbs.

swim	catch	run	race	shout
pick	ride	sing	jump	listen

11. _____

12. _____

13. _____

14. _____

15. _____

Name _____

Linking Verbs pages 80–81

> ● A **linking verb** connects the subject with other words in the predicate. It tells what the subject is or was. Forms of *be* are often used as linking verbs.
> *EXAMPLES:* am, is, are, was, were

A. Read each sentence. Draw two lines under the linking verbs.

1. The Fourth of July is my favorite holiday.
2. It is the birthday of the United States of America.
3. My friends and I are musicians.
4. I am a drummer in one of the bands.
5. The band members are boys and girls.
6. My sister is a baton twirler.
7. All the costumes are very colorful.
8. Her hat was red.
9. The fire engines were the best part of the parade.
10. Everyone in our town was happy.

B. Complete each sentence. Use *am, is,* or *are.*

11. Today _____ Thanksgiving.
12. Thanksgiving _____ a holiday.
13. This year I _____ an actress in the Thanksgiving play.
14. I _____ a Pilgrim in the play.
15. _____ you a character too?

C. Complete each sentence. Use *was* or *were.*

16. I _____ an actor last year.
17. Last year I _____ a Delaware Indian.
18. All the costumes _____ colorful.
19. Mine _____ the most colorful of all.
20. Hal and Miki _____ announcers.

Name _____

Helping Verbs   pages 82–83

> ● A **helping verb** helps the main verb express an action or make a statement.
> *EXAMPLES:* am, is, are, was, were, have, has, had, will

A. Read each sentence. Draw two lines under the helping verbs.

1. Angela and Gina are planting a garden.
2. Gina has filled a bucket with good soil.
3. Angela has plowed the ground with a little hand plow.
4. They have worked hard in the hot sun.
5. They will put the seeds in the soil this afternoon.
6. Angela's father was helping them decide what to plant.
7. They will grow tomatoes, green beans, and lettuce.
8. Their families will eat lots of fresh salad this summer.
9. Angela is picking the weeds every day.
10. The girls will work in the garden and enjoy the harvest.

B. Use each main verb with a helping verb. Write sentences.

11. cleaning	12. polishing	13. wash	14. fix
15. scrub	16. sewn	17. dusted	18. mending

11. _____

12. _____

13. _____

14. _____

15. _____

16. _____

17. _____

18. _____

Name _____

Verb Tenses pages 84–86

- The time expressed by a verb is called the **tense.** There are three main tenses.

- **Present tense** shows action that is happening now or that happens regularly.
EXAMPLE: Paul <u>cooks</u> his dinner.

- **Past tense** shows action that happened in the past. Many verbs that tell about past time end in *ed.*
EXAMPLE: Yesterday Paul <u>cooked</u> his dinner.

- **Future tense** shows action that will happen in the future. Many verbs that tell about future time have the helping verb *will.*
EXAMPLE: Paul <u>will cook</u> his dinner tomorrow.

A. Draw two lines under the verb in each sentence. Then write *past, present,* or *future* to tell the tense of the verb.

_____ 1. I visited my Aunt Kate.

_____ 2. Martha will clean her closet.

_____ 3. I baby-sit for Matthew and Ronnie.

_____ 4. My friends will drive to Detroit.

_____ 5. My father and I constructed a bookshelf.

_____ 6. We cook pizza for dinner.

B. Write two sentences in the present tense. Tell about something you are doing right now.

7. _____

8. _____

Write two sentences in the past tense. Tell about something you did last weekend.

9. _____

10. _____

34 UNIT 3: Workbook

Spelling Past Tense Verbs pages 88–89

- **Some verbs end in a consonant and *y*. To form the past tense, change *y* to *i*. Then add *ed*.**
  EXAMPLE: dry—dried

- **Some verbs have one syllable and end with a consonant, vowel, consonant. To form the past tense, double the final consonant. Then add *ed*.**
  EXAMPLE: step—stepped

A. Write the past tense of each verb.

1. mop _____   2. hum _____

3. ferry _____   4. clap _____

5. tarry _____   6. worry _____

7. plot _____   8. try _____

9. bury _____   10. drop _____

B. Read about Nicky's garden. Fill in each blank with the past tense of the verb in parentheses ( ).

11. Nicky _____ his garden.   (plan)

12. First he _____ a sunny place for it.   (spot)

13. Next he _____ to get his hoe.   (hurry)

14. He _____ the hoe to the garden.   (carry)

15. He _____ and turned the soil.   (jab)

16. He _____ to smooth the soil.   (try)

17. Next Nicky _____ his packet of seeds.   (empty)

18. Into the ground Nicky _____ seeds.   (drop)

19. He gently _____ soil over the seeds.   (tap)

20. Then he _____ on the grass and rested.   (flop)

Irregular Verbs pages 90–91

Verbs that do not add *ed* to show the past tense are called **irregular verbs**. Study the chart of irregular verbs.

Verb	Present	Past	Past with have, has, or had
come	come(s)	came	come
run	run(s)	ran	run
go	go(es)	went	gone
begin	begin(s)	began	begun
sing	sing(s)	sang	sung
ring	ring(s)	rang	rung

A. Underline the verb that will correctly complete the sentence.

1. Last week I (went, gone) to glee club for the first time.
2. I had (ran, run) all the way because I was late.
3. The lesson had already (began, begun).
4. The teacher stopped class and (come, came) up to me.
5. "Have you ever (sang, sung) before?" she asked.
6. I answered, "I once (sung, sang) in my school choir."
7. Everyone else had (began, begun) the song.
8. I began to sing, but the school bell (rang, rung).
9. "Next time please (come, came) on time," said the teacher.
10. Then I quickly (ran, run) to my next class.

B. Write a sentence using each of these verb forms correctly. Remember to use *has, have,* or *had* if necessary.

came, begun, sung, ran, went

11. _____

12. _____

13. _____

14. _____

15. _____

36 UNIT 3: **Workbook**

Name _____

Other Irregular Verbs pages 92–93

Many verbs do not form the past tense by adding *ed*.
These are called **irregular verbs**. The following chart lists more
irregular verbs.

Verb	Present	Past	Past with have, has, or had
do	do(es)	did	done
write	write(s)	wrote	written
give	give(s)	gave	given
take	take(s)	took	taken
grow	grow(s)	grew	grown

Grandpa Bill

A. Underline the verb that will correctly complete the
sentence.

1. Luke has (wrote, written) a story.
2. It's about his Grandpa Bill who (grew, grown) up in Scotland.
3. A few hours ago Luke (wrote, written) part of it.
4. His father (gave, given) him a lot of information.
5. Grandpa has (wrote, written) a diary about his early life.
6. For his first job he (did, done) work as a tailor.
7. Luke and his sister have (grew, grown) up knowing Grandpa.
8. Luke (took, taken) his story to school when he finished.

B. Use four different verbs from the chart at the top of the
page. Write four sentences about a story you have read or
written.

9. _____

10. _____

11. _____

12. _____

The Dictionary pages 96–101

A **dictionary** contains words listed in alphabetical order. There are **guide words** at the top of every page. They tell the first and last word on the page. The part of the dictionary explaining the word is called the **entry**. The **entry word** appears in dark type followed by its **pronunciation**. After the pronunciation the **part of speech** is listed. Then the **definitions** of the word are given, sometimes with **examples**.

Kenya

Ken·ya [kĕn′yə *or* kĕn′yə] *n.* A country in eastern Africa, a member of the British Commonwealth of Nations.

Kep·ler [kĕp′lər], **Johann,** 1571–1630, German astronomer.

kept [kĕpt] Past tense and past participle of KEEP: She *kept* a parrot for years.

ker·chief [kûr′chif] *n.* 1 A piece of fabric, usually square, worn over the head or around the neck. 2 A handkerchief.

ker·nel [kûr′nəl] *n.* 1 A seed or grain, as of wheat or corn. 2 The soft, often edible part inside a nut or fruit pit. 3 The central part, as of a plan or theory; nucleus; gist.

ker·o·sene [kĕr′ə·sēn] *n.* A thin oil made from petroleum, used as in fuel lamps, stoves, etc.

ketch [kĕch] *n.* A vessel with a tall mast forward and a shorter one aft.

ketch·up [kĕch′əp] *n.* A thick red sauce made with tomatoes and spices.

kidney

key² [kē] *n., pl.* **keys** A low island, especially one of coral, along a coast: the Florida *Keys*.

key·board [kē′bôrd′] *n.* The row or rows of keys, as in a piano or typewriter.

key·hole [kē′hōl′] *n.* A hole for a key, as in a lock or door.

key·note [kē′nōt′] *n.* 1 The note that a musical key is named after and based upon. 2 The basic idea or principle of a speech, philosophy, policy, etc.: Friendship was the *keynote*.

key·stone [kē′stōn′] *n.* 1 The middle stone at the top of an arch, serving to lock the other stones in place. 2 A basic or fundamental part, as of a science.

khak·i [kak′ē] *n., pl.* **khak·is,** *adj.* 1 *n., adj.* Yellowish brown. 2 *n.* A strong cotton cloth of this color. 3 *n.* (*pl.*) A uniform made of khaki.
Khaki, which describes an earthy color, comes from a Persian word meaning *dust.*

khan [kän] *n.* 1 A title once used by Mongol rulers. 2 A title for a ruler or high ranking official in central Asia, Afghanistan, and Iran.

Use the dictionary page to help you answer the questions. Write the answers in complete sentences.

1. Would you find this page in the beginning, middle, or end of the dictionary?

2. What are the guide words on this page?

3. What is the entry word after *ketch?*

4. How many syllables are in the word *kerosene?*

5. How many entry words begin with the letters *key?*

_____

6. Which word comes first on the page: *keynote, ketch,* or *kept?*

_____

7. Are the vowels *e* and *o* in the word *keynote* long or short?

_____

8. What part of speech is the word *keystone?*

_____

9. How many definitions does the word *kernel* have?

_____

10. What is the example sentence for the second meaning of *keynote?*

_____

11. What word does this respelling show? kûr′chif

_____

12. What words on the page have three definitions?

_____

13. Which of these words will also be found on this page?
    kale   kickoff   keep

_____

14. What part of speech is the word *kernel?*

_____

Read the story below.

A big cat downed everything Fred Green had in Jack's kitchen—like my nice oatmeal pancakes—quite rapidly! She took Uncle Vernon's white xylophone yesterday. *Zany!*

The story has twenty-six words—one for each letter of the alphabet. Try to write your own "alphabet" story with one word, in order, for each letter of the alphabet.

Friendly Letters   pages 102–103

Study this example of a friendly letter. Notice the five parts of a letter, the capitalization, and the punctuation.

Heading →	5 Somerset Lane Omaha, Nebraska 68122 January 16, 19__
Greeting →	Dear Eloise,
Body →	I read a book that I think you might like. It's called *How to Eat Fried Worms*. Maybe you can find it in your school library. Get ready to laugh! Let me know how you like it. What books have you been reading?
Closing →	Your friend,
Signature →	Margo

Write a friendly letter using these parts. Use a separate piece of paper. Finish the body of the letter. Remember to put capital letters and commas where they belong.

Heading   24 delgado avenue
tallahassee florida   32304
november 3 19—

Greeting   dear Captain WI-12-RQ

Body   I do not miss my galaxy so much.
I am staying with a very nice Earth family.
They live in a warm place called Florida.
Last week we did a most exciting thing.

*(Finish the paragraph. Tell what the space
visitor might have done in Florida.)*

Closing   your faithful flier

Signature   LA-44-VX

Name _____

Invitations   pages 108–109

    An invitation is a short letter asking a person to come somewhere. An invitation has five parts. It has a date, a greeting, a body, a closing, and a signature. It should contain all the information a guest needs to know.

A. **Pretend you are having a birthday party. Write a letter of invitation to your best friend. Make up this information in your invitation.**

1. For whom is the invitation? _____

2. What is the date? _____

3. When does the party begin and end? _____

4. Where is it? _____

5. What special information is needed by the guest? _____

_____

B. **Write your invitation on the lines below.**

_____

_____

_____

_____

_____

_____

_____

_____

_____

Editing Invitations page 110

Copyright © 1983 by Harcourt Brace Jovanovich, Inc.
All rights reserved.

Edit an invitation before you send it. Check to see that all important information is included. Use editing marks to show changes and corrections.

Editing Marks	
≡	capitalize
⊙	make a period
∧	add something
⌄	add a comma
⌄⌄	add quotation marks
✄	take something away
◯	spell correctly
¶	indent the paragraph
/	make a lower case letter
tr ∩	transpose

A. Read the invitation. Use editing marks to correct all the mistakes.

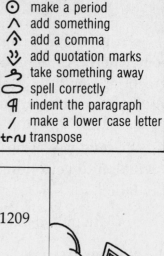

> 7901 fourth avenue
>
> brooklyn, new york 11209
>
> october 22, 19___
>
> dear rita,
>
>   i am having a costume party this halloween, and I would like you to come. It will be at my house from 2:00 p m to 6:00 p m the saturday after halloween. you cannot get in without a costume, so start creating right away!
>
>   your friend,
>
>   brent fink

B. Recopy the edited invitation correctly.

_____

_____

_____

_____

_____

_____

_____

_____

_____

Writing Place Names   page 111
Mechanics Practice

- Begin each important word in the name of a town, city, state, and country with a capital letter.

- Begin each important word in the names of streets and their abbreviations with capital letters.

- Use a period after an abbreviation of a place name.

- Use a comma in an address to separate the city and state or the city and country.

EXAMPLES: My best friend lives at 235 Sherman Avenue in Atlanta, Georgia. My aunts live on Park Street and on Northern Boulevard in New York.

A.   Correct the mistakes in these addresses.

1. 13 putnam ave.

   valley stream new york 11580

2. 1400 washington ave

   albany ny 12210

3. 3000 north carstairs place

   fort lauderdale florida 33313

4. 201 east 35 st

   chicago il 60604

5. 14-67 main street

   atlanta georgia 30735

6. 867 jefferson blvd

   st.louis missouri 65205

B.   Show where capital letters, periods, and commas are needed in these sentences. Write the sentences correctly on a separate piece of paper.

7. Our new museum is on park avenue in union city

8. Turn right at dogwood avenue and drive one mile

9. We have art classes with teachers from new orleans and memphis

10. New teachers are coming soon from new jersey and california

11. They are stopping at scottsdale arizona on the way

12. The guest speaker came here from milan italy

A Play pages 112–119

A **play** is a story that is acted out. The people in a play are the **characters**. Where the play happens is the **setting**. The conversations between the characters are the **dialog**. Directions that tell a character how to act or move are **stage directions**.

Read the beginning of a play called *The Wishing Well*.

The Wishing Well

Characters: Nicole   Scott
                   Dana   Wishing Well Voice

Setting: A deep forest. A wishing well is to one side.

Nicole: Let's hurry home. This forest is getting spooky.

Dana: (*Noticing wishing well*): Look! What's this?

Scott: (*Points to sign on well*): It's a wishing well, of course. Do you think it's a real one?

Nicole: That only happens in fairy tales. Come on.

Dana: What can it hurt to try just one wish? (Digs a penny out out of her pocket. She tosses it in the well. She whispers something over the side.)

Wishing
Well Voice: (*Deep, hollow-sounding*): WHAT? SPEAK UP! I CAN'T HEAR YOU! WHAT'S THAT YOU SAY?

Scott: (*Rolls eyes, looks shocked*): Did I hear what I think I heard? (*All look at each other*)

A.   Complete each of the following statements.

1.   The title of this play is _____ .

2.   The four characters in the play are _____

_____

3.   The setting of this play is _____ .

4.   The first character to speak is _____ .

5.   Underline some examples of dialog in the play.

6.   The stage direction for the WISHING WELL VOICE is _____

_____

7. Who might speak next in this play? Write the name of the character in capital letters. Give stage directions in parentheses (   ). Make up some dialog for the character to say.

_____

_____

_____

_____

B. **Make up a setting for each list of characters.**

8. Characters: Wizard, Frog, Prince, Soldiers

   Setting: _____

6. Characters: Lion, Mouse

   Setting: _____

10. Characters: Giant Egg, Dinosaur

    Setting: _____

11. Characters: Pilot, Flight Engineer, Flight Attendant

    Setting: _____

C. **Make up some characters for each setting.**

12. Setting: a flying saucer, deep in outer space

    Characters: _____

13. Setting: a long-lost island

    Characters: _____

14. Setting: the school gym

    Characters: _____

15. Setting: a hospital emergency room

    Characters: _____

D. **Choose a set of characters and a setting from Practice B or Practice C. Think of some ideas for a play you could write about them. On a separate piece of paper, write five sentences to tell what will happen in the play.**

Name _____

Unit Review

A. Draw two lines under the action verb in each sentence.

1. The quarterback scampers back.
2. He clutches the ball under his arm.
3. Then he flings the ball into the air.
4. The crowd roars.

B. Draw two lines under the linking verb in each sentence.

5. Andrew is black.
6. I am sad.
7. We are Andrew's owners.
8. Andrew is our cat.

C. Draw two lines under the main verb and its helping verb. Then circle the helping verb.

9. The plumber has changed the pipes.
10. She was working on the job all day.
11. We were watching her.
12. Later we will wash the dishes.

D. Draw two lines under the verb in each sentence. Then write *past, present,* or *future* to tell the tense of each verb.

_____ 13. Last year we camped on our vacation.

_____ 14. We loved the trip.

_____ 15. Today we plan for our next family trip.

_____ 16. We will travel to Florida.

E. Write the past tense of each verb.

17. copy _____
18. hop _____
19. skip _____
20. hurry _____
21. marry _____
22. shop _____

F. Underline the correct past tense verb to complete each sentence.

23. We have (wrote, written) the letter.
24. She has (took, taken) it to the post office.
25. The mail carrier (came, come) back with the letter.

Name _____

G. Look at the first word in each row. Then look at the guide words from the dictionary. Underline the guide words that the first word would come between.

26. cork	copy–corner	Columbus–come	cup–curb
27. mail	machine–mad	maid–make	me–measles
28. today	tissue–toe	tooth–torn	touch–town

H. Put a check next to the facts that belong in an invitation.

29. _____ The date of the party.

30. _____ Where the person goes to school.

31. _____ Where the party will take place.

32. _____ The time of the party.

I. Read the beginning of the play. Then answer the questions.

The Boy Next Door

Characters: Ellen York, Mrs. York, Mrs. Wills
Setting: the living room of the York house

Mrs. Wills: I really have to go now, Mrs. York, but I can't tell you how much I enjoyed my visit.
Mrs. York: It was nice seeing you again, Mrs. Wills. Please come soon, won't you? (<u>turns to window</u>) Ellen, Ellen! (<u>Ellen continues to stare out of the window.</u>) Ellen!
Ellen (<u>turning quickly</u>): Yes, Mother?
Mrs. York: Mrs. Wills is ready to leave now.

33. How many characters are in the play _____

34. What is the setting of the play? _____

35. Which character speaks first? _____

Paragraphs and Main Ideas pages 126–127

To form a good paragraph the sentences must be related. They must all tell about one main idea. The first line of a paragraph is indented. Other lines of the paragraph begin at the left margin.

Read the following groups of sentences. Put a check mark next to each group that would make a good paragraph. On the line below each good paragraph, write its main idea.

_____ 1.   When Navajo children are about seven years old, these boys and girls learn to tend sheep. Girls learn to weave and cook. Boys learn to farm and to make silver jewelry.

_____

_____ 2.   Silver jewelry is beautiful. Some Navajos can make it. The Navajos learned about raising sheep from the Spanish settlers. Women have an important place in Navajo life.

_____

_____ 3.   Early Navajos traveled on foot. Navajos began trading at the trading post. Have you any silver jewelry? Navajo weavers are known for their beautiful baskets.

_____

_____ 4.   A puffed bread the Navajos eat is called fry bread. It is made with flour, salt, baking powder, milk, and butter. The batter is mixed and kneaded. Then it is fried. Sometimes fry bread is covered with honey and eaten for dessert.

_____

Name _____

Topic Sentences pages 128–129

> ● The **topic sentence** expresses the main idea of the paragraph. It is often the first sentence of the paragraph.

Underline the sentence that would make the best topic sentence for each paragraph.

1. A quarter has 119 grooves around it. A dime has 1 less. The faces on most coins look to the left. Only one does not. Do you know which one? Look at some coins to find out.

    a. A quarter is worth more than a dime.
    b. Coins are interesting to look at.
    c. Presidents' faces are on some coins.

2. The doctor's name was Sylvester Graham. He thought that whole wheat flour was more healthful for people to eat than white flour. Using wheat flour, he made delicious crackers. They became known as graham crackers.

    a. Sylvester Graham enjoyed baking.
    b. The graham cracker is made from wheat flour.
    c. The graham cracker was named after a doctor.

3. Theodore Roosevelt was once given a koala bear. He talked about it so much that it became very popular. A copy of the bear was made as a children's toy. It was called a teddy bear.

    a. Theodore Roosevelt loved animals.
    b. The teddy bear was named for President Theodore Roosevelt.
    c. The teddy bear is still a popular toy.

Name _____

Details in Paragraphs pages 130–131

Details explain, expand, or develop the topic sentence of a paragraph. They help the reader understand more about the main idea.

A. Look at the pictures below. Write a sentence under each picture to tell what Andy is doing.

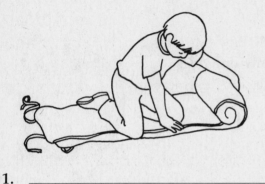 

1. _____   2. _____

_____ .   _____ .

3. _____   4. _____

_____ .   _____ .

B. Use your sentences as detail sentences. Add them to the topic sentence to make a paragraph.

Andy is getting ready for a camping trip. He _____

_____

_____

_____

_____

50 UNIT 4: Workbook

Name _____

Sentence Order in Paragraphs
pages 132–133

Sentences in a paragraph must be in the right order. If they are not, the paragraph will not make sense.

A. Estelle is making a peanut butter and jelly sandwich. Number the pictures to show the correct order.

B. Now write a sentence for each picture. Add them to the topic sentence below. Be sure to write them in the correct order. Use time-order clues such as *first, then,* and *finally.*

Estelle is making a peanut butter and jelly sandwich. _____

_____

_____

_____

C. Now help Estelle make a milk shake. Number the sentences in the correct order. Circle the time-order clues.

_____ Blend the milk, ice cream, and flavoring.

_____ First take out the milk, ice cream, and flavoring.

_____ Then pour the milk into the blender.

_____ Finally clean up the kitchen.

_____ Next add ice cream to the milk in the blender.

_____ Add your favorite flavoring to the milk and ice cream.

_____ Pour the mixture into a glass and enjoy your milk shake.

Keeping to the Topic pages 134–135

Every sentence in a paragraph should keep to the topic. The topic sentence states the main idea. Every other sentence should give details about the topic sentence.

A. Read the paragraphs. Underline the sentence in each that does not keep to the topic.

1.   Diane planted a vegetable garden. She planted peas, squash, and lettuce. After a few weeks the seeds began to grow. The potatoes have eyes, the corn has ears, and the beans talk. In a few more weeks the vegetables were almost ready to eat. Diane couldn't wait to harvest her crop!

2.   Our dog is called Spot because of his color. It was a little horse. Spot is white. He has two brown patches. One is on his head and one is on his belly.

3.   Debra and her father were making a doghouse for their dog, Harvey. Debra was in charge of holding the nails and helping to hammer them. I like it closed. Her father carried the heavy pieces of lumber into the backyard. When it was finished, they painted it red.

Now look at the sentences you underlined. Read each question below. Then write each sentence under the question that it answers. You will have three jokes to tickle your funny bone.

1. Why is it dangerous to tell a secret on a farm? _____

_____

_____

2. Why couldn't the pony talk? _____

_____

3. What did Johnny say when his grandfather asked

    him how he liked school? _____

Parts of a Book pages 138–141

A **title page** lists the title of the book, the author, and the publisher. The **table of contents** contains the chapters or units in the book and their page numbers. A **glossary** is a small dictionary of special words used in the book. An **index** is an alphabetical list of all the topics in a book and their page numbers.

Use these terms to answer the following questions.

title page   table of contents   glossary   index

_____ 1. Where would the author's name appear?

_____ 2. Where is the title of the book printed?

_____ 3. Where would you find a list of all the topics in a book?

_____ 4. Where is a list of chapters or units in the book?

_____ 5. On what page would you find the publisher's name?

_____ 6. Where would you find a definition of the word *tadpole*?

_____ 7. Where would you find the title of the third chapter?

_____ 8. Where would you find a list of the special words used in the book?

_____ 9. Where would you find the pages on which a certain topic is mentioned?

_____ 10. Where would you find the name of the chapter that begins on page 89?

The Encyclopedia pages 142–143

A good place to look for information on many subjects is an **encyclopedia**. An encyclopedia is usually a set of books. Each book is called a volume. The volumes contain articles. They are arranged in alphabetical order.

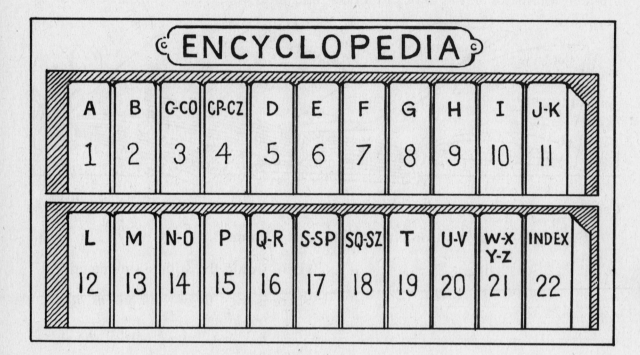

In what encyclopedia volume would you find information on the following subjects?

_____ 1. chromosome   _____ 2. Jupiter

_____ 3. Prometheus   _____ 4. algebra

_____ 5. sonata   _____ 6. electricity

_____ 7. quinine   _____ 8. Kentucky

_____ 9. submarine   _____ 10. linden

_____ 11. Seth Thomas   _____ 12. flag

_____ 13. astronomy   _____ 14. Woodrow Wilson

_____ 15. Youngstown   _____ 16. bluefish

_____ 17. insect   _____ 18. Eleanor Roosevelt

_____ 19. cloud   _____ 20. Susan B. Anthony

Direction Paragraphs   pages 146–147

When you write a direction paragraph, begin with a good topic sentence. Add detail sentences to tell the steps in the directions. Use words such as *first, second, third, next,* and *last* or *finally* to show the correct order.

It is Allison's birthday. For her party she will fold napkins so that they make pockets. Look at the pictures. They show how to fold the napkin.

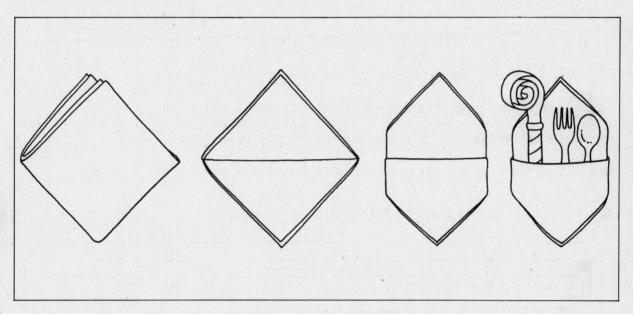

Read the paragraph. The sentences are out of order. Rewrite the paragraph putting the steps in the correct order. Be sure to add words such as *first, second, next,* and *finally.*

Fold the top layer of the napkin down. Here's how to make a pocket out of a napkin. Fold the napkin in fours. Fold the side points under. Fold the top layer of the napkin down. Slip a fork, a spoon, and a party favor into the pocket.

_____

_____

_____

_____

Editing Direction Paragraphs page 148

Edit direction paragraphs so that your directions are simple and clear. Be sure the steps are in the correct order.

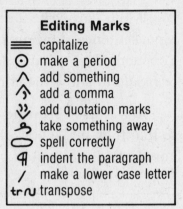

Editing Marks

≡ capitalize
⊙ make a period
∧ add something
⋏ add a comma
⋰⋰ add quotation marks
⸲ take something away
◯ spell correctly
¶ indent the paragraph
/ make a lower case letter
tr~ transpose

A. Read this paragraph about how to dial a pay telephone. Correct the sentence order. Add words like *first, second, next,* and *finally.* Cross out the sentences that are not needed. Use the editing marks you have learned.

Finally finish the call and hang up the receiver.

Here's how to use a pay telephone. Have you ever used one? Take the receiver off the hook. After you put in your money, wait for the dial tone. Second put your dime in the slot. My phone at home has push buttons. Dial the number.

B. Write your edited paragraph correctly

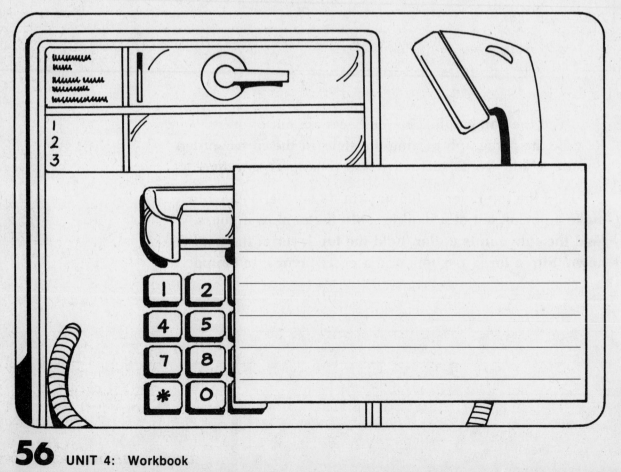

Writing Days, Months, and Holidays
Mechanics Practice

- Begin the name of a day of the week with a capital letter.

- Begin the name of a month with a capital letter.

- Begin each important word in the name of a holiday or special day with a capital letter.

- Use a period after an abbreviation of a day or month.

EXAMPLES: The first Monday in September we will celebrate Memorial Day.   Tues., Aug. 4

A.   Write these days, months, and holidays correctly.

1. wednesday _____

2. mother's day _____

3. may _____

4. lincoln's birthday _____

5. saturday _____

6. sept. _____

7. tues. _____

8. fourth of july _____

9. labor day _____

10. dec. _____

B.   Show where capital letters and periods are needed by using editing marks in these sentences. Write the sentences correctly on a separate piece of paper.

11.   My sister was born in january.

12.   Some people think of memorial day as the start of summer.

13.   My birthday is monday, may 1.

14.   may 1 is celebrated as may day all over the world.

15.   Don't forget mother's day on sunday, may 10.

16.   My class is going to dress up for halloween this year.

17.   On thursday my brother received his first birthday card.

18.   This card was sent on tuesday, february 13.

An Adventure Story   pages 150–153

Adventure stories are about people who do unusual or exciting things. The story usually begins with a problem or a challenge. The main character tries to solve the problem or meet the challenge. As you read this story, decide whether Dian Fossey met her challenge successfully.

Gorillas

by Kay McDearmon

Five roaring giant gorillas came charging toward the young woman. Their leader was only three feet away from her when she calmly spread out her arms and yelled, "Whoa!" All five gorillas stopped in their tracks.

The woman was Dian Fossey, an American scientist, now a famous expert on gorillas. When she first came to the mountains of central Africa to study these hairy black apes, the frightened animals ran screaming into the forest.

When Dian Fossey first went into Rwanda she didn't even take a noisemaker with her to protect herself. While studying gorillas in the mountains there, she has rarely seen them get excited. When they did, she realized later that she had alarmed them by coming too close to their young.

Over the years, Dian slowly won the complete trust of the animals in her study groups. It took her five years of living close to them to accustom them to her presence. To help them accept her, she "acted like a gorilla." She imitated their sounds. She chewed leaves and wild celery stalks as she crawled around the rain forest.

As the gorillas began to trust her, Dian moved closer and closer to them. Soon they allowed their youngsters to move closer to her. To her surprise, they examined her camera and played with the laces on her boots. Once a male she called Diget teasingly grabbed her pen and notebook; then he quickly returned them to her.

One day another gorilla—one she named Peanuts—suddenly appeared behind a rock. She offered him two berries on the palm of her hand, not really expecting him to take them. But he grabbed the fruit and ate it.

Another time she was lying down near a tree when Peanuts, then a hefty 250-pounder, approached her. When she scratched herself, he copied her gesture. Then she held out her hand, and he slowly reached over and touched her fingers. This was the closest any wild gorilla had come to holding hands with a human being.

1. Underline three details in the story that describe the setting.

2. Put a check next to the facts about Dian Fossey you know are true from the story.

_____ Dian Fossey is an American scientist.

_____ Dian remained calm when gorillas came charging toward her.

_____ Dian carried a gun for protection.

_____ Dian is a famous expert on gorillas.

_____ Dian is the mother of three children.

_____ Dian imitated gorillas to win their trust.

3. What was Dian Fossey's adventure? _____

_____

4. The title of an adventure story may tell about the plot. What would be another good title for this adventure story?

_____ Living in Africa

_____ Studying Gorillas in Africa

_____ African Wildlife

_____ Scientists Have Adventures

5. On a separate piece of paper describe another adventure Dian Fossey might have while studying gorillas.

Name _____

Unit Review

A. Read the paragraph and answer the questions.

My sister and I look very different. She has straight hair and mine is
very curly. I am very tall, but she is the shortest one in her class. Most of the
time I wear jeans and T-shirts, but my sister likes to wear dresses.

1. What is the main idea of the paragraph? _____

_____

_____

2. What is the topic sentence? _____

3. What are two details that tell more about the topic sentence? _____

_____

**B. Number the sentences below so that they are in the
correct order.**

_____ 4. Orangutans use their arms and fingers to swing through the trees.

_____ 5. If you have, you know that these apes have long arms.

_____ 6. Have you ever seen an orangutan?

_____ 7. At the end of their arms are long fingers.

**C. Read the paragraph. Underline the sentence that does not
keep to the topic.**

8.   Last year our class went to a Fire Engine Museum. We took a long bus
ride to the museum. Last year I joined the soccer team. A guide took us
around the museum. There were fire trucks of all kinds and sizes. We rang the
bell on each and every fire truck.

**D. Read the list. Write *T* next to each item that would be
found on a title page. Write *TOC* next to each item that
would be found in a table of contents.**

9. _____ title of the book   10. _____ publisher of the book

11. _____ titles of each chapter   12. _____ author of the book

60 UNIT 4: **Workbook**

Name _____

E. Look at part of an index and answer the questions.

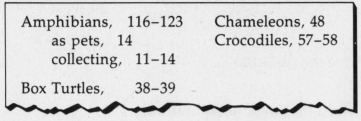

Amphibians, 116–123   Chameleons, 48
    as pets, 14   Crocodiles, 57–58
    collecting, 11–14

Box Turtles,   38–39

13. On which pages will you find information about crocodiles? _____

14. On which pages will you find out about collecting amphibians? _____

F. 15. Read the paragraph. Add words such as *first, second, third, next,* and *last* to show the order of the directions.

    I made hamburgers yesterday. I rolled the meat between my

hands. I patted down each ball of meat into a pattie. I put the

patties into a pan on the stove. I turned on the heat and fried the patties.

    I turned them with a spatula and finished cooking them.

G. Read the beginning of this adventure story. Then answer the questions.

    The wind howled. Stacey stood on the bank. She looked down into
the river. Swirling rapids thundered over the rocks. Icy spray filled the air. Stacey
sloshed through the mud to the canoe. Where could Mark be?

16. Who is the main character? _____

17. What is the setting of the story? _____

18. What is the challenge that Stacey must face? _____

Name _____

Adjectives pages 162–163

(● An **adjective** is a word that describes a noun.
EXAMPLE: The <u>red</u> rose opened under the <u>hot</u> sun.)

A. Underline the adjectives in the following sentences.

1. A daisy is a white flower with a yellow center.
2. It grows in wide grassy meadows.
3. Flowers have soft petals and beautiful colors.
4. The rose is a famous flower.
5. It has a thorny stem and grows on a tall bush.
6. Some flowers grow on low green bushes.
7. Some flowers are grown from fat little bulbs.
8. The tulip grows from a small bulb and comes in many different colors.
9. Azaleas come in pink, purple, red, and lilac shades.
10. Sunflowers have thick strong stems and large flowers.

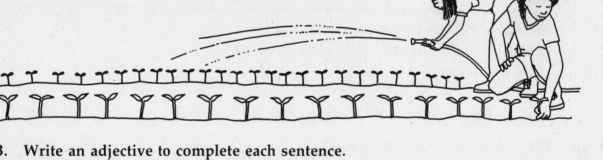

B. Write an adjective to complete each sentence.

11. I am growing _____ roses this year.

12. I need _____ soil and _____ sun to make my flowers grow.

13. _____ days also help because my flowers need water.

14. After weeding my garden, I come in with _____ hands and _____ pants.

15. But the _____ soil feels good to me.

Name _____

Adjectives That Compare   pages 164–166

An adjective is a word that describes a noun. Adjectives
can also describe by comparing two or more nouns. One-syllable
adjectives usually use *er* or *est* to make comparisons. Use *er*
to compare two nouns. Use *est* to compare more than two nouns.

EXAMPLES: This rose is bigger than that rose.
This rose is the biggest of all the roses.

Adjectives of two or more syllables usually use *more* or *most*
to make comparisons. Use *more* to compare two nouns. Use
most to compare more than two nouns.

EXAMPLES: This rose is more beautiful than that rose.
This rose is the most beautiful of all the roses.

**A.   Look at the picture of the three sleds and three hills.
Underline the words to complete each sentence correctly.**

1. Flyer is the (smaller, smallest) of the three sleds.
2. Zoom is (bigger, biggest) than Flyer.
3. Whizzer is the (larger, largest) of all the sleds.
4. Zoom is (faster, fastest) than Whizzer.
5. Flyer is (slower, slowest) than Zoom.
6. Crash is a (more difficult, most difficult) hill than Bash.
7. Point is the (more dangerous, most dangerous) of all the hills.
8. Crash is (steeper, steepest) than Bash.
9. Bash is the (smoother, smoothest) of the three hills.
10. Point is (more slippery, most slippery) than Crash.

B.   Fill in the following chart with the correct adjectives.

11.	_____	_____	most serious
12.	fast	_____	_____
13.	_____	more colorful	_____
14.	_____	_____	most thoughtful
15.	_____	tougher	_____

Name _____

Adverbs   pages 168–169

> ● An **adverb** is a word that tells more about a verb.
> Adverbs can tell *how*, *when*, or *where*.
>
> *EXAMPLES:* Thelma talks <u>excitedly</u>.   (how)
> <u>Then</u> her mother says she will go.   (when)
> Thelma can ride <u>far</u> on her bike.   (where)

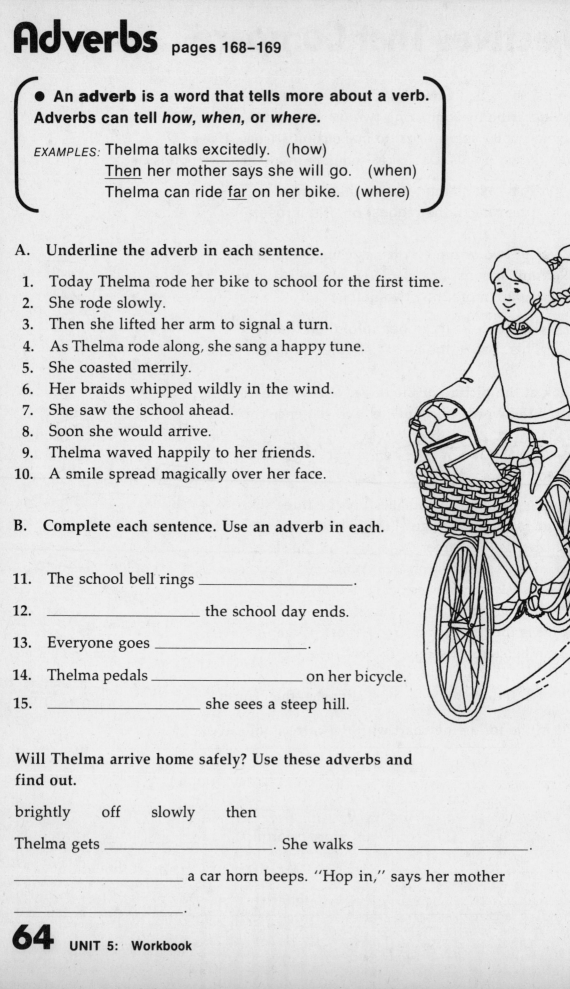

A. Underline the adverb in each sentence.

1. Today Thelma rode her bike to school for the first time.
2. She rode slowly.
3. Then she lifted her arm to signal a turn.
4. As Thelma rode along, she sang a happy tune.
5. She coasted merrily.
6. Her braids whipped wildly in the wind.
7. She saw the school ahead.
8. Soon she would arrive.
9. Thelma waved happily to her friends.
10. A smile spread magically over her face.

B. Complete each sentence. Use an adverb in each.

11. The school bell rings _____.

12. _____ the school day ends.

13. Everyone goes _____.

14. Thelma pedals _____ on her bicycle.

15. _____ she sees a steep hill.

**Will Thelma arrive home safely? Use these adverbs and
find out.**

brightly   off   slowly   then

Thelma gets _____. She walks _____.

_____ a car horn beeps. "Hop in," says her mother

_____.

64   UNIT 5: Workbook

Name _____

Adverbs That Tell
How, When, and Where pages 170–171

An adverb is a word that tells more about a verb. Some adverbs tell *how* an action happens. Most of these adverbs end with the letters *ly*.

EXAMPLES: slowly, neatly, cleverly, loudly

Other adverbs tell *when* or *where* an action happens.

EXAMPLES: never, later, often, soon, here, around, over, down

A. Underline the adverb in each sentence. Then write whether the adverb tells *how, when,* or *where*.

_____ 1. Yesterday Mitsy and I went for a walk.

_____ 2. We met eagerly at the elevator in our building.

_____ 3. Down we went in the elevator.

_____ 4. Soon we were on the main floor.

_____ 5. Mitsy raced wildly to the front door.

_____ 6. I followed briskly.

_____ 7. Outside a breeze blew.

_____ 8. It tugged playfully at our hair.

_____ 9. We skipped gleefully along the street.

_____ 10. There we saw an amazing thing.

B. Complete the sentences with adverbs that tell *how, when* or *where*.

11. A man walked _____ with a duck.   (where)

12. He looked so funny we laughed _____.   (how)

13. People stopped _____ to look at them.   (where)

14. _____ the man popped a rabbit out of his pocket.   (when)

15. He held it _____ in his hand.   (how)

Name _____

Adjectives and Adverbs pages 172–173

Adjectives and adverbs are describing words. Adjectives describe nouns. Adverbs tell more about verbs. Use an adjective when you are describing a noun. Use an adverb when you are telling about a verb.

A. Underline the adjective or adverb to complete each sentence correctly.

1. The bus zoomed by (quick, quickly).
2. Jonathan, a (good, well) runner, chased after it.
3. At the next block the (heavy, heavily) bus stopped at a light.
4. The driver took a (quick, quickly) look in her mirror.
5. She saw Jonathan dashing (wild, wildly) to catch the bus.
6. The bus turned (slow, slowly) into the bus stop.
7. The (friend, friendly) driver opened the door.
8. Jonathan poked his hand (slow, slowly) into his pocket.
9. "Oh, no," he said (sad, sadly). "My money is gone."
10. "Don't worry," said the (nice, nicely) driver. "You worked hard for this ride so you ride free."

B. Tell whether each underlined word is an adjective or adverb.

_____ 11. finally left	_____ 12. drove well
_____ 13. the kindest boy	_____ 14. a yellow ticket
_____ 15. an old bus	_____ 16. the heaviest suitcase
_____ 17. a good seat	_____ 18. waited outside
_____ 19. walked carefully	_____ 20. a good trip

C. Use some of the sentence parts from Practice B. Write a short story about a bus ride.

_____

_____

_____

_____

Name _____

Homographs pages 176–177

⎧ ● **Homographs** are words that have the same
  spelling. They have different meanings. Sometimes
  homographs have different pronunciations.

  EXAMPLE: The <u>wind</u> blew the line as I tried to <u>wind</u> in my
            fishing reel. ⎫

A. Choose the correct definition of the word *bowl* from these
dictionary entries. Write the definition on the line.

1. The <u>bowl</u> was filled with apples.

   _____

2. I <u>bowl</u> a score of 135.

   _____

> **bowl**[1] [bōl] *n.* 1 A rounded,
> rather deep dish. 2 The
> amount a bowl will hold: a
> *bowl* of water. 3 Anything
> shaped like a bowl: the *bowl*
> of a pipe. —**bowl′ful′** *n.*
> **bowl**[2] [bōl] 1 *v.* To play at
> bowling or bowls. 2 *n.* The
> ball used in bowls. 3 *v.* To
> move swiftly: to *bowl along.*
> —**bowl′·er** *n.*

B. Underline the homographs in the following sets of
sentences.

3. A live coal shot from the fireplace.
   I live in a house on Perry Street.
4. The dog's bark frightened the child.
   The bark of this tree is rough and bumpy.
5. Is it fair to make him stay at home?
   The county fair is the event of the year in my town.
6. The fine for parking here is five dollars.
   It was a fine, sunny day.

C. Choose two homographs from the list. Write two sentences
for each using different meanings of the word.

   tire   wound   bow   wind   match   fan

7. _____

   _____

8. _____

   _____

Name _____

Synonyms and Antonyms pages 178–181

> ● **Synonyms** are words having the same or almost the same meaning. **Antonyms** are words having opposite meanings.
>
> *EXAMPLE:* The words friend and pal are synonyms. The words friend and enemy are antonyms.

A. Match the synonyms.

1. cap   money   4. jump   leap   7. pick   platter
2. big   large   5. keep   nearly   8. plate   untrue
3. cash   hat   6. almost   save   9. false   choose

B. Match the antonyms.

10. full   open   13. win   tell   16. lose   loud
11. closed   empty   14. rapid   lose   17. soft   sell
12. lead   follow   15. ask   slow   18. buy   find

C. Write a synonym (S) or an antonym (A) for each word.

19. cowardly _____ (A)   20. discover _____ (S)

21. above _____ (S)   22. question _____ (A)

23. automobile _____ (S)   24. weary _____ (S)

25. absent _____ (A)   26. most _____ (A)

Make the *cowardly* lion *bold!*   L I O N
Change only one letter for each new word.

A bird (rhymes with *moon*):   __ __ __ __

Stop, _____, and listen: __ __ __ __

Catch a fish with a _____: __ __ __ __

The engine is under the _____ of a car   __ __ __ __
(rhymes with *good*):

I want to _____ your hand: __ __ __ __

The antonym of *cowardly*:   __ __ __ __

Name _____

Combining Sentences with Adjectives pages 182–183

When adjectives in several sentences describe the same noun, you can combine the sentences. Use all the adjectives in one sentence. Use commas to separate three or more adjectives in a row.

EXAMPLE: The apple is <u>red</u>.
The apple is <u>shiny</u>.
The apple is <u>crisp</u>.
The apple is <u>red</u>, <u>shiny</u>, **and** <u>crisp</u>.

Combine each set of sentences into one sentence. Write the sentence on the line.

1. I am a round fruit.
    I am an orange fruit.
    I am a juicy fruit.

    _____

    _____

2. Slice me from a long loaf.
    Slice me from a fat loaf.
    Slice me from a soft loaf.

    _____

    _____

3. This fizzy drink is cold.
    This refreshing drink is cold.
    This orange drink is cold.

    _____

    _____

4. Scoop me into a cone in different flavors.
    Scoop me into a cone in frosty flavors.
    Scoop me into a cone in delicious flavors.

    _____

    _____

Name _____

5. This tasty drink is hot.
   This chocolate drink is hot.

   _____

   _____

6. I am a potato fried into narrow strips.
   I am a potato fried into crisp strips.
   I am a potato fried into salty strips.

   _____

   _____

7. I am a smooth spread for bread.
   I am a sticky spread for bread.
   I am a peanutty spread for bread.

   _____

   _____

8. My crust is covered with red sauce.
   My crust is covered with tomato sauce.

   _____

   _____

9. This fruit is long.
   This fruit is thin.
   This fruit is yellow.

   _____

   _____

10. Use three adjectives to write a sentence about
    your favorite food or drink.

    _____

    _____

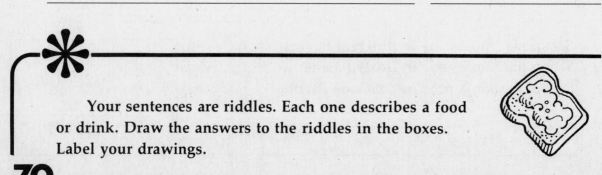

Your sentences are riddles. Each one describes a food
or drink. Draw the answers to the riddles in the boxes.
Label your drawings.

Descriptive Paragraphs pages 184–185

When you write a descriptive paragraph, remember to indent the first sentence. Begin with a topic sentence telling what the paragraph is about. Add detail sentences. In them use colorful and lively words to describe the topic. Make an exact picture with the words you choose. Keep to the topic, and use good sentence order.

A. Add adjectives and adverbs to this paragraph. Use synonyms for the underlined words. You may want to use a dictionary or a thesaurus to help you.

A _____ rainstorm <u>went</u> over the _____,

_____ town. The _____ rain <u>came</u> from

the _____ sky. It swept _____ across the

_____ hills in _____ sheets.

_____ torrents of water _____ filled the

<u>roaring</u> brooks and streams before the storm _____ stopped.

B. Write a descriptive paragraph about this picture.

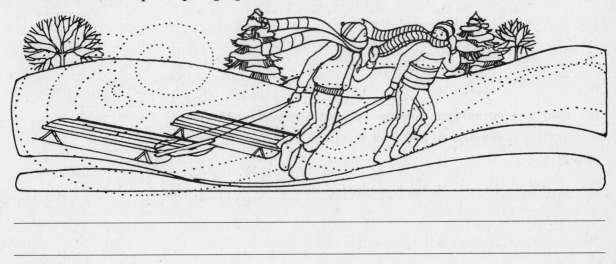

_____

_____

_____

_____

_____

_____

Name _____

Editing Descriptive Paragraphs page 186

Study the editing marks. Use them as you edit
descriptive paragraphs. Add interesting adjectives
and adverbs to make your descriptions colorful and
more exact.

Editing Marks	
≡	capitalize
⊙	make a period
∧	add something
⟨	add a comma
⟩⟩	add quotation marks
⌐	take something away
◯	spell correctly
¶	indent the paragraph
/	make a lower case letter
tr ∿	transpose

**A. This descriptive paragraph has been edited. Rewrite
it correctly. Make all the changes and additions shown.**

Bud ~~staired~~ *stared uneasily* at the funny old key. It felt heavy in his hand. What lock could it fit? ∧ *Suddenly* Bud felt as if he were being watched. He ~~looked~~ *glanced* quickly toward the ∧*attic* window. He was just in time to see the ∧*tattered* ~~curtin~~ *curtain* lowered. Bud no longer felt safe∧*calm, or sure*.

_____
_____
_____
_____
_____

**B. Edit this paragraph. Correct two misspelled words. Add
interesting verbs and describing words. Then rewrite the
paragraph.**

Bud's shirt was wet with swet. He looked behind him as

he went on. The people were coming closer. Bud felt scared .
He tried to think of a way to exscape.

_____
_____
_____
_____

Writing Dates and Times of Day

page 187

Mechanics Practice

- **Begin the name of a month with a capital letter.**

- **Put a comma between the day and the year in a date.**

- **Put a colon between the hour and the minute in the time of day.**

- **Put a period after the abbreviations A.M. and P.M.**

EXAMPLE: The record was set on June 4, 1783, at 10:00 A.M.

A. Write these dates correctly.

1. february 3 1920 _____   2. january 29 1959 _____

3. march 28 1944 _____   4. july 4 1983 _____

5. february 21 1941 _____   6. may 30 1985 _____

7. january 31 1951 _____   8. january 1 2000 _____

B. Write these times correctly.

9. 8 00 am _____   10. 12 00 pm _____   11. 11 45 pm _____

12. 2 45 pm _____   13. 1 15 pm _____   14. 4 30 pm _____

C. Show where capital letters, periods, and commas are needed in these sentences. Write the sentences correctly on a separate piece of paper.

15. I visit my grandfather in Oregon every january.

16. Around 8 15 am Grandpa takes me for a ride.

17. We go to a fruit stand that has been there since july 4 1929.

18. We play shuffleboard from 10 00 am until 12 00 pm.

19. At 12 00 pm Grandpa makes sandwiches.

20. Then at 1 30 pm every day he does volunteer work.

Name _____

Description in Poetry pages 188–189

Poets use words to describe ordinary things in a new or different way. Read this descriptive poem.

Giraffes

I like them.
Ask me why.
    Because they hold their heads so high.
    Because their necks stretch to the sky.
    Because they're quiet, calm, and shy.
    Because they run so fast they fly.
    Because their eyes are velvet brown.
    Because their coats are spotted tan.
    Because they eat the tops of trees.
    Because their legs have knobby knees.
    Because
    Because
    Because. That's why
I like giraffes.

MARY ANN HOBERMAN

A. Answer each question with a complete sentence. Tell how the poet describes each part of the giraffe.

1. How do giraffes hold their heads? _____

_____

2. How do giraffes run? _____

3. What do the giraffe's eyes look like? _____

_____

4. What does the giraffe's coat look like? _____

_____

5. What do the giraffe's legs look like? _____

_____

B. Think of an animal you like. Write five words to describe this animal. Then use the words in a poem of your own. Write the poem on a separate piece of paper.

74 UNIT 5: Workbook

Comparison in Poetry pages 190–191

A poet sometimes describes things by comparing them. If two things have something in common, they can be compared. Some comparisons use the words *like* or *as*.

A.   Read this poem about the sun. Then answer the questions using complete sentences.

Sun

The sun
Is a leaping fire
Too hot
To go near,

But it will still
Lie down
In warm yellow squares
On the floor

Like a flat
Quilt, where
The cat can curl
And purr.

VALERIE WORTH

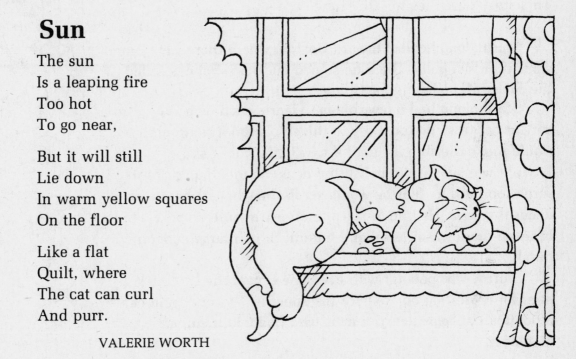

1.   In the first four lines, with what is the sun compared?

_____

2.   How are these two things alike?

_____

3.   In the next eight lines with what is the sun compared?

_____

4.   How does the poem say these two things are alike?

_____

B.   Read these groups of words. Use adjectives to complete the comparisons.

5.   as _____ as a kitten   6.   as _____ as a rock

Name _____

Description in a Tall Tale pages 192–195

Tall tales are stories that stretch the truth. When you stretch a fact so much that it can no longer possibly be true, you are exaggerating.

Read this tall tale about Alfred Bulltop Stormalong. He became a Massachusetts sea captain. He was a very big man. This story describes his first time on a ship.

Stormalong headed toward Boston, where there were more ships than sea gulls. There he signed on to a schooner called the *Silver Maid,* bound for China.

Stormalong had a few things to learn, such as being careful not to stand too close to the ship's rail. His weight would make the ship list until it was in danger of sinking. When it was his turn to polish the deck, he took pains not to scrub too hard for fear he would scrub the whole ship out from under the crew. He had to sleep in an extra-large lifeboat because there wasn't a sailor's hammock half large enough for him.

Stormy was popular with everyone except the cook. It was hard for a growing boy to curb his appetite. Stormy could eat a boatload of eggs, plus the hens who had laid them, for breakfast.

ADRIEN STOUTENBURG

Read these facts about Stormalong. After each one tell how the author exaggerated the fact.

1. Stormalong was strong. _____

_____

2. Stormalong was big. _____

_____

3. Stormalong liked to eat. _____

_____

4. Stormalong weighed a lot. _____

_____

Name _____

Unit Review

A. Underline the adjectives in each sentence.

1. Hal had fifty balloons for his party.
2. There were red and blue balloons.
3. Hanging from the high ceiling were striped balloons.
4. Hal had a delicious cake and cold ice cream.

B. Underline the correct adjective in each sentence.

5. Yesterday was the (hotter, hottest) day of the summer.
6. We wore our (lighter, lightest) clothes.
7. Today I stayed at the beach (longer, longest) than yesterday.

C. Fill in the blanks with the correct articles.

8. _____ men came to move the house.

9. They used machines to lift it onto _____ truck.

10. The truck started up and turned at _____ angle.

D. Underline the adverb in each sentence. Then write whether it tells *how, when,* or *where*.

11. The puck slid smoothly across the ice. _____

12. Amy skated quickly after it. _____

13. Karen awoke early. _____

14. She sat up in bed. _____

E. Use *good* or *well* in each sentence.

15. Dr. Steven's patient had a _____ day.

16. He had eaten a _____ dinner.

17. He slept _____ last night.

F. Underline the words that are homographs in the sentences.

18. She held a plaster palm tree in the palm of her hand.
19. He will rest while the rest of us go to lunch.
20. The innkeeper was host to a host of people.

Name _____

Unit Review

G. Write *antonym* next to each pair of antonyms. Write *synonym* next to each pair of synonyms.

21. yell/scream _____

22. mild/spicy _____

23. bad/awful _____

24. dark/light _____

H. Use commas and the word *and* where needed. Combine these sentences into one sentence.

25. Jessica has blue crayons. Jessica has yellow crayons.

Jessica has orange crayons. _____

_____

_____

26. The maple syrup was warm. The maple syrup was sticky. The maple

syrup was delicious. _____

_____

_____

I. Complete these comparisons.

27. as tall as _____

28. as sticky as _____

29. as rich as _____

30. as green as _____

31. as heavy as _____

J. Complete these exaggerations about tall tale characters.

32. Paul Bunyan was so hungry _____

_____

33. Paul's ox Babe was so strong _____

_____

78 UNIT 5: Workbook

Name _____

Pronouns pages 202–203

> ● A **pronoun** is a word used in place of a noun or nouns. The words *I, me, you, it, he, she, her, him, they,* and *them* are pronouns.
> *EXAMPLE:* Jesse cut the pictures, and then <u>he</u> pasted <u>them</u>.
> The words *he* and *them* are pronouns. *He* stands for *Jesse. Them* refers to *pictures.*

A.   Underline the pronouns in the sentences.

1.   Inez smiled as she turned the finished pages of the scrapbook.
2.   She showed me the three pages with pictures from summer camp.
3.   They were pictures of her and me in costumes.
4.   Jesse laughed at them.
5.   We noticed he quickly turned the pages that had pictures of him.
6.   Inez and I like to decorate the scrapbook pages with crayons.
7.   You should see the fancy lettering we have done on some pages.
8.   It really makes the pages colorful, so reading them is more fun.
9.   She told us about a special handwriting course she was taking.
10.   I asked her if I could take it too.

B.   Read these pairs of sentences. In the second sentence of each pair underline the pronoun. Then write the pronoun and the noun for which it stands.

11.   Geoffrey collects baseball cards. He has 58 cards.

_____

12.   Anita's teammates won all their games. They are league champions.

_____

Name _____

Subject Pronouns pages 204–205

● Sometimes a pronoun takes the place of the subject of the sentence. The words *I, you, he, she, we, they,* and *it* are **subject pronouns.**

EXAMPLES: <u>Max</u> is so excited.
<u>He</u> is going to the circus on Saturday.

A.   Read each sentence. Use a subject pronoun to replace the underlined noun or nouns.

_____   1.   <u>Max and his brother</u> went to the circus.

_____   2.   <u>Max</u> heads directly for the magician's tent.

_____   3.   Max thought to himself, "<u>My brother</u> really wants to see the lions instead."

_____   4.   "<u>The magician's tent</u> is over here," Max said.

_____   5.   "<u>The magician</u> is really super. I've seen her perform before," Max told his brother.

B.   Use a subject pronoun in the second sentence of each pair.

6.   <u>The magician and her helper</u> came onto the stage.

_____ bowed to the audience.

7.   <u>The magician</u> took out a magic hat.

_____ showed it to the audience.

8.   <u>The hat</u> was black.

_____ was empty inside.

9.   <u>The magician's helper, Sid,</u> took the hat.

_____ held it as the magician tapped it three times.

10.   <u>A rabbit</u> popped out of the hat.

_____ hopped off the stage.

80   UNIT 6:   Workbook

Name _____

Pronouns After Action Verbs
pages 206–207

> ● Sometimes pronouns replace nouns that follow action verbs. The words *me, you, him, her, it, us,* and *them* are pronouns that follow action verbs.
>
> EXAMPLES: Sal saw <u>Jason and Al</u>. Sal saw <u>them</u>.
> Sal told <u>Jason</u> about the game. Sal told <u>him</u> about the game.

A. Underline the pronoun that follows the action verb in each sentence.

1. Mother helped me pack for my trip.
2. She and Dad drove us to the station.
3. Jill and I thanked them.
4. Then we watched them through the window of the train.
5. They saw us waving as the train left for San Francisco.

B. Use a pronoun after the action verb in the second sentence of each pair.

6. My cousin Sal met <u>Jill and me</u> in San Francisco.

   Sal took _____ everywhere.

7. We saw <u>boats and trolleys</u>.

   We rode _____ too.

8. Sometimes we left <u>Sal</u>.

   We would meet _____ later in the day.

9. Jill and I wandered all over <u>the city</u>.

   In no time we knew _____ very well.

10. One day by chance I spotted my long lost friend, <u>Elsie</u>.

    I was thrilled to see _____.

11. When I returned home I said good-by to <u>Jill</u>.

    I was sad to leave _____.

12. I told my <u>mother, father, sister, and brother</u> about the trip.

    I told _____ about the city.

Name _____

Possessive Pronouns
pages 208–209

> ● Some pronouns show who or what owns or has something. These are called **possessive pronouns.** They are used in place of possessive nouns. The words *my, your, his, her, our, their,* and *its* are possessive pronouns.
>
> EXAMPLES: Marie said, "I lost <u>my</u> notebook."
> Phil answered, "I think it is in <u>your</u> locker."

A. Read the sentences. Underline the correct possessive pronoun.

1. Marie: Hi Peter. Are you ready for (our, her) gym class?
2. Peter: Yes, except I can not find (their, my) tennis racket.
3. Marie: There's Phil. Why don't you borrow (its, his) racket.
4. Peter: You know (its, our) teacher likes us to remember our things.
5. Marie: Then let us go find Mr. Franks. Maybe it is in (his, their) Lost and Found closet.

B. Rewrite the sentences. Use possessive pronouns for the underlined words.

6. Karen and Seth found <u>Karen and Seth's</u> bat.

   _____

7. I am Emily. I found <u>Emily's</u> boot.

   _____

8. Peter found <u>Peter's</u> paintbrush.

   _____

9. Mr. Kilpatrick found <u>Mr. Kilpatrick's</u> wallet.

   _____

10. Mrs. Drake found <u>Mrs. Drake's</u> key.

   _____

Look at the picture again. Find the team's baseball bat, Emily's boot, Peter's paintbrush, Mr. Kilpatrick's wallet, and Mrs. Drake's key. Circle these items as you find them.

Choosing a Topic pages 216-217

Remember when you choose a report topic to choose a topic that interests you. Limit your topic so that it is not too big or too small. The whole report should be about the topic. Be sure you can tell about your topic in a short report. Ask yourself this question: Can I tell about this topic in two or three paragraphs?

A. For each group choose the topic that would make the best short report.

1. The Story of Birds
   Nest Building of the Barn Swallow
   Bird Migration

2. Desert Plants
   Growing Plants
   The Saugaro Cactus

3. Sports
   The Boyhood of Lee Trevino
   Golf Throughout History

4. Famous Singers
   Ella Fitzgerald
   Women Singers

5. Flowering Plants
   The American Beauty Rose
   Kinds and Colors of Roses

6. Dogs That Work
   Guide Dogs for the Blind
   Breeds of Dogs

B. For each idea write a smaller topic that you could use for a report.

7. Water Sports _____

8. Astronauts _____

9. Games _____

10. Kinds of Food _____

11. The Olympics _____

12. Hobbies _____

13. Forms of Travel _____

14. Places to Visit _____

15. Pets _____

16. Careers _____

17. Winter Sports _____

18. Kinds of Music _____

Name _____

Taking Notes pages 218–219

Remember to do these things when you take notes. List the title of the book, the author, and the page number on which you find information. Write only facts you want to include in your report. Write the information in your own words. Write sentences or write short groups of words.

A. Read the paragraph. Write five facts you could use in a report about the jobs of a uniformed police officer.

Officers in uniform have many duties. Most important of all is to help protect people. Officers direct traffic and help children get to and from school. They also enforce parking, speed, and safety laws. Some of these officers keep crowds in order.

1. _____

2. _____

3. _____

4. _____

5. _____

B. Read the paragraph. Write five facts you could use in a report about the training of a police officer.

It takes a lot of hard work and training to become a police officer. The first step is to attend the police academy. Here men and women learn wrestling, judo, first aid, and the law of their area. They learn how to defend themselves, gather clues, and take fingerprints. Some police officers learn special skills such as how to pilot a helicopter, or how to ride a horse or a motorcycle.

6. _____

7. _____

8. _____

9. _____

10. _____

_____

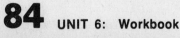
84 UNIT 6: Workbook

Making an Outline pages 220–221

An **outline** is a way to organize notes for a report. The title tells the topic of the report. Main topics are listed with a Roman numeral and a period. They begin with a capital letter. Subtopics are the facts about each main topic. Subtopics are indented under the main topic. They are listed with a capital letter and a period.

A. Use the notes. Fill in the outline.

Title: Flatboats
Main topics: How flatboats move
How parts of the flatboat are used

Subtopics:
Small wooden cabin where family lives
Furniture and food stored in cabin
Carried by river current
Livestock carried on deck
Long pole used to push and guide
Has no motor or sails

_____

I. _____

   A. _____

   B. _____

   C. _____

II. _____

   A. _____

   B. _____

   C. _____

Name _____

B. Read each set of notes. For each, write the title, main
topics, and subtopics in outline form.

1. Title: Canoes   **Subtopics:**
   Main Topics: Bow stroke moves canoe forward
   How a canoe is paddled   Life jacket or float pillow
   Equipment for a canoe   Coffee can or pump for bailing
                                    J-stroke helps hold a straight course

_____

I. _____

   A. _____

   B. _____

II. _____

   A. _____

   B. _____

2. Title: Tankers   **Subtopics:**
   Main topics: Liquefied natural gas carriers
   Kinds of tankers   Deckhouse for crew
   Structure of tankers   Many tanks in hull for cargo
                                    Oil tankers for oil, gasoline, kerosene
                                    Pumps and pipes on main deck
                                    Oil and bulk-oil carriers for oil and coal

_____

I. _____

   A. _____

   B. _____

   C. _____

II. _____

   A. _____

   B. _____

   C. _____

Name _____

Research Reports   pages 222–223

When you write a research report, use the title and notes from your outline. Write a paragraph for each main topic in your outline. Write a topic sentence for each main topic. Write detail sentences for the subtopics. Indent the first word of each paragraph.

Read the outline about chimpanzees. Write a report using the outline. Remember to begin a new paragraph for each main topic.

Chimpanzees

I. How a chimpanzee looks
   A. Vary in height from 3¼ feet to 5½ feet
   B. Weigh 90 to 110 pounds
   C. Body is covered with long black hair
   D. Have no tails
II. Chimpanzee communication
   A. Communicate with noises such as barks, grunts, and screams
   B. Hoot loudly when food is found
   C. Use facial expressions to show fear and anger

_____

_____

_____

_____

_____

_____

_____

_____

_____

_____

_____

Editing Reports page 224

Edit your research reports after you write them. Check all your facts, especially numbers, names, and dates. Use editing marks to show changes and corrections.

	Editing Marks
≡	capitalize
⊙	make a period
∧	add something
⋏	add a comma
⌄⌄	add quotation marks
ꝺ	take something away
◯	spell correctly
¶	indent the paragraph
/	make a lower case letter
tr ∼	transpose

A.   Study this part of an outline for a report.

Fire Fighters Yesterday and Today
I. History of fire fighting
   A. Ancient Egypt had volunteer fire fighters
   B. London fire in 1666 destroyed 13,000 buildings
   C. Steam fire engine used in Ohio in 1852 to
   ~~D. Helped~~ get water to fires more quickly

B.   Read the first paragraph of the report based on the outline above. Recopy the edited paragraph correctly.

Fire Fighters Yesterday and Today

People have always known about the danger of fire. Ancient ~~Greece~~ (Egypt) had ~~voluntere~~ (volunteer) fire fighters. In ~~1699~~ (1666) a fire in London destroyed ~~1300~~ (13,000) buildings. Not until 1852 was a steam (fire) engine used in ~~Iowa~~ (Ohio). It helped get water to fires (much more quickly).

_____

_____

_____

_____

_____

_____

_____

Writing Titles page 225
Mechanics Practice

● **Use a capital letter to begin the first, last, and all important words in the title of a book, report, story, poem, song, or television show.**

● **Underline the title of a book or report.**

● **Put quotation marks before and after the title of a story, poem, song, or television show.**

EXAMPLE: In the book <u>Songs America Sings</u> there is a song called "Clementine."

A. Write these titles correctly.

1. ecology today (book)

_____

2. sesame street (TV show)

_____

3. making time count (report)

_____

4. a spring day (poem)

_____

5. frontier world (TV show)

_____

6. barbara allen (song)

_____

7. profiles in sports (book)

_____

8. tomorrow (song)

_____

9. anne of green gables (book)

_____

10. microscopic animals (report)

_____

B. Add capital letters, underlines, and quotation marks where they are needed. Then write the sentences correctly on a separate piece of paper.

11. We are reading the book rabbit hill in class.

12. Every evening at camp we sing god bless america.

13. Do you know the poem the children's hour?

14. Last year we read the story my first friend.

A Magazine Article   pages 228–231

Magazines have a variety of features. They have stories, poems, even puzzles and games. They also have articles. An **article** is a nonfiction feature. Articles give interesting information about many different topics.

Read the article. Then answer the questions.

What Makes Rainbows?

by Mark C. Blazek

How many times have you seen a rainbow appear magically in the sky? Of course, it isn't really magic. A rainbow forms when the sun is shining at the same time that rain is falling. Rainbows are seen only when the sun is low in the sky. An afternoon rainbow means that the sun is shining in the west and that showers are falling in the east. A morning rainbow appears when there is rain in the west.

Rainbows form because sunlight is really a mixture of many colors. When a ray of sunlight shines on a raindrop, the raindrop acts like a prism, a tool used to separate the colors of sunlight. A prism breaks the light apart. The raindrops break the sunbeam up into these colors: red, orange, yellow, green, blue, indigo, and violet. Then these colors are reflected back to you as by a mirror.

When a single rainbow arches across the sky, red is always on the outside of the band and violet is always on the inside. If you are lucky, you might see a second rainbow form outside the first. This second rainbow is always fainter than the first one, with red on the INSIDE of the color band.

If you are on a high mountain late in the afternoon, you can even see a rainbow in the form of a full circle.

A rainbow forms only when all the conditions are just right. It is one of the most beautiful sights in nature. According to an old legend, at the end of every rainbow there is a pot of gold. But who needs a pot of gold when we have the beauty of the rainbow itself?

Name _____

A. **Answer each question using information from the article.**

1. Which would be a good title for a report based on this article?

    _____ Sunlight in a Mixture of Colors

    _____ How Rainbows Are Formed

    _____ A Pot of Gold

2. Which three of these statements might be used in a factual report about rainbows?

    _____ There are always the same colors in a rainbow.

    _____ Rainbows form when it is raining while the sun is shining.

    _____ There may be a pot of gold at the end of a rainbow.

    _____ Rainbows are seen only when the sun is low in the sky.

3. Which two topics could you write about using facts from this article?

    _____ When Rainbows Appear   _____ What Makes a Rainbow

    _____ The Gold Diggers   _____ Where the Rainbow Ends

4. If you were writing a report about why rainbows form, which paragraph

    would you use? _____

5. If you were writing a report about morning and afternoon rainbows, which

    paragraph would you use? _____

6. If you were writing a report about double rainbows, which paragraph

    would you use? _____

7. If you were writing a report about how a raindrop acts like a prism, which

    paragraph would you use? _____

B. **To show that you learned the way sunlight separates, draw
    and color a rainbow using the information from the article.**

Name _____

Unit Review

A. Underline the pronoun in each sentence.

1. After the holiday party we went home.
2. He had eaten too much.
3. She had eaten three pieces of pie.
4. Ted told them not to eat so much.

B. Write a subject pronoun that stands for the word in parentheses ( ).

5. _____ went to the swimming pool. (Mary)

6. _____ was there and so was Sophie. (Carlos)

7. Then _____ arrived. (Ted and Art)

8. _____ was filled with people. (the swimming pool)

9. Maggie lent _____ a magazine. (Anne)

10. Agnes gave _____ the book. (Richard)

11. Otto brought _____ the same book. (Ted and me)

12. I borrowed _____ from the library. (the book)

C. Underline the possessive pronoun in each sentence.

13. Is that your collie?
14. My dog is in the car.
15. We thought her poodles were lost.

D. Underline the topic in each group that would be the best topic for a short report.

16. Tigers of the World   17. How a Baseball Is Made
     Where Tigers Live   All About Baseball
     Tigers   Sports in Today's World

E. Pretend you are writing a report about the training of a knight. Check two questions that relate to the topic.

18. _____ What did knights have to learn about using a bow and arrow?

19. _____ How many battles did knights fight in?

20. _____ How did knights protect the castle?

21. _____ What did knights have to learn about riding horses?

F. 22. On a separate piece of paper write an outline from these notes.

Main Topics:
Learning about the bow and arrow
Learning about riding horses

Subtopics:
Bow was called a crossbow
Knights learned to ride with one hand to
keep the weapon arm free
Knights trained horses not to fear loud noises
Knights learned to use crossbows in battle
Knights learned to ride wearing clumsy armor

G. 23. Write a two-paragraph report from your outline about the training of a knight. Write the report on a separate piece of paper. Include a title for your report.

H. Read this article to find information on tigers as hunters.

  Many tigers live in the jungle. Tigers are beautiful animals. They eat other animals. They have soft padded toes so that they can sneak up on these animals. Hidden in these toes are the tiger's sharp claws. When the tiger needs its claws to catch prey, they are ready and sharp.

Check each fact from the article you would use to write a report called Tigers as Hunters.

24. _____ Tiger's toes are soft so that they can sneak up on other animals.

25. _____ Tigers have sharp claws.

26. _____ Tigers live in the jungle.

27. _____ Tigers are beautiful animals.

Name _____

Simple Subjects   pages 240–241

> ● The **simple subject** is the one word that tells
> whom or what the sentence is about. It may name a
> person, place, or thing.
> *EXAMPLE:* A big <u>storm</u> ended our game.
> *Storm* is the simple subject. *A big storm* is the complete
> subject.

A. Draw a line under the complete subject in each sentence.
Then circle the simple subject.

1. The big jet landed at the airport.
2. A furry panda was taken off the plane.
3. The panda's name was Cha-Cha.
4. He was going to the San Diego Zoo.
5. The people were very excited.
6. Most Americans had few chances to see panda bears.
7. Poor little Cha-Cha was very frightened at first.
8. He missed his home at the zoo in China.
9. Cha-Cha was as happy as could be a few days later.
10. Ling-Ling was waiting for him in San Diego.

B. Add a complete subject to each sentence. Then underline
the simple subject of each sentence.

11. _____ have interesting pets.
12. _____ is a colorful bird.
13. _____ own snakes and lizards.
14. _____ sleeps during the day.
15. _____ lives in a fish tank.
16. _____ is my favorite pet.

Name _____

Simple Predicates pages 242–243

> • The **simple predicate** is the key word or words in
> the complete predicate. The simple predicate is an
> action verb or a linking verb together with any helping
> verbs.
> *EXAMPLE:* Jesse and I will shop for my mom.
> *Will shop* is the simple predicate. *Will shop for my mom*
> is the complete predicate.

A. Draw two lines under the complete predicate in each
sentence. Then circle the simple predicate.

1. Chin stays at my house. (4)
2. He and I go to the grocery store. (2)
3. Chin uses my brother's bike. (1)
4. We raced all the way over. (2)
5. Many people are there already. (2)
6. Everyone likes the new grocery carts. (4)
7. A clerk grinds coffee for the customer. (1)
8. Chin carried a large package home. (3)
9. He eats an apple every day. (1)
10. He has a pear too. (2)
11. I try the peaches instead. (1)

B. Add a complete predicate to each sentence. Then draw
two lines under the simple predicate of each sentence.

12. This Saturday I _____.

13. At the store we _____.

14. The store _____.

Look at the number after each sentence in Practice A. If it is a 1,
circle the first letter in the simple predicate in that sentence. If it is a 2,
circle the second letter. If it is a 3, circle the third letter. If it is a 4,
circle the fourth letter. Do all eleven. What do the letters spell?

___ ___ ___ ___   ___ ___ ___ ___ ___ ___ ___.

Name _____

Subject-Verb Agreement
pages 244–245

- Most verbs have one form that agrees with singular subjects. Another form agrees with plural subjects.
EXAMPLE: John <u>looks</u> at the sunset.
John and Jane <u>look</u> at the sunset.

- Most present tense verbs agree with singular subjects by adding s. EXAMPLE: John <u>looks</u> at the sunset.

- Present tense verbs that end in ss, ch, x, or sh agree with singular subjects by adding es.
EXAMPLE: John <u>washes</u> the car.

A. Underline the form of the verb that agrees with the subject. Choose from the words in parentheses ( ).

1. Every year the Animal Help House (hold, holds) a party.
2. Staff members (invite, invites) everyone to attend.
3. The party (begin, begins) at 3:00 P.M.
4. The Animal Help House (stand, stands) at 49 Center Avenue.
5. The president, Mr. Fernandez, (plan, plans) to give a short speech.
6. Then a tour (begin, begins).
7. Forty dogs now (stay, stays) in the main building.
8. Some cats (live, lives) there too.
9. We (hope, hopes) to find all of them homes.
10. After the tour we (ask, asks) guests to stay for refreshments.

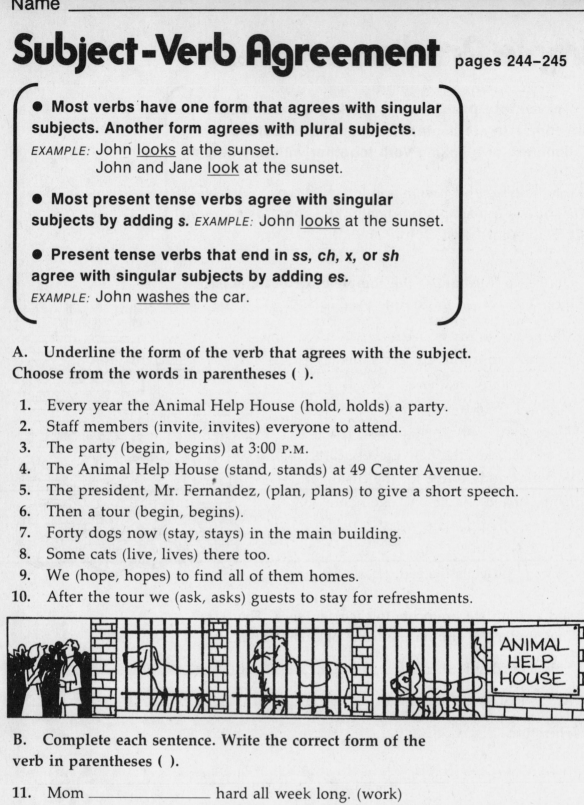

B. Complete each sentence. Write the correct form of the verb in parentheses ( ).

11. Mom _____ hard all week long. (work)

12. We _____ her study door on tiptoe. (pass)

13. My little sister Pat sometimes _____ the door open. (push)

14. She _____ Mom working at her desk. (see)

15. Sometimes Pat _____ Mom to play with her. (ask)

96 UNIT 7: Workbook

Name _____

Word Order in Sentences pages 246–247

Sometimes you can change the order of the words in a sentence. You can make a statement using words from a question.

EXAMPLE: Will Hilda sing the song? Hilda will sing the song.

The words *yes* or *no* are sometimes included in answers to questions. A comma follows the words *yes* or *no*.

EXAMPLE: Yes, Hilda will sing the song.

A. Write an answer to each question by changing the word order. Begin your answer with *yes* or *no*.

1. Is Hilda going to be in the play? (yes) _____

_____

2. Will she sing with Antonio? (no) _____

_____

3. Are they going to play instruments? (yes) _____

_____

4. Will Hilda play the piano? (no) _____

_____

5. Has Antonio found his guitar? (yes) _____

_____

6. Was it in the hall closet? (yes) _____

_____

B. Write two yes/no questions about a talent of someone you know. Then write two statements that answer the questions.

7. _____

_____

8. _____

_____

Name _____

Prefixes and Suffixes pages 250–253

(• A **prefix** is a letter or group of letters added to
the beginning of a base word. *EXAMPLE:* <u>un</u>kind

• A **suffix** is a letter or group of letters added to
the end of a base word. *EXAMPLE:* watch<u>ful</u>)

Prefixes and suffixes can change the meaning of the base word.

A. Underline each base word. Circle each prefix or suffix.

1. disconnect
2. impatient
3. breakable
4. incorrect
5. singer
6. helpful
7. misprint
8. careless
9. director
10. nonfiction
11. prepaid
12. reread

B. Choose a word from Practice A to use in each sentence.

13. This delicate vase is very _____ .

14. The tickets for the train ride were _____ .

15. Please _____ the toaster before you clean it.

16. A biography will always be in the _____ section.

17. Sometimes I am _____ with my little brother.

18. You had better _____ the chapter before the test.

19. "I believe this total is _____," said the banker.

20. You have been very _____ to me with this job.

21. I think there is a _____ on this page.

22. Charlie is the most _____ person I know.

23. She is studying to be a great opera _____ .

24. Who is the _____ of the new movie?

Name _____

Compound Words pages 254-255

Some words are made by putting two smaller words together. The new word is a **compound word**.

A. Underline the compound words in the story.

"You are lower than an earthworm," Toby Tyler told Maggie. "You are a real rattlesnake in the crabgrass."

"I did not take your goldfish, Toby," said Maggie. "Do not try to put me in handcuffs."

"Well, who was the underhanded groundhog that did it?" Toby asked.

"It was your greyhound dog," Maggie answered. "She ate your whole fishbowl this afternoon."

B. Complete each sentence with a compound word. Put two words together from the box to make each compound word.

roof	coats
every	berry
out	body
rain	doors
blue	top

1. _____ come into the house.

2. It is raining too hard _____.

3. Put your _____ on the porch to dry.

4. We will make a _____ pie.

5. Listen to the rain on the _____.

C. Write a paragraph. Use these and other compound words.
classroom, chalkboard, afternoon, bookcase, workbook

_____

_____

_____

_____

_____

_____

_____

Name _____

Homophones pages 256–257

> ● **Homophones** are words that sound alike. They are spelled differently and have different meanings.
>
> *EXAMPLES:* too, to, two; its, it's

A. Find a homophone in the puzzle for each of these words. Circle the homophone. (Hint: The words are printed down, across, or diagonally.)

1.	be	2.	weight	3.	sail	4.	knot	5.	pear	6.	two
7.	blew	8.	flour	9.	sun	10.	beet	11.	by	12.	they're
13.	pale	14.	reed	15.	dear	16.	stare	17.	see	18.	do
19.	night	20.	scene	21.	through	22.	rode	23.	hear	24.	sore

```
D W B A U P A I R T S S
B A E S O N E N O B U Y
E I A P L X I O W D A B
E T T W R P H T D E E R
X F M S O A R T H R E W
S A L E A I W Y S E E N
T F T L D L F L O W E R
A B L U E Q W S H E R E
I X E T H E R E R S E A
R Q K N I G H T U A D D
```

B. Write a homophone for each of the words in the box.
Then write a sentence using one of the homophones in each pair.

to –	25. _____
there –	26. _____
ate –	27. _____
no –	28. _____
eye –	29. _____
one –	30. _____

100 UNIT 7: **Workbook**

Name _____

Combining Subjects and Predicates with <u>and</u>   pages 258–259

If the predicates of two sentences are the same, the subjects can often be combined using the word *and*. The verb must agree with the plural subject of the new sentence.

EXAMPLE: <u>Mary</u> <u>likes apples</u>. <u>Mark</u> <u>likes apples</u>.
<u>Mary</u> and <u>Mark</u> <u>like apples</u>.

If the subjects of two sentences are the same, the predicates can often be combined using the word *and*.

EXAMPLE: <u>Farmers</u> <u>grow fruit</u>. <u>Farmers</u> <u>harvest it</u>.
<u>Farmers</u> <u>grow fruit and harvest it</u>.

A.   Combine the subjects of these sentences with the word
and. **Write the new sentence.**

1.   Apples grow best in a region not too hot or too cold. Pears grow best in a region not too hot or too cold.

   _____

   _____

2.   Strawberries like this kind of climate too.
Raspberries like this kind of climate too.

   _____

   _____

3.   Peaches need a warmer place to grow.
Grapes need a warmer place to grow.

   _____

   _____

Name _____

4. Oranges require a hotter climate.
   Lemons require a hotter climate.

   _____

   _____

5. Bananas must have a tropical climate.
   Pineapples must have a tropical climate.

   _____

   _____

**B. Combine the predicates of these sentences
with the word *and*. Write the new sentences.**

6. Fruit trees are planted.
   Fruit trees grow year after year.

   _____

   _____

7. Trees are fertilized.
   Trees are sprayed.

   _____

   _____

8. Insects attack fruit trees.
   Insects sometimes kill them.

   _____

   _____

9. Fruit bruises easily.
   Fruit ripens quickly.

   _____

   _____

10. Workers pick the fruit.
    Workers pack it carefully.

    _____

    _____

Varying Sentences pages 260–261

One way to make sentences more interesting is to add details that tell *how, when, why,* or *where.* Another way to vary your sentences is to begin them in different ways. Do not always begin with the subject.

A. Change the way each sentence begins by moving the words that tell *when, where, how,* or *why.* Write the new sentences.

1. I found a key in my room. _____

_____

2. I tucked the key into my pocket. _____

_____

3. I went downstairs soon afterward. _____

_____

4. I had an idea just then. _____

_____

5. I looked endlessly for a secret room. _____

_____

6. I finally found it because I am so smart. _____

_____

7. I quietly slid the key into the lock. _____

_____

B. Add words to the beginning or end of each sentence. Tell *where, why,* or *how.* Write the new sentences.

8. There were boxes. (where) _____

_____

9. I shouted to my brother. (how) _____

_____

10. We were both surprised. (why) _____

_____

Editing for Sentence Variety page 262

Edit your sentences to make them more interesting. Add words that tell *how, when, where,* and *why* to make sentences colorful and more exact. Begin your sentences in different ways. Do not always begin with the subject.

Editing Marks	
☰	capitalize
⊙	make a period
∧	add something
⋋	add a comma
∜	add quotation marks
⅌	take something away
◯	spell correctly
¶	indent the paragraph
/	make a lower case letter
tr ⟲	transpose

A. This paragraph has been edited. Rewrite it correctly.

Many fire departments have rescue companies. Rescue workers go to large fires. *to assist fire fighters* They help get people out of burning buildings. *When people are overcome by smoke* They give first aid. [They rush people—in emergencies] to hospitals ⊙

_____
_____
_____
_____
_____

B. Edit this paragraph. Add interesting words that tell *how, when, where,* and *why.* Begin your sentences in different ways. Then rewrite the paragraph.

The fire fighters went to the building. The flames rose. The roof fell. The crowd could not get very close.

_____
_____
_____
_____

Using Commas page 263
Mechanics Practice

- **Use a comma to separate three or more words in a series.**

- **Use a comma after the words *yes* and *no* when they begin a statement.**

EXAMPLE: Yes, I hiked with Victor, Paul, and Francine.

Show where commas are needed in these sentences. Write the sentences correctly on a separate piece of paper.

1. No we did not go to the shore this weekend.
2. No we did not stay at home either.
3. Yes we did go to the mountains.
4. We hiked through the cool green and leafy forest.
5. Yes we wore backpacks.
6. We filled them with cold drinks sandwiches and fruit.
7. The rabbits squirrels and deer avoided us.
8. Yes we stopped by a splashing stream on the way.
9. We looked at the small smooth and shiny pebbles.
10. No we do not climb with ropes.
11. We wear good boots high socks and gloves.
12. My cousins Victor Paul and Francine came with us.
13. Yes we finally stopped to eat.
14. Victor sang played his harmonica and whistled.
15. We enjoyed the warm sun cool grass and tall trees.
16. Yes we had to climb down the mountain before dark.
17. We had lighter backpacks tired feet and full stomachs.
18. No we will not go again next weekend.
19. Yes we will do spring cleaning then.
20. Please come over to help us wash windows polish cars and clean garages.

Name _____

A fable pages 264–267

A **fable** is a short story that teaches a lesson or moral. Often the characters are animals.

Read this fable. Answer the questions that follow it.

The Horse and the Donkey

Each week a peddler took his horse and donkey to market. The horse was a fine animal. Its jet-black coat was always carefully brushed. The donkey was small and thin.

Early in the morning the peddler loaded the donkey with baskets of vegetables, sacks of grain, pottery from his shop, and many other things he hoped to sell. The horse was only asked to carry its master.

Today the donkey's load was especially heavy. It spoke to the horse about it. "Please, friend, you can see the size of this load. I beg of you, won't you carry some of it for me? I fear my back is going to break under the weight!"

The horse only tossed its head impatiently and said, "I really haven't time to listen to your troubles. You have your work and I have mine."

With that, the three of them began their journey to market. The donkey tried its best to keep up, but finally it could go no further. Halfway up a steep mountain path, its thin legs gave way.

The master was very cross. "You there! Get up, donkey!" But even he could see how tired it was. He looked at his horse. There it stood, tossing its mane proudly, hardly sweating at all.

"You look fit and strong," said the peddler. "You will have no trouble carrying my goods to market!" The horse watched in horror as its master piled its back high with the basket of vegetables, the sacks of grain, the pottery from his shop, and many other things. Finally, on the very top, the peddler laid the tired little donkey.

"If only I had helped you before," said the horse to the donkey. "Not only must I carry the master's things. Now I must carry you as well!" The donkey smiled and settled back to enjoy the ride.

Moral: Being unhelpful only hurts you in the end.

106 UNIT 7: Workbook

Name _____

1. Write the moral of the fable in your own words.

   _____

   _____

2. Write a sentence that describes the donkey.

   _____

   _____

3. Write a sentence that describes the horse.

   _____

   _____

4. Why was the donkey smiling at the end of the fable?

   _____

   _____

5. What makes this story a fable?

   _____

   _____

6. Write a word that describes how each animal might act in a fable. For
   example, in most fables a goat is a silly or careless animal.

   a. lion _____   b. ant _____

   c. monkey _____   d. fox _____

   e. peacock _____   f. owl _____

7. Read this list of morals. Underline the one that states the moral of this fable
   in another way.
   a. When you help others you help yourself.
   b. One good turn deserves another.
   c. It is foolish to wish you were someone else.
   d. Don't believe everything you hear.

Name _____

Unit Review

A. Draw one line under the simple subject in each sentence. Draw two lines under the simple predicate.

1. The three friends were driving to California.
2. Many cars passed them.
3. They looked at all the license plates.
4. Arthur stopped the car suddenly.
5. A little chipmunk scurried across the road.

B. Underline the correct form of the verb. The verb should agree with the subject of the sentence.

6. Every cold winter day Barry (go, goes) skating.
7. All of his friends (meets, meet) at the pond.
8. They (brings, bring) their skates.
9. Barry (race, races) home for dinner.

C. Write an answer to each question. Begin your answer with *yes* or *no*.

10. Did Jackie and Roger go sledding? (yes)

_____

11. Was it Roger who fell first? (yes)

_____

12. Did Jackie help Roger get up? (no)

_____

D. Underline the base word. Circle the prefix or suffix in each word.

13. restate   14. careless   15. preplan
16. pitcher   17. guilty   18. nonfiction
19. untidy   20. quickly   21. impossible

E. Underline the correct homophone for each sentence.

22. (You're, Your) going downtown.
23. Will they be (there, their)?

24. Are you going to take the bus (to, too)?
25. We know (they're, their) here.

F. Underline the compound words in each sentence.

26. Liza brought her pillowcase into the bedroom.
27. The silverware is in the dishwasher.
28. Take the clothesline from the workbench.

G. Combine the subjects or predicates of each pair of sentences. Write the new sentence.

29. Ted watched the launching of the space shuttle.
    Abby watched the launching of the space shuttle.

    _____

30. The engines smoke.
    The engines shoot out flames.

    _____

H. Read the fable. Then underline the answer to complete each statement correctly.

Every animal in the forest busily bragged about its many children.

"I have five," said the squirrel. "But they never remember where they bury their food."

"I have six," said the raccoon. "But they don't wash when I tell them to."

After a while the rabbit asked the lioness, "How many children do you have?"

The lioness replied proudly, "I have only one, but that child is a fine lion."

31. Characters in a fable are usually
    a. people   b. animals   c. monsters
32. The moral of this fable is
    a. More is not always better.
    b. Bragging is bad.

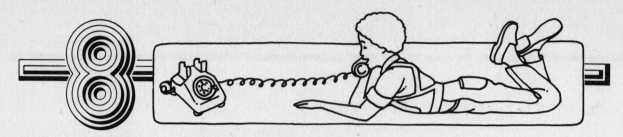

Using the Telephone pages 276–277

When you take a telephone message, write down the details. Write the time and date of the call. Tell the name of the person called and the person who is calling. Write the message and your name.

When you report an emergency, give your name. Describe the problem and give the location of the emergency.

A. Pretend you are working in an office at 500 Central Avenue. Write whom you would call and what you would say when you discover a small fire in an elevator in the hallway.

_____

_____

_____

_____

_____

_____

B. Write the messages for these telephone calls.

Gordon Eldridge (calling at 11:04 A.M.): Good morning. This is Gordon Eldridge calling. Is Ms. Levy in?

Operator: Yes, but she is in a meeting right now. May I take a message?

Gordon Eldridge: Yes, please tell her the report is ready. She can send a messenger to pick it up at 480 Main Street.

_____

_____

_____

_____

Listening to a Guest Speaker   pages 278–279

The high school baseball team has just won the state championship. Ruth's class has invited the star pitcher to visit as a guest speaker. Ruth is making a list of questions to ask. The class will ask questions that relate to the speaker's subject. The words *who, what, where, when,* and *how* are good words with which to begin questions.

A. Read Ruth's list of questions. Check the nine questions that would be good questions to ask the star pitcher. For each one you do not check, think about why it was not a good question.

1. _____ How long have you been playing baseball?

2. _____ Do you like other sports too?

3. _____ Did the team practice a lot for the championship?

4. _____ Do you have any girl friends?

5. _____ Do you play other positions on the team?

6. _____ Who is the worst player?

7. _____ Did you have a plan for winning?

8. _____ What do you eat for breakfast?

9. _____ When was the game played?

10. _____ Where was the game played?

11. _____ What was the best play of the game?

12. _____ How did you feel when you won?

13. _____ Do you have a car?

B. Now write two more questions to ask the speaker.

14. _____

_____

15. _____

_____

Following Directions pages 280–281

When you fill out a form, remember to read the form over once. Write or print clearly. Give all the information requested. Be sure that all the information is in the right place.

A. You are going to enter your apple pie in the 4-H County Fair baking contest. Fill out this entry form.

Print all information clearly.

Name: _____ Age: _____

Address: _____ Home Telephone: _____

Kind of baked good: _____

Booth number (leave blank): _____

B. You are going to order a basketball uniform. Fill out this form.

Name: _____ Date: _____

Address: _____
      Street   City   State   Zip Code

Height: _____ Weight: _____ Size: _____

School Name: _____

School or Team Colors: _____

Date of Order: _____

Name _____

Listening Critically pages 282–283

    Some parts of ads give **facts.** A statement of fact can be checked. It can be proved true or false.

EXAMPLE: E-Z Grow plant food is a house plant fertilizer.

    Some parts of ads give **opinions.** A statement of opinion tells what someone thinks or feels. It cannot be proved true or false.

EXAMPLE: E-Z Grow plant food will give you prize-winning
             plants.

A. Write *fact* under each person who states a fact. Write *opinion* under each person who states an opinion.

1. _____ 2. _____ 3. _____ 4. _____

B. Read this ad. Write *fact* or *opinion* next to each statement.

_____ 5. Frieda's Famous Figs are fresh.

_____ 6. Frieda's Famous Figs will sweeten your snack time.

_____ 7. Frieda's Famous Figs have all natural ingredients.

_____ 8. Your kids will say, "We want Frieda's Famous Figs!"

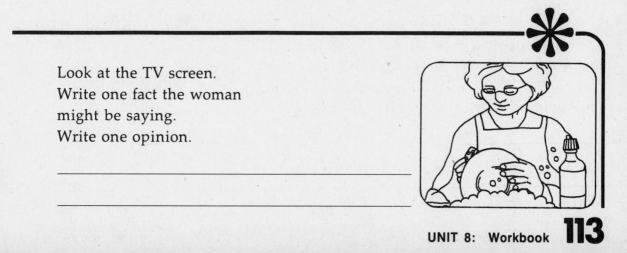

Look at the TV screen.
Write one fact the woman
might be saying.
Write one opinion.

_____

_____

Using an Atlas pages 288–289

An **atlas** is a book of maps.
Each map has a **legend** or **key**
to explain the map symbols.
A **direction symbol** tells which
way is north, south, east, and
west on the map. A **distance scale**
shows the distance between places
in miles and kilometers.

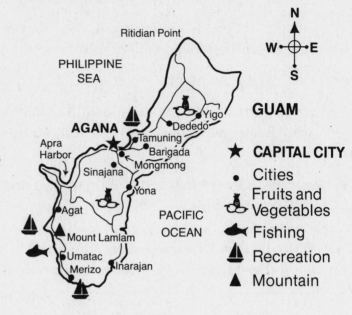

**Study the map of Guam. Then read each question. Check
the correct answer.**

1. What is the capital city of Guam?

    _____ Agana   _____ Merizo

2. What is the northernmost point of Guam called?

    _____ Umatac   _____ Ritidian Point

3. Tamuning borders on what body of water?

    _____ Philippine Sea   _____ Pacific Ocean

4. Near what two northern cities are fruits and vegetables grown?

    _____ Dededo and Yigo   _____ Agat and Yona

5. What is the name of the mountain on the island?

    _____ Mongmong   _____ Mount Lamlam

6. Yona is located on what body of water?

    _____ Pacific Ocean   _____ Philippine Sea

7. About how far is it from Inarajan to Yona?

    _____ 15 kilometers   _____ 10 kilometers

8. How many cities are shown on this map?

    _____ 11   _____ 12

Name _____

Writing Conversation pages 290–292

When you write conversation, place quotation marks before and after the quotation. Begin the first word of a quotation with a capital letter. Use a comma to separate a quotation from the rest of the sentence unless a question mark or exclamation point is needed. Start a new paragraph for each new speaker. Use descriptive words to show how a person speaks.

EXAMPLES: "I love to travel," said Roseann excitedly.
Gary asked, "What trips have you taken?"

Write these quotations correctly.

1. My family is going on a trip roseann told her class

_____

2. where are you going asked her teacher

_____

3. we're going to the Lilac Festival roseann answered.

_____

4. She said the Lilac Festival is in Rochester, New York

_____

5. What will you see asked her friend niki

_____

6. There will be a parade, bands, and fireworks roseann said

_____

7. roseann told her friends the first Lilac Festival was held in 1905.

_____

_____

8. thousands of people come to see over 500 kinds of lilacs she continued

_____

_____

Name _____

Ordering Events in a Story pages 293–295

Every good story has three parts. The beginning is the **introduction.** In it the main characters and setting are introduced. The middle of the story is the **development.** It tells about a problem or challenge for the main characters. The end, or **conclusion,** of a story usually tells how the problem is solved.

A.   Read these paragraphs from a short story. Put the paragraphs in the correct order by numbering them 1, 2, 3, and 4. Then write a title for the story.

_____

_____ Anna's mother turned to her and said, "Anna, how would you like to go for a horseback ride?"

_____ Anna and her mother were taking a walk in the city park one Sunday. Everyone was enjoying the beautiful spring day. People were riding bicycles, roller skating, jogging, and even horseback riding.

_____ Anna's mother smiled. A few minutes later they went around a curve of the path. There before them was a carousel. Anna was going to ride on a horse after all!

_____ Anna cried, "How can I? I do not know how to ride. And besides, we are wearing our good clothes."

B.   Use this story beginning. Add at least two more paragraphs. Develop the problem in the middle part. Then tell how the main characters solve the problem in the conclusion. Finish the story on a separate piece of paper.

One fine, sunny day Matt asked Joe to walk along the beach with him. They strolled on the deserted beach for about twenty minutes. Suddenly, Matt pointed to an unusual patch of sand.

"Look! There is something in the sand," Matt shouted.

The boys quickly uncovered an old bottle crusted with sand. Matt took the bottle to the water's edge and washed it. The boys noticed a piece of paper inside the bottle.

"Open it! Hurry!" urged Joe.

The paper had writing on it. With Joe looking over his shoulder, Matt slowly began to read: "To the Lucky Person Who Finds This Bottle..."

Editing Conversation
page 296

Edit stories after you write them. Pay special attention to conversations between characters. Capitalize the first word of a quotation. Use quotation marks to separate it from the rest of a sentence. End it with a punctuation mark. Always begin a new paragraph each time a new character speaks.

Editing Marks	
≡	capitalize
⊙	make a period
∧	add something
∧	add a comma
ᵛᵛ	add quotation marks
ᴣ	take something away
◯	spell correctly
¶	indent the paragraph
/	make a lower case letter
tr ∿	transpose

EXAMPLE: Jenny whispered, "We have trapped the bandits this time."

A. These quotations have been edited. Follow the editing marks. Write the conversations correctly.

1. can you show me how to use the cowboy puppet? asked Robert

2. it's not as hard as it looks, answered Jenny.

3. first be sure the strings are untangled, she said.

4. Jenny continued, then try to move different parts of ~~him~~ it.

5. oh, look how I can make him dance! ~~said~~ exclaimed Robert.

6. Jenny asked, would you like to give a puppet show?

B. Edit this conversation among three people. Then rewrite it correctly on a separate piece of paper. Remember to begin a new paragraph each time a different character speaks.

why don't we do a puppet show about the Old West asked Lorna. Robert said good idea! We'll make some scenery that looks like a ghost town .   Jenny looked at them both. She said let's dress up this puppet to be Calamity Jane, a cowgirl!

Writing Quotations page 297

Mechanics Practice

- Begin the first word of a quotation with a capital letter.

- Put quotation marks before and after a direct quotation.

- Put a comma between a quotation and the rest of the sentence unless a question mark or exclamation point is needed.

- Begin a new paragraph each time a different character speaks.

EXAMPLES: "Can you do macrame?" asked Rita.
Harry replied, "My mom is teaching me."

A. Add capital letters and punctuation marks to these sentences. Write the sentences correctly on a separate piece of paper.

1. Harold said what shall our next project be

2. why don't we make Mother's Day presents   said Peter.

3. we could make flower arrangements   he said.

4. my mom would like that   said Dibe.

5. yes   let's do that   exclaimed Harold.

6. why don't we make whatever we want   said Ted.

7. that way we can make what we really want   he said.

8. let's go   everyone yelled.

B. Write this conversation correctly. Add quotation marks and capital letters. Begin new paragraphs for each new speaker.

did you finish your flower arrangement asked Peter.
no i'm having a lot of trouble with it answered Dibe. i'll
help you said Peter. where do we start laughed Dibe.

_____

_____

_____

A Story pages 298–301

In stories that are **fiction,** characters and events come from the author's imagination.

Read this part of a story about a boy named Peter. Think about the characters, setting, and plot of the story.

Tales of a Fourth Grade Nothing

by JUDY BLUME

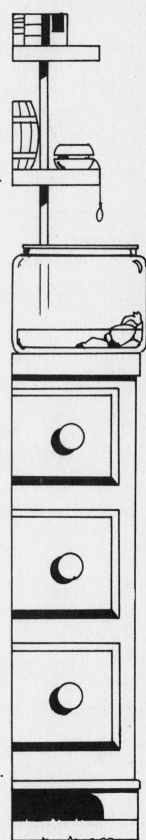

The first thing I noticed was my chain latch. It was unhooked. My bedroom door was open. And there was a chair smack in the middle of my doorway. I nearly tumbled over it. I ran to my dresser to check Dribble, my turtle. He wasn't there! His bowl with the rocks and water was there—but Dribble was gone.

I got really scared. I thought, MAYBE HE DIED WHILE I WAS AT SCHOOL AND I DIDN'T KNOW ABOUT IT. So I rushed into the kitchen and hollered, "Mom . . . where's Dribble?" My mother was baking something. My brother sat on the kitchen floor, banging pots and pans together.

"You mean he's not in his bowl?" my mother asked.

I shook my head.

"Oh dear!" my mother said. "I hope he's not crawling around somewhere. You know I don't like the way he smells. I'm going to have a look in the bedrooms. You check in here, Peter."

My mother hurried off. I looked at my brother. He was smiling. "Fudge, do you know where Dribble is?" I asked calmly.

Fudge kept smiling.

"Did you take him? Did you, Fudge?" I asked not so calmly. Fudge giggled and covered his mouth with his hands.

I yelled. "Where is he? What did you do with my turtle?"

No answer from Fudge. He banged his pots and pans together again. I yanked the pots out of his hand. I tried to speak softly. "Now tell me where Dribble is. Just tell me where my turtle is. I won't be mad if you tell me. Come on, Fudge . . . please."

Fudge looked up at me. "In tummy," he said.

"What do you mean, in tummy?" I asked, narrowing my eyes.

Fudge stood up. He jumped up and down and sang out, "I ATE HIM . . . ATE HIM . . . ATE HIM!"

My mother came back into the kitchen. "FUDGE ATE

DRIBBLE!" I screamed.

My mother moaned and picked up my brother. "Oh no! My angel! My precious little baby! OH . . . NO . . ."

My mother didn't stop to think about my turtle. She didn't even give Dribble a thought. She didn't even stop to wonder how my turtle liked being swallowed by my brother. She ran to the phone with Fudge tucked under one arm. I followed. Mom dialed the operator and cried, "Oh help! This is an emergency. My baby ate a turtle . . . STOP THAT LAUGHING," my mother told the operator. "Send an ambulance right away; 25 West 68th Street."

A. Tell about the story. Use complete sentences.

1. Who are the characters in the story? _____

_____

2. What is the setting for this part of the story? _____

_____

3. What is Peter's problem? _____

_____

4. Where do you think the next setting will be? _____

_____

5. How do you think Peter's problem will be solved? _____

_____

B. Tell how each character acted in the emergency.

6. How did Peter act when his mother was concerned only with Fudge?

_____

_____

7. How did Peter's mother act when she found out Fudge ate the turtle?

_____

_____

8. How did Fudge act when Peter kept asking about Dribble?

_____

Name _____

Unit Review

A. Pretend you are working in a store at 757 Third Avenue. James Carl, a customer, becomes very ill. Write whom you would call and what you would say.

_____

_____

_____

_____

B. Pretend a veterinarian is coming to speak to your class. Check the questions that would be good ones to ask.

_____ 1. What did you do to learn how to become a veterinarian?

_____ 2. Do you like to read?

_____ 3. How many animals do you care for each day?

C. 4. Follow the directions to fill out the form.

```
┌──────────────────────────────────────────────────────────────┐
│                                                                │
│                      LIBRARY SURVEY                            │
│                                                                │
│                 (Please print all information.)                │
│                                                                │
│  Name: _____ Age: _____        │
│  Your favorite kind of book. Circle one only:                  │
│                                                                │
│     biography     sports     mystery     humor     fiction     │
│                                                                │
│     other _____                                │
│  How often do you visit the library? Check one:                │
│     ☐ once a week   ☐ once a month   ☐ once every few months   │
│                                                                │
│  Do you have a library card? Write yes or no. _____  │
│                                                                │
└──────────────────────────────────────────────────────────────┘
```

Name _____

Unit Review

D. Read the ad for Bubble Better Shampoo. Write *fact* next to each statement of fact. Write *opinion* next to each statement of opinion.

_____ 5. Bubble Better is a shampoo and cream rinse all in one.

_____ 6. Its gleaming gold color will add shine to every strand of your hair.

_____ 7. Bubble Better will not sting your eyes.

_____ 8. It is sold at drugstores and department stores.

E. Show where quotation marks, end punctuation marks, and capital letters belong. Then write the sentences correctly.

9. i don't want to go to the race said Craig.

_____

10. you already signed up replied Nan.

_____

11. Craig said maybe so, but i feel sick.

_____

12. Do you think some water will help asked Nan.

_____

F. Tell what happens in each part of a story.

13. introduction _____

_____

14. development _____

_____

15. conclusion _____

_____

122 UNIT 8: **Workbook**

ANSWER KEY FOR WORKBOOK

UNIT 1

Workbook 1
A. 1, 4, 7, 8, 10

B. 11.–15. Answers will vary. Possible answers include: **11.** Insects have hard outer shells. (2) **12.** Some insects are protected by their color. (3) **13.** A bee or a wasp can sting. (5) **14.** These insects sting you to protect themselves. (6) **15.** Grasshoppers can jump away from their enemies. (9)

Workbook 2
A. 1.–3. Answers will vary. Check for complete declarative sentences.

B. Answers will vary. Check for complete interrogative sentences. Possible answers include: **4.** How many legs does it have? **5.** How many eyes does it have. **6.** What kind of hat does it wear?

Special Feature: Answers may vary. Possible answer is given. The outside of the chicken has the most feathers.

Workbook 3
A. 1. exclamatory (!) **2.** imperative (.) **3.** imperative (.) **4.** imperative (.) **5.** exclamatory (!)

B. Answers will vary. Possible answers include: **6.** Sit up. **7.** Bring me the newspaper. **8.** Roll over. **9.** Eat your dog food. **10.** Don't chew the furniture.

C. Answers will vary. Possible answers are given. **11.** What a great pet I have! **12.** Wow, my pet does wonderful tricks! **13.** How smart my pet is! **14.** How much food that pet eats!

Workbook 4
A. 1. Ling-Ling is a giant panda. **2.** She is in the Washington Zoo. **3.** She is eating bamboo shoots. **4.** Ling-Ling weighs almost 300 pounds. **5.** Her keeper is with Ling-Ling.

B. 6.–8. Answers will vary.

Workbook 5
A. 1. <u>Our class</u> <u>went on a nature hike</u>. **2.** <u>The clear stream</u> <u>trickled over the rocks</u>. **3.** <u>Several small insects</u> <u>crawled over a log</u>. **4.** <u>The galloping horses</u> <u>raced across the field</u>. **5.** <u>Cheerful birds</u> <u>chirped a sweet song</u>. **6.** <u>Three rabbits</u> <u>hopped across the meadow</u>.

B. 7.–12. Answers will vary.

Workbook 6
A. 1. a. Hershell H. Nixon b. S. H. Burchard c. Carolyn Meyer **2.** a. *Oil and Gas* b. *Dorothy Hamill* c. *Stitch by Stitch* **3.** a. oil and gas b. Dorothy Hamill c. needlecrafts

B. 4. P **5.** W **6.** B **7.** G **8.** C **9.** C **10.** L

Workbook 7
1. It was lunchtime, and children filled the school cafeteria. **2.** Walter opened his lunch bag, and he took out a peanut butter sandwich. **3.** Greta brought fried chicken to eat, but she forgot to bring napkins. **4.** Brenda ate a hot dog, and she munched a cookie for dessert. **5.** Fred and Brian bought hot lunches, and they carried them to a table. **6.** The students could buy hot lunches, or they could buy sandwiches. **7.** Brian chewed on a carrot, but he didn't like it very much.

Workbook 8
8. The boys and girls finished their lunches, and they cleared the tables. **9.** They played outside in the yard, or they went to the gym. **10.** The bell rang, and it was time for class again. **11.** Samuel went to class, but he did not feel well. **12.** Karen took Samuel's hand, and she took him to the nurse. **13.** Samuel could lie down in the nurse's office, or he could call his mom. **14.** Soon Samuel felt better, and he returned to class.

Workbook 9
A. Check for correct editing marks. **1.** Some new neighbors moved into the house next door. **2.** Their last name is Mahnster. **3.** Their best friends are Mr. and Mrs. Ghoolie. **4.** Lately I've heard strange noises at night. **5.** Sometimes I play with their son, Harry Mahnster. **6.** He has four pet spiders and a black cat. **7.** You should see their house on Halloween. **8.** Harry's mother, Ima Mahnster, doesn't need a costume. **9.** Watching their home movies is always exciting. **10.** Once they invited me over for bat stew.

B. Sentences will vary.

Workbook 10
1. A little sand crab skittered along the sand. **2.** How angry it looked! **3.** Four sea gulls soared overhead. **4.** Do you know what they were looking for? **5.** How hungry the little babies are! **6.** Do you know why the sea animals are hiding?

Workbook 11
A.   Summer Songs

By the sand between my toes,
By the waves behind my ears,
By the sunburn on my nose.
By the little salty tears
That make rainbows in the sun
When I squeeze my eyes and run,
By the way the seagulls screech,
Guess where I am? At the . . . . . !
By the way the children shout
Guess what happened? School is . . . . !
By the way I sing this song
Guess if summer lasts too long:
You must answer Right or . . . . . !

B. Probable answers are: **1.** beach **2.** out **3.** wrong

C. Answers will vary. Possible answers include: **4.** band, tanned, land, hand **5.** peach, reach, teach **6.** brave, cave, Dave, gave **7.** bell, sell, tell, well, smell. Poems will vary.

Workbook 12
A. 1. hushes 2. shushes
B. 3. whack 4. click 5. rumble 6. thump
C. 7. laughs a lovely whiteness 8. whitely whirs
away.

Workbook 13
A. 1. Our classroom is very large. 2. Thirty students
are in the class. 3. Our plants grow on the
windowsill.
B. 4. (.) 5. (?) 6. (.) 7. (!) 8. (.) 9. (.)
C. 10. George Washington was our first President.
11. Betsy Ross made America's first flag.
12. Paul Revere is famous for his warning that
British troops were coming.
D. 13. The warm rain falls on fields and trees.
14. Max and I got dressed to go out. 15. We wear
boots, rain hats, and raincoats.

Workbook 14
E. 16. biography 17. nonfiction 18. reference
19. fiction 20. reference
F. 21. Marcie raced off, and I raced after her.
22. She had a good lead, but I was gaining on her.
23. Would Marcie win the race, or would I win?
G. 24.–27. Answers will vary.
H. 28. two

UNIT 2
Workbook 15
A. 1. Bananas, kind, fruit 2. grapefruit, day, Florida
3. Sam, salad, potatoes, onions, celery 4. kinds,
apples 5. tomato, fruit
B. Answers will vary but may include those given.
6. clerk, child, boy/girl, woman/lady 7. market,
sidewalk, storefront, store 8. apples, shelves,
boxes, peaches, fruit, cartons, oranges, signs,
strawberries, carts

Workbook 16
A. 1. boxes 2. princesses 3. wrenches
4. leashes 5. crayons 6. dishes 7. babies
8. ferries 9. notebooks 10. bandages
B. 11. foxes 12. bushes 13. cities 14. desks
15. berries. Sentences will vary.

Workbook 17
A. Across: moose, trousers, men, mice
Down: feet, women, oxen, sheep, deer
B. 10.–14. Answers will vary.

Workbook 18
1. Marcy Russo and her family went on a trip across
the United States. 2. They began in the state of
Maine and ended in the state of California. 3. They
crossed the Mississippi River and many other small
rivers. 4. Marcy Russo liked crossing the Mojave
Desert. 5. John Russo was most excited about
going over the Rocky Mountains. 6. As they
crossed the country, the Russos went through towns
and cities. 7. On the Fourth of July they watched
fireworks in Denver, Colorado. 8. The Russos
enjoyed their vacation.

Special Feature: Answers will vary. Be sure the
students supply a proper noun for each symbol.

Workbook 19
A. 1. Sen. Robin Horn 2. Gov. Esther A. Jones
3. Mr. Harold Papas 4. Miss A. A. Reed
5. Mrs. Rosa Sanchez 6. Gov. Kevin G. Goodwin
7. Dr. Frank J. Purcell 8. Mr. Les Roy
9. Ms. Mary I. Proto 10. Mrs. Ruth Roth
B. 11. Gov. M. A. Tobian 12. Mr. H. L. Tolman
13. Sen. A. M. Bianco 14. Dr. D. M. Starr
15. Miss P. M. Owens 16. Dr. P. M. Gomez

Workbook 20
A. 1. Tom Hart lives on Cherry St. 2. You can shop at
Harry's Shoe Store on Main St. 3. Jenny Martino
lives on Clinton Ave. 4. Littletown, Idaho, is in the
United States of America.
B. 5.–6. Answers will vary. Be sure the students label
the map.

Workbook 21
A. 1. gull's 2. starfish's 3. clam's 4. oyster's
5. cockle's
B. 6. children's 7. fishermen's 8. gulls' 9. sand
crabs' 10. divers'

Workbook 22
C. 11. The lobsters' claws are tools to get food.
12. The sponge's home is in wet places.
13. Shells are the sand crabs' homes. 14. The
jellyfish's sting is caused by cells that blow up.
15. The geese's wings were dark against the sky.
D. 16. boat's/boats' 17. fish's/fishes'
18. lifeguard's/lifeguards'
19. swimmer's/swimmers'
20. captain's/captains' 21. box's/boxes'
22. clam's/clams' 23. gull's/gulls'
24. shark's/sharks' 25. tooth's/teeth's

Workbook 23
1. c 2. a 3. c 4. c

Workbook 24
A. 1. opinion 2. fact 3. opinion 4. opinion
5. opinion 6. fact 7. opinion
B. 8.–10. Answers will vary.

Workbook 25
A. 1. Hortense the Hippo 2. The Disappearing Dog Catcher 3. The Book of Baby Animals 4. The Tale of the Mountain Goat 5. A Rabbit Named Red
B.   Book Report
TITLE Misunderstood Animals

AUTHOR Sara L. Fernandez

SUMMARY This book is about animals such as the wolf, the bat, and the octopus. The book says that these animals have frightened people for centuries. It explains why people have been afraid of them. The book says that many of these animals are actually helpful.

OPINION I enjoyed this book because it told many interesting facts about animals.

Workbook 26
A. Edited version should reflect appropriate editing marks.
B. Final version is as follows:
TITLE Baney's Lake

AUTHOR Nan Hayden Agle

SUMMARY Eleven-year-old Baney Trimble buys some land from Miss Luke. Baney discovers that a lake and a dam will soon be built on the land. He tries to save his land by going to court and talking to Judge Grimes. Baney loses his case, but the story has a happy ending anyhow.

OPINION I think Baney's Lake was interesting because the reader didn't know if Baney would be able to keep his land.

Workbook 27
A. 1. Dr. Anna Bianco 2. Prince Charles 3. Spot 4. Ms. Chung Lee 5. Mr. A. L. Lewis 6. Bruce T. Wilks
B. Be sure the students use editing marks. 7. This morning I was running with my dog. 8. I didn't see the groundhog hole, but Buttons did. 9. Dad took me to see Dr. Antonio Madrid. 10. Dr. Madrid told me I had sprained my ankle. 11. His partner, Dr. Marta Roja, will wrap my ankle. 12. She asked me how Buttons was doing.

Workbook 28
1. a biography 2. Yes 3. Elizabeth Blackwell
4. She was the first woman doctor in America.
5. Dr. Elder 6. He let her study his medical books and helped her write letters to medical schools.
7. Details are underlined. Accept any five details.
8. She studied hard, searched for two years for a medical school she could attend, graduated first in her class, and went to Europe to practice.

Workbook 29
A. 1. Mack 2. brother, store 3. boy 4. friend, Bonnie, telephone
B. 5. dragons 6. beaches 7. buses 8. boys 9. sheep 10. women 11. boxes 12. mice
C. 13. Maryvale Street is the street where we live.
14. It is in the town of Sacramento. 15. On a holiday such as Labor Day we have fun.
D. 16. King Ferdinand 17. Dr. Les Green 18. Mrs. G. L. Lopez 9. London, England 20. Stevens Blvd. 21. Heathcote Rd.
E. 22. Leslie's 23. players' 24. catchers'

Workbook 30
F. 25. Marty takes good care of his dog. 26. Detail sentences are underlined.
G. 27. fact 28. fact 29. opinion
H. Items 30, 31, and 33 are true.
I. 34. Elizabeth 35. Answers will vary. Possible answers include: sad, sorry, determined.

UNIT 3
Workbook 31
A. 1. visited 2. chopped 3. cooked, cleaned 4. rode 5. jumped, galloped 6. brush, groom 7. learned 8. returned 9. sat 10. enjoyed.
B. 11.–15. Answers will vary.

Workbook 32
A. 1. is 2. is 3. are 4. am 5. are 6. is 7. are 8. was 9. were 10. was
B. 11. is 12. is 13. am 14. am 15. Are
C. 16. was 17. was 18. were 19. was 20. were

Workbook 33
A. 1. are 2. has 3. has 4. have 5. will 6. was 7. will 8. will 9. is 10. will
B. 11.–18. Answers will vary.

Workbook 34
A. 1. visited, past 2. will clean, future 3. baby-sit, present 4. will drive, future 5. constructed, past 6. cook, present
B. 7.–10. Answers will vary.

Workbook 35
A. 1. mopped 2. hummed 3. ferried 4. clapped 5. tarried 6. worried 7. plotted 8. tried 9. buried 10. dropped
B. 11. planned 12. spotted 13. hurried 14. carried 15. jabbed 16. tried 17. emptied 18. dropped 19. tapped 20. flopped

Workbook 36
A. 1. went 2. run 3. begun 4. came 5. sung 6. sang 7. begun 8. rang 9. come 10. ran
B. 11.–15. Answers will vary.

Workbook 37

A. 1. written 2. grew 3. wrote 4. gave
   5. written 6. did 7. grown 8. took
B. 9.–12. Answers will vary.

Workbook 38–39

Be sure that the students write complete sentences.
   1. middle 2. Kenya/kidney 3. ketchup
   4. three 5. five 6. kept 7. long 8. noun
   9. three 10. Friendship was the keynote.
   11. kerchief 12. kernel, khaki 13. kickoff
   14. noun
Special Feature: Answers will vary.

Workbook 40

                    24 Delgado Avenue
                    Tallahassee, Florida 32304
                    November 3, 19--

Dear Captain WI-12-RQ,
   I do not miss my galaxy so much. I am staying with a
very nice Earth family. They live in a warm place called
Florida. Last week we did a most exciting thing.
(Answers will vary.)

                    Your faithful flier,
                    LA-44-VX

Workbook 41

A. 1.–5. Answers will vary.
B. Answers will vary.

Workbook 42

A. Be sure that the students use correct editing marks.
B.   7901 Fourth Avenue
                    Brooklyn, New York 11209
                    October 22, 19--

Dear Rita,
   I am having a costume party this Halloween, and I
would like you to come. It will be at my house from 2:00
P.M. to 6:00 P.M. the Saturday after Halloween. You cannot
get in without a costume, so start creating right away!

                    Your friend,
                    Brent Fink

Workbook 43

A. 1. 13 Putnam Ave.
      Valley Stream, New York 11580
   3. 3000 North Carstairs Place
      Fort Lauderdale, Florida 33313
   5. 14-67 Main Street
      Atlanta, Georgia 30735
   2. 1400 Washington Ave.
      Albany, NY 12210
   4. 201 East 35 St.
      Chicago, IL 60604
   6. 867 Jefferson Blvd.
      St. Louis, Missouri 65205
B. 7. Our new museum is on Park Avenue in Union
   City. 8. Turn right at Dogwood Avenue and drive
   one mile. 9. We have art classes with teachers
   from New Orleans and Memphis. 10. New
   teachers are coming soon from New Jersey and
   California. 11. They are stopping at Scottsdale,
   Arizona, on the way. 12. The guest speaker came
   here from Milan, Italy.

Answer Key for Workbook

Workbook 44

A. 1. The Wishing Well 2. Nicole, Scott, Dana, and
   the Wishing Well Voice 3. a deep forest
   4. Nicole 5. Be sure the students underline only
   dialog. 6. (deep, hollow-sounding) 7. Any
   character but Scott may speak next. Be sure
   students provide stage directions and dialog.

Workbook 45

B. Answers will vary. Possible answers are given.
   8. an ancient castle, an enchanted forest 9. a
   forest, a zoo, a circus 10. a prehistoric cave, a
   far-away planet 11. airplane, airport
C. Answers will vary. Possible answers include:
   12. 4 Martians, Commander, and Navigator
   13. Shipwrecked Family, Various Animals
   14. Group of Fourth-Graders, Basketball Team
   15. Nurse, Doctor, Patient
D. Answers will vary.

Workbook 46

A. 1. scampers 2. clutches 3. flings 4. roars
B. 5. is 6. am 7. are 8. is
C. 9. The plumber has changed the pipes. 10. She
   was working on the job all day. 11. We were
   watching her. 12. Later we will wash the dishes.
D. 13. *camped*, past 14. *loved*, past 15. *plan*,
   present 16. *will travel*, future
E. 17. copied 18. hopped 19. skipped
   20. hurried 21. married 22. shopped
F. 23. written 24. taken 25. came

Workbook 47

G. 26. copy–corner 27. maid–make 28. tissue–toe
H. Items 29, 31, and 32 belong in an invitation.
I. 33. 3 34. the living room of the York house
   35. Mrs. Wills

UNIT 4

Workbook 48

Items 1 and 4 make good paragraphs. A possible main
idea for paragraph 1 is: Navajo children have many
tasks to do. A possible main idea for paragraph 4 is: Fry
bread is an important Navajo food.

Workbook 49

   1. b 2. c 3. b

Workbook 50

A. 1. Andy is rolling up his sleeping bag. 2. Andy is
   packing food. 3. Andy is packing his clothes.
   4. Andy is putting on his boots.
B. Paragraphs will vary.

Workbook 51

A. The correct order is: 2, 1, 4, 3.
B. Paragraphs will vary. Be sure that the students
   include details from the pictures and use time-order
   words.
C. The correct order is: 5, 1, 2, 7, 3, 4, 6. The time-order
   clues are: First, Then, Finally, Next.

Workbook 52

1. The potatoes have eyes, the corn has ears, and the beans talk.   2. It was a little horse.   3. I like it closed.

Special Feature: 1. The potatoes have eyes, the corn has ears, and the beans (s)talk.   2. It was a little horse (hoarse).   3. I like it closed.

Workbook 53

1. title page   2. title page   3. index   4. table of contents   5. title page   6. glossary   7. table of contents   8. glossary   9. index   10. table of contents

Workbook 54

1. 3   2. 11   3. 15   4. 1   5. 17   6. 6   7. 16   8. 11   9. 18   10. 12   11. 19   12. 7   13. 1   14. 21   15. 21   16. 2   17. 10   18. 16   19. 3   20. 1

Workbook 55

Here's how to make a pocket out of a napkin. First fold the napkin in fours. Second fold the top layer of the napkin down. Next fold the side points under. Finally slip a fork, a spoon, and a party favor into the pocket.

Workbook 56

A. Be sure that students use correct editing marks.

B. Here's how to use a pay telephone. First take the receiver off the hook. Second put your dime in the slot. After you put in your money, wait for the dial tone. Then dial the number. Finally finish the call and hang up the receiver.

Workbook 57

A. 1. Wednesday   2. Mother's Day   3. May   4. Lincoln's Birthday   5. Saturday   6. Sept.   7. Tues.   8. Fourth of July   9. Labor Day   10. Dec.

B. 11. My sister was born in January.   12. Some people think of Memorial Day as the start of summer.   13. My birthday is Monday, May 1.   14. May 1 is celebrated as May Day all over the world.   15. Don't forget Mother's Day on Sunday, May 10.   16. My class is going to dress up for Halloween this year.   17. On Thursday my brother received his first birthday card.   18. This card was sent on Tuesday, February 13.

Workbook 59

1. Details are underlined. Answers will vary.

2. Dian Fossey is an American scientist. Dian remained calm when gorillas came charging toward her. Dian is a famous expert on gorillas. Dian imitated gorillas to win their trust.   3. She studied gorillas in Africa and was finally able to touch one.   4. Studying Gorillas in Africa   5. Answers will vary.

Workbook 60

A. 1. Answers will vary. The students should indicate that the main idea concerns how different the two sisters are.   2. My sister and I look very different.   3. Accept any two sentences except the first sentence.

B. 4. 4   5. 2   6. 1   7. 3

C. Last year I joined the soccer team.

Workbook 61

D. 9. T   10. T   11. TOC   12. T

E. 13. 57–58   14. 11–14

F. 15. I made hamburgers yesterday. First I rolled the meat between my hands. Second I patted down each ball of meat into a pattie. Third I put the patties into a pan on the stove. Next I turned on the heat and fried the patties. Last I turned them with a spatula and finished cooking them.

G. 16. Stacey   17. in a storm near a river   18. to find Mark

UNIT 5

Workbook 62

A. 1. white, yellow   2. wide, grassy   3. soft, beautiful   4. famous   5. thorny, tall   6. low, green   7. fat, little   8. small, many, different   9. pink, purple, red, lilac   10. thick, strong, large

B. 11.–15. Answers will vary. Possible answers include: 11. beautiful   12. rich, hot   13. Wet   14. dirty, muddy   15. warm

Workbook 63

A. 1. smallest   2. bigger   3. largest   4. faster   5. slower   6. more difficult   7. most dangerous   8. steeper   9. smoothest   10. more slippery

B. 11. serious, more serious   12. faster, fastest   13. colorful, most colorful   14. thoughtful, more thoughtful   15. tough, toughest

Workbook 64

A. 1. Today   2. slowly   3. Then   4. along   5. merrily   6. wildly   7. ahead   8. Soon   9. happily   10. magically

B. Answers will vary. Possible answers include: 11. loudly   12. Then   13. outside   14. away   15. Then

Special Feature: off, slowly, Then, brightly

Workbook 65

A. 1. *Yesterday*, when   2. *eagerly*, how   3. *down*, where   4. *Soon*, when   5. *wildly*, how   6. *briskly*, how   7. *outside*, where   8. *playfully*, how   9. *gleefully*, how   10. *There*, where

B. Answers will vary. Possible answers include: 11. along   12. gleefully   13. there   14. Soon   15. neatly

Workbook 66

A. 1. quickly   2. good   3. heavy   4. quick   5. wildly   6. slowly   7. friendly   8. slowly   9. sadly   10. nice

B. 11. adverb   12. adverb   13. adjective   14. adjective   15. adjective   16. adjective   17. adjective   18. adverb   19. adverb   20. adjective

C. Answers will vary.

Workbook 67

A. 1. a rounded, rather deep dish   2. to play at bowling or bowls

B. live/live   4. bark/bark   5. fair/fair   6. fine/fine

C. 7.–8. Sentences will vary.

Workbook 68

A. 1. cap/hat 2. big/large 3. cash/money
  4. jump/leap 5. keep/save 6. almost/nearly
  7. pick/choose 8. plate/platter 9. false/untrue

B. 10. full/empty 11. closed/open
  12. lead/follow 13. win/lose 14. rapid/slow
  15. ask/tell 16. lose/find 17. soft/loud
  18. buy/sell

C. Answers will vary. Possible answers include:
  19. brave 20. find 21. over 22. answer
  23. car 24. tired 25. present 26. least

Special Feature: LOON LOOK HOOK HOOD
HOLD BOLD

Workbook 69

  1. I am a round, orange, and juicy fruit. 2. Slice
  me from a long, fat, and soft loaf. 3. This fizzy and
  refreshing orange drink is cold. 4. Scoop me into a
  cone in different, frosty, and delicious flavors.
  5. This tasty, chocolate drink is hot.

Workbook 70

  6. I am a potato fried into narrow, crisp, and salty
  strips. 7. I am a smooth, sticky, peanutty spread
  for bread. 8. My crust is covered with red tomato
  sauce. 9. This fruit is long, thin, and yellow.
  10. Answers will vary.

Special Feature: orange, bread slices, orange drink, ice
cream cone, french fries, peanut butter, pizza, banana

Workbook 71

A. Answers will vary. Possible answers include:
  A huge rainstorm went (traveled) over the tiny,
  unprotected town. The cold rain came (poured) from
  the leaden gray sky. It swept angrily across the misty
  hills in gusty sheets. Huge torrents of water quickly
  filled the (raging) brooks and streams before the
  storm finally stopped.

B. Answers will vary.

Workbook 72

A. Bud stared uneasily at the funny old key. It felt
  heavy in his hand. What lock could it fit? Suddenly
  Bud felt as if he were being watched. He glanced
  quickly toward the attic window. He was just in time
  to see the tattered curtain lowered. Bud no longer
  felt safe, calm, or sure.

B. Answers will vary. Be sure the students use editing
  marks correctly. Possible changes include:
  Bud's shirt was wet with sweat. He looked
  desperately behind him as he (raced) on. The
  (menacing) people were coming closer. Bud felt
  scared (, tired, and helpless). He tried to think of a
  way to escape.

Workbook 73

A. 1. February 3, 1920 2. January 29, 1959
  3. March 28, 1944 4. July 4, 1983 5. February
  21, 1941 6. May 30, 1985 7. January 31, 1951
  8. January 1, 2000

B. 9. 8:00 A.M. 10. 12:00 P.M. 11. 11:45 P.M.
  12. 2:45 P.M. 13. 1:15 P.M. 14. 4:30 P.M.

C. 15. I visit my grandfather in Oregon every
  January. 16. Around 8:15 A.M. Grandpa takes me
  for a ride. 17. We go to a fruit stand that has been
  there since July 4, 1929. 18. We play shuffleboard
  from 10:00 A.M. until 12:00 P.M. 19. At 12:00 P.M.
  Grandpa makes sandwiches. 20. Then at 1:30 P.M.
  every day he does volunteer work.

Workbook 74

A. 1. They hold their heads so high. 2. They run so
  fast they fly. 3. Their eyes are velvet brown.
  4. Their coats are spotted tan. 5. Their legs have
  knobby knees.

B. Answers will vary.

Workbook 75

A. 1. It is compared with a leaping fire. 2. They are
  both hot and glowing. 3. It is compared with a
  quilt. 4. Both lie down in warm yellow squares on
  the floor.

B. Answers will vary. Possible answers include:
  5. soft, furry 6. hard

Workbook 76

  1. If he scrubbed too hard, he would scrub away the
  ship. 2. He had to sleep in an extra-large
  lifeboat. 3. He could eat a boatload of eggs plus
  the hens that laid them. 4. If he stood too near the
  rail, the ship might tip over.

Workbook 77

A. 1. fifty 2. red, blue 3. high, striped
  4. delicious, cold

B. 5. hottest 6. lightest 7. longer

C. 8. The 9. a, the 10. an

D. 11. *smoothly*, how 12. *quickly*, how 13. *early*,
  when 14. *up*, where

E. 15. good 16. good 17. well

F. 18. palm/palm 19. rest/rest 20. host/host

Workbook 78

G. 21. synonym 22. antonym 23. synonym
  24. antonym

H. 25. Jessica has blue, yellow, and orange crayons.
  26. The maple syrup was warm, sticky, and
  delicious.

I. Answers will vary. Possible answers include: 27. a
  mountain, the Empire State Building 28. glue,
  melted candy, gum 29. a king, a queen, a
  millionaire 30. grass, spring leaves 31. lead,
  bricks

J. 32.–33. Answers will vary.

UNIT 6

Workbook 79

A. 1. she 2. she, me 3. They, her, me 4. them
  5. We, he, him 6. I 7. You, we 8. It, them
  9. She, us, she 10. I, her, I, it

B. 11. He—Geoffrey 12. They—Anita's teammates

Workbook 80
A. 1. They 2. He 3. He 4. It 5. She
B. 6. They 7. She 8. It 9. He 10. It

Workbook 81
A. 1. me 2. us 3. them 4. them 5. us
B. 6. us 7. them 8. him 9. it 10. her
   11. her 12. them

Workbook 82
A. 1. our 2. my 3. his 4. our 5. his
B. 6. their 7. my 8. his 9. his 10. her
Special Feature: Be sure students circle the baseball bat, the boot, the paintbrush, the wallet, and the key.

Workbook 83
A. 1. Nest Building of the Barn Swallow 2. The Saguaro Cactus 3. The Boyhood of Lee Trevino 4. Ella Fitzgerald 5. The American Beauty Rose 6. Guide Dogs for the Blind
B. Answers will vary. Possible answers include:
   7. Skin Diving, Swimming 8. John Glenn, The First Astronauts 9. Chess, Checkers, Tag 10. Making Egg Rolls, Baking Bread 11. The Marathon Race, The Decathlon 12. Reading, Crafts, Painting, Collecting 13. The Automobile, The Train 14. The Beach, The Mountains 15. My Dog, My Horse 16. Dentist, Engineer, Mechanic 17. Skiing, Ice Skating 18. Popular, Jazz, Opera

Workbook 84
A. 1. protect people 2. direct traffic 3. help children get to and from school 4. enforce parking, speed, and safety laws 5. keep crowds in order
B. 6. attend police academy 7. learn wrestling, judo, first aid, laws 8. learn self-defense 9. learn to gather clues and take fingerprints 10. learn how to pilot a helicopter or how to ride a horse or motorcycle

Workbook 85
A.   Flatboats

   I. How flatboats move
      A. Carried by river current
      B. Long pole used to push and guide
      C. Has no motor or sails
   II. How parts of the flatboat are used
      A. Small wooden cabin where family lives
      B. Furniture and food stored in cabin
      C. Livestock carried on deck

Workbook 86
B. 1.   Canoes

   I. How a canoe is paddled
      A. Bow stroke moves a canoe forward
      B. J-stroke helps hold a straight course
   II. Equipment for a canoe
      A. Life jacket or float pillow
      B. Coffee can or pump for bailing
   2.   Tankers
   I. Kinds of tankers
      A. Liquified natural gas carriers
      B. Oil tankers for oil, gasoline, kerosene
      C. Oil and bulk-oil carriers for oil, coal, grain, iron

   II. Structure of tankers
      A. Deckhouse for crew
      B. Many tanks in hull for cargo
      C. Pumps and pipes on main deck

Workbook 87
Paragraphs will vary. Be sure students include all information from the outline and that facts are stated accurately.

Workbook 88
                Fire Fighters Yesterday and Today
   People have always known about the danger of fire. Ancient Egypt had volunteer fire fighters. In 1666 a fire in London destroyed 13,000 buildings. Not until 1852 was a steam fire engine used in Ohio. It helped get water to fires much more quickly.

Workbook 89
A. 1. Ecology Today 2. "Sesame Street" 3. Making Time Count 4. "A Spring Day" 5. "Frontier World" 6. "Barbara Allen" 7. Profiles in Sports 8. "Tomorrow" 9. Anne of Green Gables 10. Microscopic Animals
B. 11. We are reading the book Rabbit Hill in class. 12. Every evening at camp we sing "God Bless America." 13. Do you know the poem "The Children's Hour"? 14. Last year we read the story "My Friend Flicka."

Workbook 91
   1. How Rainbows Are Formed 2. There are always the same colors in a rainbow. Rainbows form when it is raining while the sun is shining. Rainbows are seen only when the sun is low in the sky. 3. When Rainbows Appear, What Makes a Rainbow 4. paragraph 2 5. paragraph 1 6. paragraph 3 7. paragraph 2
Special Feature: Colors include: red, orange, yellow, green, blue, indigo, and violet.

Workbook 92
A. 1. we 2. He 3. She 4. them
B. 5. She 6. He 7. they 8. It 9. her 10. him 11. us 12. it
C. 13. your 14. My 15. her
D. 16. Where Tigers Live 17. How a Baseball Is Made
E. Items 18 and 21 relate to the topic.

Workbook 93
F. 22. I. Learning about the bow and arrow
         A. Bow was called a crossbow
         B. Knights learned to use crossbows in battle
      II. Learning about riding horses
         A. Knights learned to ride with one hand to keep the weapon arm free
         B. Knights trained horses not to fear loud noises
         C. Knights learned to ride wearing clumsy armor
G. Reports will vary. Be sure that the students include all the information from the outline and that they title the report.
H. Items 24 and 25 are facts for the report.

Answer Key for Workbook

UNIT 7

Workbook 94

A. 1. The big jet landed at the airport.   **2.** A furry panda was taken off the plane.   **3.** The panda's name was Cha-Cha.   **4.** He was going to the San Diego Zoo.   **5.** The people were very excited.
6. Most Americans had few chances to see panda bears.   **7.** Poor little Cha-Cha was very frightened at first.   **8.** He missed his home at the zoo in China.   **9.** Cha-Cha was as happy as could be a few days later.   **10.** His new neighbor, Ling-Ling, was waiting for him in San Diego.
B. 11.–16. Answers will vary.

Workbook 95

A. 1. Chin stays at my house.   **2.** He and I go to the grocery store.   **3.** Chin uses my brother's bike.
4. We raced all the way over.   **5.** Many people are there already.   **6.** Everyone likes the new grocery carts.   **7.** A clerk grinds coffee for the customer.
8. Chin carried a large package home.   **9.** He eats an apple every day.   **10.** He has a pear too.   **11.** I try the peaches instead.
B. 12.–14. Answers will vary.

Special Feature: $\underset{1}{Y}\ \underset{2}{O}\ \underset{3}{U}\ \underset{4}{A}\ \underset{5}{R}\ \underset{6}{E}\ \underset{7}{G}\ \underset{8}{R}\ \underset{9}{E}\ \underset{10}{A}\ \underset{11}{T}$

Workbook 96

A. 1. holds   **2.** invite   **3.** begins   **4.** stands   **5.** plans   **6.** begins   **7.** stay   **8.** live   **9.** hope   **10.** ask
B. 11. works   **12.** pass   **13.** pushes   **14.** sees   **15.** asks

Workbook 97

A. 1. Yes, Hilda is going to be in the play.   **2.** No, she will not sing with Antonio.   **3.** Yes, they are going to play instruments.   **4.** No, Hilda will not play the piano.   **5.** Yes, Antonio has found his guitar.   **6.** Yes, it was in the hall closet.
B. 7.–8. Answers will vary.

Workbook 98

A. 1. disconnect   **2.** impatient   **3.** breakable
4. incorrect   **5.** singer   **6.** helpful   **7.** misprint
8. careless   **9.** director   **10.** nonfiction
11. prepaid   **12.** reread
B. 13. breakable   **14.** prepaid   **15.** disconnect   **16.** nonfiction   **17.** impatient   **18.** reread   **19.** incorrect   **20.** helpful   **21.** misprint   **22.** careless   **23.** singer   **24.** director

Workbook 99

A. earthworm, rattlesnake, crabgrass, goldfish, handcuffs, underhanded, groundhog, greyhound, fishbowl, afternoon
B. 1. Everybody   **2.** outdoors   **3.** raincoats   **4.** blueberry   **5.** rooftop
C. Paragraphs will vary.

Workbook 100

A. 1. bee   **2.** wait   **3.** sale   **4.** not   **5.** pair   **6.** to, too   **7.** blue   **8.** flower   **9.** son   **10.** beat   **11.** buy   **12.** there   **13.** pail   **14.** read   **15.** deer   **16.** stair   **17.** sea   **18.** due   **19.** knight   **20.** seen   **21.** threw   **22.** road   **23.** here   **24.** soar
B. 25. too, two   **26.** their, they're   **27.** eight   **28.** know   **29.** I   **30.** won
Sentences will vary.

Workbook 101

A. 1. Apples and pears grow best in a region not too hot or too cold.   **2.** Strawberries and raspberries like this kind of climate too.   **3.** Peaches and grapes need a warmer place to grow.

Workbook 102

4. Oranges and lemons require a hotter climate.
5. Bananas and pineapples must have a tropical climate.
B. 6. Fruit trees are planted and grow year after year.   **7.** Trees are fertilized and sprayed.
8. Insects attack fruit trees and sometimes kill them.   **9.** Fruit bruises easily and ripens quickly.
10. Workers pick the fruit and pack it carefully.

Workbook 103

A. 1. In my room I found the key.   **2.** Into my pocket I tucked the key.   **3.** Soon afterward I went downstairs.   **4.** Just then I had an idea.
5. Endlessly I looked for a secret room.
6. Because I am so smart I finally found it.   **7.** Into the lock I quietly slid the key.
B. 8.–10. Answers will vary.

Workbook 104

A. Many fire departments have rescue companies. Rescue workers go to large fires to assist fire fighters. They help get people out of burning buildings. When people are overcome by smoke they give first aid. In emergencies they rush people to hospitals.
B. Answers will vary.

Answer Key for Workbook

Workbook 105

1. No, we did not go to the shore this weekend.
2. No, we did not stay at home either. 3. Yes, we did go to the mountains. 4. We hiked through the cool, green, and leafy forest. 5. Yes, we wore backpacks. 6. We filled them with cold drinks, sandwiches, and fruit. 7. The rabbits, squirrels, and deer avoided us. 8. Yes, we stopped by a splashing stream on the way. 9. We looked at the small, smooth, and shiny pebbles. 10. No, we did not climb with ropes. 11. We wear good boots, high socks, and gloves. 12. My cousins Victor, Paul, and Francine came with us. 13. Yes, we finally stopped to eat. 14. Victor sang, played his harmonica, and whistled. 15. We enjoyed the warm sun, cool grass, and tall trees. 16. Yes, we had to climb down the mountain before dark.
17. We had lighter backpacks, tired feet, and full stomachs. 18. No, we will not go again next weekend. 19. Yes, we will do spring cleaning then. 20. Please come over to help us wash windows, polish cars, and clean garages.

Workbook 107

1. Answers will vary. The students should indicate that you make more work for yourself by refusing work initially. 2. Answers will vary. The students should indicate that the donkey is small, thin, hardworking, and helpful. 3. Answers will vary. The students should indicate that the horse is proud, unhelpful, lazy, and vain. 4. Answers will vary. The students should indicate that the donkey rode on the animal who had refused to help. 5. The characters are animals. The story teaches a lesson or moral.
6. Possible answers include: a. brave, wise b. busy, hardworking c. clever or foolish d. clever, sly e. proud, vain f. wise, helpful
7. a.

Workbook 108

A. 1. The three friends were driving to California.
2. Many cars passed them. 3. They looked at all the license plates. 4. Arthur stopped the car suddenly. 5. A little chipmunk scurried across the road.

B. 6. goes 7. meet 8. bring 9. races
C. 10. Yes, Jackie and Roger did go sledding.
11. Yes, it was Roger who fell first. 12. No, Jackie did not help Roger get up.
D. 13. restate 14. careless 15. preplan
16. pitcher 17. guilty 18. nonfiction
19. untidy 20. quickly 21. impossible

Workbook 109

E. 22. You're 23. there 24. too 25. they're
F. 26. pillowcase, bedroom 27. silverware, dishwasher 28. clothesline, workbench
G. 29. Ted and Abby watched the launching of the space shuttle. 30. The engines smoke and shoot out flames.
H. 31. b. animals 32. a. More is not always better.

UNIT 8

Workbook 110
A. Call the fire department. Report your name, the nature of the emergency, and the location.
B. Call for Ms. Levy at 11:04 A.M. Mr. Eldridge called to say that your report is ready. A messenger can pick it up at 480 Main Street. Call taken by (pupil's name).

Workbook 111
A. Answers will vary, but suggested answers include: 1, 2, 3, 5, 7, 9, 10, 11, 12.
B. 14.–15. Answers will vary.

Workbook 112
A. Answers will vary.
B. Answers will vary.

Workbook 113
A. 1. fact 2. fact 3. opinion 4. fact
B. 5. fact 6. opinion 7. fact 8. opinion
Special Feature: Answers will vary.

Workbook 114
1. Agana 2. Ritidian Point 3. Philippine Sea
4. Dededo and Yigo 5. Mount Lamlam
6. Pacific Ocean 7. 15 kilometers 8. 12

Workbook 115
1. "My family is going on a trip," Roseann told her class. 2. "Where are you going?" asked her teacher. 3. "We're going to the Lilac Festival," Roseann answered. 4. She said, "The Lilac Festival is in Rochester, New York." 5. "What will you see?" asked her friend Niki. 6. "There will be a parade, bands, and fireworks," Roseann said.
7. Roseann told her friends, "The first Lilac Festival was held in 1905." 8. "Thousands of people come to see over 500 kinds of lilacs," she continued.

Workbook 116
A. 2, 1, 4, 3
B. Titles will vary.

Workbook 117
A. 1. "Can you show me how to use the cowboy puppet?" asked Robert. 2. "It's not as hard as it looks," answered Jenny. 3. "First be sure the strings are untangled," she said. 4. Jenny continued, "Then try to move different parts of it."
5. "Oh, look how I can make him dance!" exclaimed Robert. 6. Jenny asked, "Would you like to give a puppet show?"
B. Check for correct editing marks.
  "Why don't we do a puppet show about the Old West?" asked Lorna.
  Robert said, "Good idea! We'll make some scenery that looks like a ghost town."
  Jenny looked at them both. She said, "Let's dress up this puppet to be Calamity Jane, a cowgirl!"

Answer Key for Workbook

Workbook 118

A. 1. Harold said, "What shall our next project be?"
2. "Why don't we make Mother's Day presents?" said Peter. 3. "We could make flower arrangements," he said. 4. "My mom would like that," said Dibe. 5. "Yes, let's do that!" exclaimed Harold. 6. "Why don't we make whatever we want?" said Ted. 7. "That way we can make what we really want," he said. 8. "Let's go!" everyone yelled.

B.   "Did you finish your flower arrangement?" asked Peter.

"No, I'm having a lot of trouble with it," answered Dibe.

"I'll help you," said Peter.

"Where do we start?" laughed Dibe.

Workbook 120

A. 1. Peter, Fudge, and Mom are the main characters. 2. The setting for this part of the story is the bedroom and kitchen of Peter's house.
3. His pet turtle Dribble has disappeared. 4. The next setting will be in the hospital. 5. Answers will vary.

B. 6. He became upset and worried about Dribble.
7. She became upset. She thought Fudge might be in danger and called for an ambulance. 8. He laughed and thought it was funny.

Workbook 121

A. Call the hospital or an ambulance. Report your name, the nature of the emergency, and the location.
B. Questions 1 and 3 would be appropriate.
C. 4. Answers will vary.

Workbook 122

D. 5. fact 6. opinion 7. fact 8. fact
E. 9. "I don't want to go to the race," said Craig.
10. "You already signed up," replied Nan.
11. Craig said, "Maybe so, but I feel sick." 12. "Do you think some water will help?" asked Nan.
F. 13. The author introduces characters and setting.
14. The author tells about a problem or challenge for the main character. 15. The problem usually is solved or the challenge is met.

Answer Key for Workbook

EXTRA PRACTICE MASTERS

The Extra Practice Masters that accompany this level of *Language for Daily Use, Phoenix Edition* appear on the following pages. They provide additional practice on the concepts and skills developed in the program. Reference is made in the appropriate lesson plan each time an Extra Practice Master can be assigned. Each Extra Practice Master also appears in reduced form within the lesson plan it accompanies. The answer key for these pages follows the Extra Practice Masters in this Teacher's Resource Book.

(The Extra Practice Masters also are available as separate spirit duplicating masters.)

Name _____

Sentences pages 2–3

A. Match these sentence parts to make six complete sentences.

1. The sidewalks in the city   are filled with shoppers.

2. The department stores   cook meals for the people.

3. Taxicabs   pick up people.

4. Many office buildings   are lined with people.

5. The restaurants   has some trees and a place to rest.

6. A little park   have hundreds of workers.

B. Make a check next to each group of words that is a complete sentence.

_____ 7. Makes delicious chocolate cookies.

_____ 8. In the back of the bakery large ovens.

_____ 9. My sister visits the bakery after school.

_____ 10. Eats the corn muffins first.

_____ 11. Blueberry muffins warm from the oven.

_____ 12. For my birthday we bought a clown cake.

_____ 13. My mother buys cherry cake also.

_____ 14. Every afternoon last month.

_____ 15. I love to walk past the bakery.

C. For each group of words in Practice B that is not a complete sentence, add words to make one. Write the sentences.

16. _____

17. _____

18. _____

19. _____

20. _____

Name _____

Four Kinds of Sentences pages 4–7

A. Add end punctuation marks to each sentence. Then write
declarative, interrogative, exclamatory, or *imperative* to tell the
kind of sentence it is.

1. Do not pick the daisies.

   _____

2. Where is the shovel?

   _____

3. Can you hear the woodpecker?

   _____

4. Ouch, these thorns are sharp!

   _____

5. I like to plant seeds.

   _____

6. Bring the watering can.

   _____

B. Underline the correct punctuation mark to end each sentence.
Then rewrite each sentence correctly.

7. What animals live in my garden	a. (.)	b. (?)	c. (!)
8. How colorful that snake is	a. (.)	b. (?)	c. (!)
9. A bushy-tailed squirrel hides nuts	a. (.)	b. (?)	c. (!)
10. Is that a mole's tunnel in the dirt	a. (.)	b. (?)	c. (!)
11. Rabbits munch my carrots	a. (.)	b. (?)	c. (!)
12. Look at this bird's nest	a. (.)	b. (?)	c. (!)
13. Wow, that toad jumps fast	a. (.)	b. (?)	c. (!)
14. Do bumblebees like flowers	a. (.)	b. (?)	c. (!)
15. Find some earthworms in the rich soil	a. (.)	b. (?)	c. (!)
16. All of these creatures like my garden	a. (.)	b. (?)	c. (!)
17. The leaves are falling	a. (.)	b. (?)	c. (!)
18. Where are the keys	a. (.)	b. (?)	c. (!)

C. Complete these statements about the four kinds of sentences.

19. A declarative sentence ends with a _____.

20. An interrogative sentence ends with a _____.

21. An imperative sentence ends with a _____.

22. An exclamatory sentence ends with an _____.

2 UNIT 1: Extra Practice Master

Complete Subject and Predicate pages 10–11

A. Draw one line under the complete subject of each sentence.
Draw two lines under each complete predicate.

1. Mr. Clemson took our class on a hike.
2. We saw a lot of traffic.
3. José pointed to an unusual building.
4. Three girls stopped at an old fountain.
5. The warm sun shone brightly.
6. We grew hotter and hotter.
7. Mary and Tish told Mr. Clemson.
8. He turned into a building.
9. We shrieked for joy.
10. A sign said "City Swimming Pool."

B. Match each subject in the group with its correct predicate.
Write the complete sentences.

11. The bus	soaked the garden.
12. That sailor	yapped at the mail carrier.
13. Three of my friends	picked up riders at the stop.
14. Our dog	returned to his ship.
15. The thunderstorm	went downtown together.

_____

_____

_____

_____

C. Finish each sentence. Add a complete subject or a complete predicate.

16. The baby _____

17. _____ buzzed loudly.

18. The newborn kittens _____.

19. _____ started the plane engine.

20. _____ built a tunnel.

The Library and the Card Catalog pages 14-17

A. Write the section of the library where each book can be found.
Write *fiction, nonfiction, biography,* or *reference.*

_____ 1. *Full-Court Pirate* (a story about basketball)

_____ 2. *Maria Tallchief* (a true-life story of a ballerina)

_____ 3. *Students' Encyclopedia*

_____ 4. *Life in Colonial America*

_____ 5. *The Big Book of Animal Fables* (short animal stories)

_____ 6. *Franklin D. Roosevelt* (true-life story of a President)

_____ 7. *Understanding Photography*

_____ 8. *Birds Do the Strangest Things* (facts about birds)

_____ 9. *Random House Dictionary*

_____ 10. *Steamboat South* (a story about a trip on a river)

B. Study these cards from a library card catalog. Write *title card,
author card,* or *subject card* under each card. Then answer the
questions that follow.

```
j798
 K
      Krementz, Jill
A Very Young Rider.
Illustrated by Jill Krementz
Knopf, c. 1977   128 p. illus.
```

```
j798
 K      A very young rider
Krementz, Jill
      A very young rider.
      Illustrated by Jill Krementz.
      Knopf, c. 1977   128 p. illus.
```

```
j798
 K      SHOW RIDING
      Krementz, Jill
      A very young rider.
      Illustrated by Jill Krementz
      Knopf, c. 1977   128 p. illus.
```

_____   _____   _____

11. The title of this book is _____.

12. The author's name is _____.

13. The subject of the book is _____.

C. On what kind of card would you find each book? Write *subject
card, title card,* or *author card.*

_____ 14. a book about Latin American folktales

_____ 15. a book called *How to Show Your Dog*

_____ 16. a book by Ed Emberley

Writing Sentences page 23
MECHANICS PRACTICE

A. Put the correct punctuation mark at the end of each sentence.

1. Where is my mitt
2. Today is the big game
3. I can hardly wait
4. Do not forget your hat
5. Is Uncle Mike coming
6. This is so exciting
7. We are playing the Tigers
8. Are they in third place
9. Please make room for me
10. What a huge crowd

B. Write the sentences correctly. Use capital letters and punctuation marks where they are needed.

11. i play first base and left field

_____

12. my friend Susan is our star pitcher

_____

13. how fast she can pitch

_____

14. who hit a home run in the first inning

_____

15. Richie plays on another team in the summer

_____

16. please buy me a drink

_____

17. what a great catch that was

_____

18. where is the refreshment stand

_____

19. it is near the children's playground

_____

20. is our team up at bat now

_____

21. do not forget to take pictures today

_____

22. do you think we'll win the game

_____

Name _____

Nouns   pages 36–37

A. Put an X on the words that are nouns.

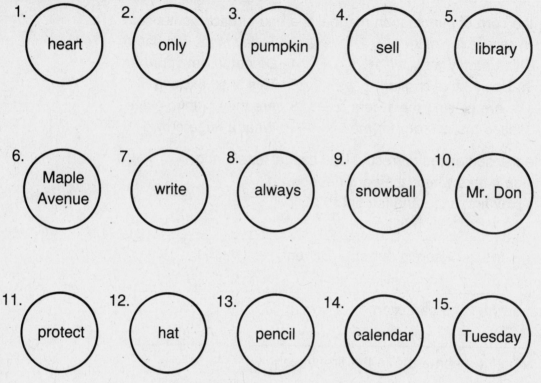

1. heart 2. only 3. pumpkin 4. sell 5. library

6. Maple Avenue 7. write 8. always 9. snowball 10. Mr. Don

11. protect 12. hat 13. pencil 14. calendar 15. Tuesday

B. Underline the nouns in each sentence.
16. Marta read an interesting book.
17. One story told about gnomes and giants.
18. Another tale told of an elf.
19. The librarian asked Harold to find some paper.
20. She wrote a list of stories for the class.

C. 21.–30. Write a noun in each blank. Make the story funny.

My sister's name is _____. My name is _____.

We rode our _____ to the _____. We saw a

strange-looking _____ there. The thing had tiny

_____ all over its _____. It was as tall as a

_____. It looked as if it were made of _____.

When we looked more closely, we saw that it was formed of

_____.

6 UNIT 2:   Extra Practice Master

Plural Nouns pages 38–39

A. Look at the first word in each row. Then underline its correct plural spelling.

1. **machine**	machinies	machiness	machines
2. **city**	citys	cities	cityes
3. **match**	matches	matchs	matchies
4. **glass**	glass	glasses	glassies
5. **quiz**	quizs	quizzes	quizies
6. **doctor**	doctors	doctories	doctores
7. **lullaby**	lullabyes	lullabies	lullabys
8. **monkey**	monkies	monkeyes	monkeys
9. **radio**	radioes	radios	radioies
10. **rash**	rashs	rashies	rashes

B. Write the plural of each of the nouns in parentheses ( ).

11. Dad and I decided to make two _____ of our special recipe.   (batch)

12. The recipe is for chocolate chip _____.   (cookie)

13. My brother and I will take them to school for our

_____.   (class)

14. We used spoons, _____, and an eggbeater.   (bowl)

15. We added flour, sugar, an egg, and _____.   (nut)

16. We got fresh eggs from the local _____.   (dairy)

17. We poured in the _____ too.   (chip)

18. When the cookies were in the oven Dad and I washed the

_____.   (dish)

19. Then we used spatulas to stack the cookies in

_____.   (box)

20. "Freeze the extras for _____," said Dad.   (party)

21. We ate _____ and grapes for dessert. (cherry)

22. Then we washed the _____. (plate)

Name _____

Other Plural Nouns   pages 40–41

A. Underline the correct plural form of the noun that belongs in each sentence.

1. Her three (grandchilds, grandchildren) came to visit.
2. A family of field (mice, mouses) ran through the garden.
3. The king greeted the (gentlemans, gentlemen) at the door.
4. On our camping trip we spotted many (deer, deers).
5. After walking through the zoo my (feet, foots) ached.
6. If you are quiet you will see three (mooses, moose) in the distance.
7. The (womans, women) worked on the construction crew.
8. At the ranch we watched many (sheeps, sheep) being sheared.
9. I hear a flock of (gooses, geese) honking in the sky.
10. On Jesse's farm the (oxen, oxes) pull heavy loads.

B. Next to each noun write its plural form.

11. scissors _____   12. Englishman _____

13. elk _____   14. glasses _____

15. child _____   16. man _____

17. tooth _____   18. deer _____

19. pants _____   20. saleswoman _____

C. Choose eight plural nouns from this page. Use each one in a sentence.

21. _____

22. _____

23. _____

24. _____

25. _____

26. _____

27. _____

28. _____

Name _____

Common and Proper Nouns pages 42–43

A. Write a proper noun next to each common noun.

1. river _____   2. day _____

3. book _____   4. person _____

5. park _____   6. holiday _____

7. month _____   8. school _____

9. country _____ 10. state _____

B. Capitalize the proper nouns. Underline the common nouns.
Then write each sentence correctly.

11. My uncle lives in a country called italy.

_____

12. It is on the continent of europe.

_____

13. He speaks a language called italian.

_____

14. A sea called the adriatic sea is on the coast.

_____

15. My uncle takes trips by car to the town of rimini.

_____

16. Then he drives through a tunnel called the apennine tunnel.

_____

17. He arrives in the town of pisa.

_____

18. He sees a famous tower called the tower of pisa.

_____

Writing Names and Titles   pages 44–45

A. In each group underline the name that is written correctly.

1. Rev T. G. Hoyt
   Rev t. g. Hoyt
   Rev. T. G. Hoyt
   rev T. G. Hoyt

2. ms. linda b. kaplan
   Ms. Linda B. Kaplan
   Ms Linda b Kaplan
   Ms. Linda b. Kaplan

3. Gov Morris S Ferguson
   gov. Morris S. Ferguson
   Gov morris s. Ferguson
   Gov. Morris S. Ferguson

4. Mr. Chan Tung Lee
   mr. Chan Tung Lee
   Mr Chan Tung Lee
   mr. chan tung lee

B. Write the sentences correctly. Use capital letters and periods where they are needed.

5. Did miss ellen powers come to Career Day?

_____

6. She and dr l w atkins train animals for television.

_____

7. They own zeke, a beagle, and miss daisy, a spaniel.

_____

8. miss janet sun spoke about art and music.

_____

9. mr and mrs ray helped with Career Day.

_____

10. My teacher, mrs conroy, met with r p ives.

_____

11. Did you enjoy the slide show given by gov scott?

_____

12. My friend, mr quincy m summers, writes her speeches.

_____

13. What did dr mae stewart and mr ed black talk about?

_____

14. Were jimmy mercer and kathy turner there?

_____

15. mrs rosa hernandez talked about careers in science.

_____

Writing Names of Places pages 46-47

A. Write these place names correctly.

1. benton harbor, michigan

2. windsor, ontario

3. tremain st

4. fisher rd

5. cleveland, ohio

6. kansas city, kansas

7. grand ave

8. acapulco, mexico

9. rome, italy

10. holmes road

11. buffalo, new york

12. ferry street

13. baltimore, maryland

14. paris, france

B. Show where capital letters and periods are needed. Then write the sentences correctly on a separate piece of paper.

15. philadelphia is a city in the state of pennsylvania

16. east river drive and west river drive follow the Schuylkill River through the city

17. watts street runs through the city past City Hall

18. There are many interesting buildings along chestnut street and walnut street

19. ardmore and lansdowne are towns near philadelphia

20. camden, new jersey, is located across the Delaware River

21. we visited lincoln center

22. my family took a boat ride up the hudson river

Possessive Nouns pages 48–51

A. Underline the possessive nouns.
1. The king's password is known.
2. Knight Roger's chances grew smaller each day.
3. The ravens' cries woke him at daybreak.
4. We must find the children's trail.
5. Will they lead us to the magician's cave?

B. Write the possessive form of the noun in parentheses ( ).

6. Can you escape the _____ curse? (goblins)

7. The _____ secrets are now yours. (women)

8. A message is in the _____ bonnet. (baby)

9. What is _____ plan? (Queen Bess)

10. The _____ armor is ready. (men)

11. The _____ horses have been saddled. (riders)

12. The _____ lands will be lost. (family)

13. Bring _____ crown to me. (King Edward)

14. The _____ nurse must not know. (children)

15. _____ hoofbeats thundered on the road. (horse)

C. Write a possessive noun for each group of words.

16. the jewels of the queen

_____

18. the horses of the knights

_____

20. the hand of the princess

_____

22. the spell of the witches

_____

24. the kindness of Queen Hilda

_____

17. the magic of the elves

_____

19. the cave of the dragons

_____

21. the castle of the duke

_____

23. the bravery of Prince Charles

_____

25. the wands of the wizards

_____

Name _____

Fact and Opinion pages 58–59

A. Read the pairs of sentences. Write *fact* before the sentence
in the pair that is a *fact.* Write *opinion* before each *opinion.*

_____ 1. Everyone likes to watch Jacques Cousteau on TV.

_____ 2. Jacques Cousteau is an underwater diver.

_____ 3. Arizona is a state.

_____ 4. Arizona has the best climate of any state.

_____ 5. This town has 30,000 people.

_____ 6. Small towns are better than cities.

_____ 7. George Washington was the greatest President.

_____ 8. George Washington was the first President of the United States.

_____ 9. The first day of winter is December 21.

_____ 10. Winter is the worst season.

_____ 11. This camera takes number 120 film.

_____ 12. Everyone should use this camera.

_____ 13. Volleyball was invented in 1895 by William Morgan.

_____ 14. Volleyball is the most fun of any sport to play.

_____ 15. In 1893 the first license plates appeared on a car.

_____ 16. The license plate for our state has the best colors of any plate.

_____ 17. Old cars are funny looking.

_____ 18. Many early model cars had a crank in the front.

_____ 19. On October 20, 1975, the world's biggest birthday cake was cut
in San Francisco, California.

_____ 20. This cake will make your taste buds tingle.

B. Write a fact about dogs. Then write an opinion about them.

21. _____

22. _____

Writing Names page 63
MECHANICS PRACTICE

A. Write these names of people and pets correctly.

1. mr ron cummings

   _____

2. sen ann dempsey

   _____

3. thunder

   _____

4. mrs l s lorenz

   _____

5. gov pat a landau

   _____

6. miss kathy kinski

   _____

7. vincent reynolds

   _____

8. dr ruth blair

   _____

9. chuckles

   _____

10. sen bill greenman

    _____

11. ms sally anderson

    _____

12. mr s m marchard

    _____

B. In each group circle the name that is written correctly.

13. gov. P. B. Armstrong
    Gov P B Armstrong
    Gov. P. B. Armstrong
    Gov P. B. Armstrong

14. Ms Kathy Warren Smith
    ms. kathy Warren Smith
    Ms. kathy warren smith
    Ms. Kathy Warren Smith

15. Rev. Chris B Cahill
    Rev Chris B. Cahill
    rev. Chris B. Cahill
    Rev. Chris B. Cahill

16. Dr. Sandra Marsilio
    dr. Sandra Marsilio
    Dr. sandra marsilio
    Dr Sandra Marsilio

C. Write the sentences correctly. Use capital letters and periods where they are needed.

17. On Monday mrs kahn's class is going to the zoo.

    _____

18. Will you talk to dr leslie jonas about his work?

    _____

19. His favorite zoo animal is a snake named slim.

    _____

20. His assistant is miss laura knowlton.

    _____

Action Verbs pages 78–79

A. Read the sentences. Draw two lines under the action verbs. Some sentences have more than one action verb.

1. The coals glowed in the fireplace.
2. Dad toasted the bread to a golden brown.
3. The colt trotted around the field.
4. Daisy, our old dog, rests under the maple tree.
5. The great eagle glided through the sky.
6. At about 8:00 P.M. every night I yawn.
7. The cars speed down the highway.
8. Leo ties the bundles of newspapers.
9. I crush cans under my foot.
10. The performers practice on the stage.
11. The dolphins swim to the side of the pool.
12. We fasten the windows and shutters.
13. Nelson looked at his watch.
14. Kim wrote a letter to her cousin in Japan.
15. I packed my clothes for the trip to Idaho.
16. My baby brother blinks and sighs in his crib.
17. Chew and swallow before you leave the table.
18. Next I roll out the dough and knead it.
19. I trained my dog and taught him well.
20. Marla slides and turns on her ice skates.

B. Use each action verb in a sentence.

21. agree _____
22. decide _____
23. teach _____
24. invite _____
25. choose _____
26. ask _____

Name _____

Linking Verbs pages 80–81

A. Draw two lines under the linking verb in each sentence.
1. Adrienne and Richard are expert skin divers.
2. The collection of shells in their house is huge.
3. Pirate's Cove and Landlubber's Reef were their favorite spots.
4. Some old sunken ships were interesting.
5. Today the ships are beautiful.
6. Now their favorite place is Flounder Bay.
7. Nearly every weekend they are tourists.
8. Their treasure is shells.
9. A few years ago Richard was a salesman in a large city.
10. Adrienne was a nurse in a busy downtown hospital.

B. Complete each sentence. Use *am*, *is*, or *are*.

11. I _____ a teacher of oceanography at the high school.

12. The ocean _____ my second home on the weekends.

13. This summer I _____ a guide for other skin divers.

14. Sea creatures _____ my underwater friends and neighbors.

15. But some of them _____ not so friendly.

C. Complete each sentence. Use *was* or *were*.

16. Deep under the ocean the water _____ very dark and cold.

17. The pressure at this level _____ tremendous.

18. The only lights _____ tiny flashes from some kinds of fish.

19. The only sound _____ the low moaning of a humpback whale.

20. She and her mate _____ happy.

D. Draw two lines under the verb in each sentence. Then write
action verb or *linking verb* to tell the kind of verb it is.

21. Whale songs travel hundreds of miles.   _____

22. These songs are unlike anything else.   _____

23. Scientists were curious about them.   _____

24. But a whale is a difficult research animal.   _____

25. These animals are huge, shy, and rare.   _____

16   UNIT 3:   Extra Practice Master

Helping Verbs pages 82–83

A. Draw two lines under each main verb and its helping verb.
Then circle the helping verb.

1. The girl on the horse will ride around the ring.
2. Kenny is hanging upside down on the monkey bars.
3. The little dog has jumped through the hoop.
4. I have gone to the circus every year.
5. My grandmother will come next week.
6. The girls have taken the bus into town.
7. We were sailing last week at the lake.
8. The truck is collecting newspapers today.
9. We will return the lawn mower this afternoon.
10. Marla had spent all her savings on a tiny radio.
11. Freddy is vacuuming the living room.
12. May had ridden in the ambulance to the hospital.
13. We were sliding down the snowy hill on a sled.
14. I am wandering down the path.
15. Jack and Missy were going to the pizza shop.
16. They will meet you there.
17. He is working hard on the reading lesson.
18. The sun is shining brightly through the window.
19. I had spoken to my friend on the telephone just yesterday.
20. I was checking for some books at the library.

B. Use these main verbs and helping verbs in sentences.

21. had run _____

22. will go _____

23. were playing _____

24. is coming _____

25. are taking _____

26. am walking _____

27. will see _____

28. has come _____

Name _____

Verb Tenses pages 84–86

Draw two lines under the verb in each sentence. Then write *past*, *present*, or *future* to tell the tense of the verb.

_____ 1. Brian mowed the lawn last week.

_____ 2. We watched the fire truck at a fire.

_____ 3. Please join our dodgeball game.

_____ 4. Mother will meet grandmother at 6:00 P.M.

_____ 5. They will fix Leo's car at the service station.

_____ 6. I will swim the backstroke in the meet.

_____ 7. The basketball game started an hour ago.

_____ 8. For our school project we collected old newspapers.

_____ 9. Mira will take the science test.

_____ 10. Alice comes with us to the lake.

_____ 11. I raised this carrot in my own garden.

_____ 12. That cloud looks like a rabbit in the sky.

_____ 13. I will buy new blue jeans and a sweat shirt.

_____ 14. My brother earned ten dollars on his paper route.

_____ 15. Roger mends the hole in his sock.

_____ 16. The workers dig a huge hole in the field.

_____ 17. At 7:30 P.M. I will watch my favorite TV show.

_____ 18. Mr. Silver reads the newspaper.

_____ 19. The pitcher will throw the ball to the catcher.

_____ 20. I tie my shoes.

_____ 21. Jason dribbled the basketball during the game.

_____ 22. The kids lick their ice cream cones.

_____ 23. Our library will show a movie this Saturday.

_____ 24. Sheila watches the ballet.

Contractions page 87

A. Underline the contractions. Then write the two words from which the contraction is made.

_____ 1. Didn't Stacey receive a new camera for her birthday?

_____ 2. She doesn't know how to use it, but May will show her.

_____ 3. Nathaniel isn't sure what shutter speed to use.

_____ 4. Won't she be pleased with this roll of pictures?

_____ 5. Her poodle wasn't sitting still for his photograph.

_____ 6. May can't seem to make him face the camera for Stacey.

_____ 7. Aren't black and white photographs easier to take?

_____ 8. I haven't learned how to take flash pictures yet.

_____ 9. Don't use this high-speed film for everyday pictures.

_____ 10. Our film hasn't come back from the developers yet.

B. Write the contraction for each pair of words.

11. are not _____   12. was not _____

13. will not _____   14. did not _____

15. have not _____   16. cannot _____

C. Write four sentences. Use at least one contraction in each sentence.

17. _____

18. _____

19. _____

20. _____

D. Fill in the blanks with the correct word.

21. A _____ is a short form of two words.

22. In a contraction an _____ takes the place of the missing letters.

Name _____

Spelling Past Tense Verbs   pages 88–89

A. Look at the first verb in each row. Underline the correct spelling of the past tense.

1. **stir**	stirred	stired	stirried
2. **hurry**	hurryed	hurried	hurred
3. **spot**	spoted	spottied	spotted
4. **dry**	dried	dryed	dryd
5. **hop**	hoped	hopped	hoppied
6. **scrap**	scrappied	scraped	scrapped
7. **empty**	emptyed	emptied	empted
8. **strum**	strummed	strumed	strumied
9. **flop**	floped	flopped	flopied
10. **try**	trid	tryed	tried

B. Fill in each blank with the past tense form of the verb in parentheses ( ).

11. The police officer _____ open the car door.   (pry)

12. They _____ their knees at the square dance.   (slap)

13. We _____ a caterpillar so we could look at it.   (trap)

14. The kitten _____ up the milk quickly.   (lap)

15. My little sister _____ that she lost my book.   (deny)

16. Michael _____ his finger in the car door.   (jam)

17. The class _____ a holiday lunch for parents.   (plan)

18. The woman _____ herself in the hot auditorium.   (fan)

19. Every year our family _____ vegetables from the garden.   (can)

20. We _____ to hurry but we were still late.   (try)

21. My cousin _____ the hedge.   (trim)

22. The blanket _____ quickly.   (dry)

Using Irregular Verbs   pages 90–93

Read each sentence. Underline the correct past form of the
verb in parentheses (   ).

1. Morning bells have (rang, rung) on the *Challenger II.*
2. Turo (gone, went) into the control room of his father's spaceship.
3. His sister, Celeste, (began, begun) her work in the solar greenhouse.
4. Her father had (gave, given) her permission to experiment there.
5. She had (grew, grown) a special kind of plant.
6. Astronauts had (took, taken) samples of the plant from the surface of Venus.
7. She had (wrote, written) careful records about the plant.
8. Celeste (did, done) not know how important the plant would soon be.
9. Suddenly one of the ship's alarm bells (rang, rung).
10. Men and women (ran, run) to their emergency stations.
11. Lights have (began, begun) to flash on the control panels.
12. Members of the crew (did, done) what they could to find the trouble.
13. "We are losing power!" cried Turo's father as he (took, taken) charge.
14. Computers (gave, given) no reason for a breakdown.
15. Then an eerie voice (came, come) through the intercom system.
16. "Earthlings, beware!" it (sang, sung) strangely.
17. The spaceship had (came, come) into the Singing Galaxy.
18. The songs here have (took, taken) over the minds of men.
19. Others (wrote, written) about the dangers in the Singing Galaxy.
20. Turo's eyes (grew, grown) wide with fear.
21. "Is there anything others have (did, done) to escape?" he asked.
22. "That is what we have (came, come) to find out," replied his father grimly.
23. The songs had (grew, grown) very loud in the spaceship.
24. Slowly their melodies (gone, went) into the minds of the crew.
25. Turo had (did, done) all he could to avoid listening.
26. More and more voices (sang, sung) around the ship.
27. The Singing Galaxy had (sang, sung) a powerful trance.
28. Celeste (ran, run) into her greenhouse to escape the sound.
29. Something very strange had (took, taken) place there.
30. Each plant had (grew, grown) to twice its size.
31. As the voices (sang, sung), the plants (grew, grown).
32. Their leaves had (began, begun) to muffle the sounds of the songs.
33. Celeste (rang, rung) the code bell for the control room.
34. Her father (took, taken) one look at the plants and (gave,
    given) an order.
35. Thanks to Celeste, they (began, begun) their escape from the
    Singing Galaxy.

Name _____

Guide Words and Alphabetical Order pages 96–97

A. Write each list of words in alphabetical order.

1. arc, arbor, arrow, art, arena

_____, _____, _____, _____, _____

2. ostrich, onion, otter, oyster, olive

_____, _____, _____, _____, _____

3. sleigh, sleep, slicker, slim, slide

_____, _____, _____, _____, _____

4. zoo, zodiac, zoom, zipper, zone

_____, _____, _____, _____, _____

5. exchange, explode, exercise, excavate, explain

_____, _____, _____, _____, _____

B. Words from three pages of a dictionary are shown in the word box. Write the words under the correct set of guide words. List them in alphabetical order.

roadside	joker	pincers	roaster
pineapple	roach	rob	pinch
pimple	Jordan	pinfeather	journal
joiner	river	pilot	roaring
	jolly	josh	

6. **joggle–journey**   7. **pillow–pinkeye**   8. **risk–robbery**

_____ _____ _____

_____ _____ _____

_____ _____ _____

_____ _____ _____

_____ _____ _____

C. Look at the guide words from a page in a dictionary. Underline the words that would be found on that page.

comforter–concern

compare   comb   comma
comeback   complain   confess
computer   community   congress

Entry Words pages 98–99

A. Use these words to label the parts of the dictionary entry.

1. entry   2. entry word   3. pronunciation

4. part of speech   5. definition   6. example

_____

_____

_____

skim [skim] *v.* **skimmed, skim·ming 1** To remove floating matter from the surface of (a liquid): to *skim* milk. **2** To remove in this way: to *skim* the cream from milk. **3** To move quickly and lightly over or near a surface; glide: skiers *skimming* over the snow. **4** To read hastily in glances, without reading every word. **5** To cover with a thin layer or film: a pond *skimmed* with ice.

_____

_____

_____

fright·en [frīt′(ə)n] *v.* **1** To fill with sudden fear; make or become afraid; scare. **2** To force or drive by scaring: He *frightened* us into agreeing; to *frighten* a thief away.

B. Use the entry word *frighten* to answer these questions.

7. Would the word *fright* come before or after *frighten* in the

dictionary? _____

8. Would the word *froth* come before or after *frighten* in

the dictionary? _____

9. How many syllables does *frighten* have? _____

10. Is *frighten* a noun or a verb? _____

11. How many definitions are listed for *frighten*? _____

12. Write the examples given for using the word *frighten*.

_____

_____

in·quire [in·kwir′] *v.* **in·quired, in·quir·ing 1** To ask in order to find out: He *inquired* the way. **2** To make an investigation or search: to *inquire* into the causes of heart disease. —**in·quir′er** *n.*

C. Use the entry word *inquire* to answer these questions.

13. Is *inquire* a noun or a verb? _____

14. How many syllables does *inquire* have? _____

15. How many definitions are listed for *inquire*? _____

16. Write two of the examples given for using the word *inquire*.

_____

_____

From THE HBJ SCHOOL DICTIONARY, copyright © 1977 by Harcourt Brace Jovanovich, Inc. Reprinted by permission of the publisher.

Writing Place Names page 111
MECHANICS PRACTICE

A. Write these place names correctly.

1. 20 cedar mill lane
   seaford new york 11783

   _____

   _____

2. 114 barron avenue
   ashland pennsylvania 17921

   _____

   _____

3. 407 buckler drive
   cody wyoming 82414

   _____

   _____

4. 7743 dela cruz st
   kaneohe hawaii 96744

   _____

   _____

5. 88 larchmont way
   chamblee georgia 30341

   _____

   _____

6. 555 estes lake drive
   rancho mirage california 92270

   _____

   _____

7. 118 wright st
   salem oregon 97310

   _____

   _____

8. 2074 north elbe blvd
   belleville illinois 62223

   _____

   _____

B. Write these sentences correctly. Use capital letters, periods, and commas where they are needed.

9. People at my school in carbondale colorado, came from all over the world.

   _____

10. One girl was from mexico city mexico. _____

    _____

11. Twin boys were from san juan puerto rico. _____

    _____

12. One day we visited the museum on high stone drive. _____

    _____

24 UNIT 3: Extra Practice Master

Paragraphs and Main Ideas pages 126–127

Make a check next to each group of sentences that is a good paragraph. Under the paragraphs you check write the main idea.

____ 1.　Did you know that the redwood is not the oldest living tree in the world? The honor goes to a tree that grows in Australia. It is called the Macrozamia tree. Most live 5,000 to 7,000 years. Some even reach their 15,000th birthday!

_____

____ 2.　A sneeze can travel up to 100 miles (160 km) per hour. Fresh air is good for a cold. A race car can also go very fast. I like to walk.

_____

____ 3.　The first telephone book came out in 1878. It listed only 50 names. It was published in New Haven, Connecticut, by the telephone company.

_____

____ 4.　The bat is the only mammal that can fly. We went to see dolphins at the aquarium. It rained. Don't get caught in the rain without an umbrella. Thunder and lightning don't scare me.

_____

____ 5.　A snake has no ears. It uses its tongue to pick up sound waves. That's why it flicks its tongue in and out. You might say that a snake "hears" with its tongue.

_____

____ 6.　When were hats first made? Some say in the 1400's. That's when the material called felt was first made. The first hat factory in the United States was started in 1780.

_____

____ 7.　Yesterday was Marie's tenth birthday. We gave her a surprise party. Balloons and streamers were hung in the dining room. We played games and won prizes. Marie opened her presents before we ate lunch.

_____

____ 8.　Sometimes dogs and cats are best friends. My cat just had seven gray kittens. We live on a farm. My mother has a horse named Cinnamon. Cats are more independent than dogs.

_____

Topic Sentences   pages 128–129

Read each paragraph. Think about the main idea. Write a topic
sentence that tells the main idea.

1. _____

_____

We always go to Saranac Lake. We set up a tent and build a campfire. For dinner
we cook stew. Later we roast delicious marshmallows.

2. _____

_____

This week Sara bought her sister a birthday present. She was able to buy a new
book. Sara also had money to get a ticket to the school carnival.

3. _____

_____

It was invented by William Morgan. Volleyball used to be called "mintonette." It was
played by hitting a basketball over a rope.

4. _____

_____

He rode on a biking trip with his mom. Casey rides across town and back again. He
rides to school. Sometimes he even takes his bike on the family vacation.

5. _____
People enjoy listening to music. They like to dance to it. Many people like to make
music themselves.

6. _____

_____

In 1974 a group made a TV survey. It found that the average three-year-old child
watches 30 hours of TV a week. Some children watch even more.

7. _____

_____

Gerbils need exercise. Their cages must be kept clean. Gerbils need raw vegetables.

Name _____

Sentence Order in Paragraphs pages 132–133

A. Number the sentences in order. Then underline the words that show time order.

1. ____ Thanksgiving is my favorite holiday.

   ____ Then the children give a holiday puppet show.

   ____ My whole family gets together for the day.

   ____ First we eat a delicious dinner.

   ____ Finally we sing and talk together.

2. ____ Then she got a fever.

   ____ Marcy has the chicken pox.

   ____ She said Marcy had to stay in bed for a week.

   ____ First she saw some little red spots on her face.

   ____ Finally the doctor came.

B. Some of the sentences from this story are missing. They are below the story. Decide where each sentence belongs in the story. Write it in the correct space.

Ginny missed the bus.

3. _____
She decided not to wait for the next bus.

4. _____
The taxi driver sped through the streets toward the theater.

5. _____
Ginny paid the driver and ran through the stage door.

6. _____
"Thank goodness you are here. How could the show go on without you?" he said.

Instead she hailed a taxi.
She worried that she would miss her play.
The driver parked at the back of the theater.
The director of the play was waiting there.

Title Page and Table of Contents   pages 138–139

Title Page   **Table of Contents**

**All
About
Spiders**

by Arlene Silver

Greene Book Company
New York   Chicago

1. Spider Relatives   3
2. Spider Webs   20
3. Spider Nurseries   39
4. Spiderlings   50
5. Spider Food   61
6. How Spiders Move   82
7. Black Widow Spiders   100
8. Tarantula Spiders   106
   Index   120

A. Answer these questions about the **title page.**

1. Where would this page appear in the book? _____

2. What is the book title? _____

3. Who is the author? _____

4. Who is the publisher? _____

5. Where is the book company located? _____

6. Might this book tell you about a wolf spider? Why? _____

_____

B. Answer these questions about the **table of contents.**

7. How many chapters are in this book? _____

8. On what page does the chapter on spiderlings begin? _____

9. Is there a chapter about spider webs? _____

10. Is there a chapter about enemies of spiders? _____

11. Does this book have a glossary? _____

12. Might this book tell you if a spider is a relative of a scorpion? How do you

know? _____

13. To find out what spiders eat, what chapter would you read? _____

14. To find out about the tarantula spider, what chapter would you read?

_____

15. What part of the book begins on page 120? _____

Glossary and Index   pages 140–141

GLOSSARY

astronomy—the science of the stars, planets, and other heavenly bodies.
meteor—a shooting star.
Milky Way galaxy—the galaxy of which our earth and sun are a part.
planet—a body that moves in a path around a sun.
solar system—a sun with all that moves in orbit around it.
star—a giant ball of gas that gives off heat and light.
telescope—an instrument that makes it easier to see far-off objects.
universe—the total of everything that exists including the earth, the stars, the planets, and outer space.

INDEX

Astronaut, 70	Planets, 48–59
Astronomer, 10	Pluto, 58
Astronomy, 12	Pulsar, 40
Black dwarf, 35	Solar System, 28–30
Black hole, 92	Spacecraft, 66
Cluster, 36	Star, 22–48
Comet, 75	Telescope, 15
Mars, 52	Universe, 83
Meteor, 20	Uranus, 55
Milky Way, 32–35	

Use the glossary and index. Write the definition of each word.
Then write the page numbers showing where that topic can be found.

1. astronomy _____

   _____

2. star _____

   _____

3. planet _____

   _____

4. universe _____

   _____

5. solar system _____

   _____

6. Milky Way galaxy _____

   _____

7. meteor _____

Name _____

The Encyclopedia pages 142–143

A. Study the subjects listed below. Write the number of the volume in which you would look for each subject.

A	B	C–Ch	Ci–Cz	D	E	F	G	H	I	J–K	L	M	N–O	P	Q–R	S–Sn	So–Sz	T	U–V	W–X Y–Z	Index
1	2	3	4	5	6	7	8	9	10	11	12	13	14	15	16	17	18	19	20	21	22

1. Clara Barton ____   2. Football ____

3. Yosemite National Park ____   4. Butterflies ____

5. Canary Islands ____   6. Clocks ____

7. John J. Audubon ____   8. Hydrogen ____

9. Pioneer Life ____   10. West Virginia ____

11. Thomas Jefferson ____   12. Photography ____

13. Emily Dickinson ____   14. Transportation ____

B. Underline the one word you would use to look up each topic in an encyclopedia.

15. The Life of Babe Ruth   16. How a Tree Grows
17. Parts of the Brain   18. Names of the Planets
19. History of Money   20. The Work of Louis Pasteur
21. Kinds of Whales   22. Inventions of Ancient China
23. State Parks of Indiana   24. How a Volcano Is Formed
25. Uses for the Peanut   26. Traditional Eskimo Clothing

C. Write the correct word in each blank. Use this list to help you.

volumes   **alphabetical**   **subjects**
information   **number**   **encyclopedia**

27. A good place to look for _____ about different

    topics is an _____.

28. The _____ of an encyclopedia are arranged in

    _____ order.

29. The spine of each volume shows a letter and a _____.

30. Information about _____ beginning with the letter
    A would be found in Volume 1 of the encyclopedia on this page.

Name _____

Writing Days, Months, and Holidays page 149
MECHANICS PRACTICE

A. Write these days, months, and holidays correctly.

1. saturday

2. valentine's day

3. tues

4. october

5. thanksgiving

6. feb

7. father's day

8. nov

9. thurs

10. june

11. halloween

12. mon

13. dec

14. wed

15. new year's day

B. Write these sentences correctly. Use capital letters and periods where they are needed.

16. On friday, january 27, we leave for a ski trip.

17. People celebrate labor day in september.

18. Is halloween on a tuesday or a wednesday?

19. The first tuesday in november is election day.

20. I help my parents cook on thanksgiving.

21. The month of february is full of holidays.

22. Valentine's day, lincoln's birthday, and washington's birthday are all in february.

Name _____

Adjectives pages 162–163

A. The underlined words are nouns. Circle the adjective that describes each noun.

1. A small <u>monkey</u> escaped from the zoo.
2. It climbed up a tall <u>tree</u>.
3. Then it jumped aboard a red <u>bus</u>.
4. The speedy <u>bus</u> turned around a sharp <u>corner</u>.
5. The monkey was thrown off the bus into a deep <u>pond</u>.
6. A sleepy <u>fisherman</u> in a boat saw the monkey.
7. He dove into the murky <u>water</u> and saved it.
8. The dripping <u>monkey</u> sat in the man's tiny <u>boat</u>.
9. They had a delicious <u>lunch</u> together.
10. The man ate a sandwich and the monkey ate a yellow <u>banana</u>.

B. Add adjectives to each sentence.

11. That afternoon the man took the _____ monkey to his

    _____ cottage.

12. It was near a _____ zoo.

13. Through the _____ window the monkey could hear

    _____ sounds.

14. First came the _____ roar of a _____ tiger.

15. Then came the sound of _____ parrots.

16. Finally came a _____ sound that the monkey knew well.

17. The sound was the _____ noise of a family of monkeys.

18. The monkey gave the _____ man a _____ kiss.

19. Then it jumped out the _____ window and climbed over a

    _____ fence.

20. In no time at all the _____ monkey was back with its

    _____ family.

C. Write adjectives to describe a monkey.

21. _____ arms   22. _____ ears   23. _____ tail

24. _____ eyes   25. _____ fur

Articles page 167

A. Underline the articles in each sentence.

1. Some of the books fell off the shelf in the school library.
2. One of the books had a beautiful picture of an eagle on the cover.
3. A few of the pages tore when the book dropped.
4. Mrs. Dario taped the pages carefully and put the book back in place on the shelf.
5. One other book, a story about an ostrich, was damaged too.
6. The book had six pages crumpled.
7. Mrs. Dario fixed the pages on this book also.
8. She asked the children to be more careful when replacing books.

B. Write *a* or *an* before each word or group of words.

9. ____ huge hippopotamus
10. ____ eagle's nest
11. ____ robin's egg
12. ____ frog's eyes
13. ____ extinct dinosaur
14. ____ alligator
15. ____ grizzly bear
16. ____ hen and her chicks
17. ____ salmon
18. ____ armadillo
19. ____ electric eel
20. ____ colorful peacock
21. ____ otter
22. ____ poodle
23. ____ baby giraffe
24. ____ large white crane

C. Underline the correct articles in each sentence.

25. Belinda wanted (a, an) good book to read over spring vacation.
26. She found a book about (a, an) lost treasure in (an, the) school library.
27. A book about (a, an) haunted house was on (a, an) bottom shelf.
28. One book told of (a, an) legend about (an, the) Egyptian pyramids.
29. Belinda chose a book about (a, an) sea monster.
30. (The, An) sea monster caused (a, an) shipwreck.
31. The puppy hid (a, an) slipper under the bed.
32. We went to visit (a, an) aunt in Omaha.

Adverbs pages 168–169

A. Underline the adverb in each sentence.

1. She neatly wrote her name on the homework paper.
2. I answered the phone politely.
3. Later Mrs. Hoolihan left to work at the office.
4. In the afternoons we usually played.
5. Sometimes we visited Schrafft's Stamp Shop.
6. We looked for old stamps there.
7. Mrs. Schrafft let us buy them cheaply.
8. We always brought her some flowers in the summertime.
9. Later we would stop at the pet store.
10. We liked to watch the gerbils sleep snugly in their nests.

B. Underline the adverb in each sentence. Then write if the adverb tells *how, when,* or *where.*

_____ 11. I often ride the subway to the river.

_____ 12. Today the subway clicks along the track.

_____ 13. Two men speak quietly in the next seat.

_____ 14. An old woman stands wearily in the aisle.

_____ 15. Finally the train pulls into a station.

_____ 16. Ten passengers leave the train and walk outside.

C. Use each of these adverbs in a sentence.

softly   **outside**   **sweetly**   **yesterday**

17. _____

_____

18. _____

_____

19. _____

_____

20. _____

_____

Adverbs and Adjectives pages 172–173

Write the adjective or adverb to complete each sentence correctly.

1. He is a _____ cook.   (good, well)

2. He cooks _____.   (good, well)

3. Margo is a _____ person.   (neat, neatly)

4. Margo writes her homework _____.   (neat, neatly)

5. The man has a _____ voice.   (sad, sadly)

6. The man answered the phone _____.   (sad, sadly)

7. Our cat, Minnie, has _____ paws.   (soft, softly)

8. Our cat, Minnie, walks _____ across the rug.   (soft, softly)

9. Tom had a _____ look on his face.   (blank, blankly)

10. Tom looked _____ at the floor.   (blank, blankly)

11. Mother walked _____ into the office.   (brisk, briskly)

12. Abigail _____ looked around.   (slow, slowly)

13. Penny is my _____ friend.   (good, well)

14. _____ the door swung open.   (Sudden, Suddenly)

15. Peter played a _____ song.   (beautiful, beautifully)

16. My little sister walks _____.   (good, well)

17. The math problem is _____.   (easy, easily)

18. He spread the frosting _____ over the cake.   (smooth, smoothly)

19. She is a _____ judge.   (fair, fairly)

20. _____ run and tell Aunt Rose.   (Quick, Quickly)

21. Richard _____ helped Leva do her homework.   (glad, gladly)

22. The plane had a _____ runway for landing.   (clear, clearly)

23. Pietra is a _____ walker.   (slow, slowly)

24. The wind blew _____.   (wild, wildly)

25. The children played _____.   (quiet, quietly)

Name _____

Homographs pages 176–177

Write the number of the correct definition for each homograph.

bridge
1. a structure built across a road
2. a card game

____ Our car crossed the bridge.

____ My parents play bridge.

fly
3. a small insect
4. to move through the air

____ I caught a fly.

____ Birds fly south in the winter.

well
5. a hole for collecting water
6. in good health

____ Mr. Potts is well today.

____ The well has gone dry.

bank
7. a place to keep money
8. to heap into a pile

____ Put your savings in the bank.

____ Bank the snow against the fence.

date
9. time of some event
10. fruit from a type of palm tree

____ The date tasted sweet.

____ My birth date is March 31.

curry
11. to rub down and clean with a currycomb
12. a seasoning for food

____ Sprinkle curry on the meat.

____ Curry the horse for the fair.

cricket
13. an outdoor game
14. an insect

____ The cricket is chirping.

____ Let's play cricket now.

bay
15. a deep bark or cry
16. an evergreen tree

____ A bay has shiny leaves.

____ The coyotes bay at the moon.

tip
17. the point or end
18. a small gift of money

____ Give the waiter a tip.

____ The arrow has a sharp tip.

36 UNIT 5:   Extra Practice Master

Name _____

Synonyms and Antonyms pages 178–179

A. Tell whether the pairs of words are synonyms or antonyms.
Write *synonyms* or *antonyms*.

1. smile, frown _____
2. heal, cure _____
3. easy, simple _____
4. clear, hazy _____
5. answer, reply _____
6. argue, disagree _____
7. old, new _____
8. left, right _____
9. ill, sick _____
10. chilly, warm _____
11. hot, cold _____
12. fast, quick _____
13. windy, breezy _____
14. stop, halt _____
15. hit, missed _____
16. whisper, shout _____
17. shiny, dull _____
18. slender, thin _____
19. nungry, full _____
20. kind, mean _____

B. Write an antonym for the word in parentheses ( ).

21. Martha took a _____ walk downtown.   (brisk)

22. On the beach Matt stood in the _____.   (shade)

23. Be sure to wear _____ clothes to the party.   (dirty)

24. We saw a lost dog that was _____.   (fat)

25. The girls dug a _____ hole in the ground.   (shallow)

26. That Thanksgiving pie was too _____ for my taste.   (sour)

27. Ramón is reading a book that has a _____ ending.   (happy)

28. James was _____ today.   (present)

29. This train goes through a _____ tunnel.   (narrow)

30. Michael _____ the ball that was thrown to him.   (dropped)

31. The train was _____.   (empty)

32. Your suitcase is _____.   (light)

Writing Dates and Times of Day page 187
MECHANICS PRACTICE

A. Write these dates correctly.

1. march 7 1940 _____
2. february 14 1876 _____

3. may 21 1939 _____
4. july 1 1963 _____

5. january 4 1801 _____
6. september 12 1917 _____

7. may 5 1922 _____
8. november 24 1889 _____

9. august 9 1981 _____
10. april 23 1950 _____

B. Write these times correctly.

11. 7 25 am _____
12. 4 33 pm _____
13. 1 09 pm _____

14. 12 45 pm _____
15. 2 22 am _____
16. 11 15 pm _____

17. 3 55 pm _____
18. 7 48 am _____
19. 6 00 am _____

C. Write the sentences correctly. Use capital letters, periods, colons, and commas where they are needed.

20. I kept a special diary from march 1 to march 15.

_____

21. Most school days I woke up at 7 15 am.

_____

22. We ate breakfast from 7 40 am to 8 00 am.

_____

23. School began at 8 20 am.

_____

24. On march 11 1981, my diary was different.

_____

25. That day I had a doctor's appointment at 10 15 am.

_____

26. I read a page of a diary written on may 1 1899.

_____

27. The writer woke up at 6 00 am to walk to school.

_____

28. She did not return home until 5 00 pm.

_____

Pronouns pages 202–203

A. Underline the pronouns in each sentence.

1. Tanya was glad when she saw the first signs of spring.
2. She thought the robins were singing songs to her.
3. Tanya's grandfather showed her signs of spring.
4. Did he show her places to look for skunk cabbage?
5. Together they planted tulip and daffodil bulbs.
6. They brought me a huge bouquet of flowers.
7. Do you plant flowers and vegetables in the spring?
8. Shall we put them in a glass vase?
9. One day I heard Canadian geese honking.
10. We spied a woodchuck looking at us.

B. Underline the pronouns in the second sentence of each pair.
Then write the pronouns and the nouns for which they stand.

11. Days are longer in spring. They are usually warmer too.

_____

12. Tanya found two baby rabbits. She brought them home.

_____

13. Tanya and Grandfather built a cage. They put the rabbits in it.

_____

14. Grandfather brought soft hay. He put it in the cage.

_____

15. Juanita found some furry pussy willows. They tickled her.

_____

16. Annie loves spring. She rides a bicycle to school.

_____

17. Paula collects flowers. She presses them for a scrapbook.

_____

18. Paula and Annie are in the same class. They wrote about spring.

_____

Subject Pronouns and Pronouns
After Action Verbs   pages 204–207

A. Use a subject pronoun in the second sentence of each pair.
The subject pronoun should take the place of the underlined words.

1. Carla and I went to a movie yesterday.

   _____ saw *The Lady and the Tramp.*

2. Billy plays soccer almost every day.

   _____ has become an expert player.

3. Peanuts came to America on sailing ships from Africa.

   _____ were used as cheap food.

4. My grandfather makes his own peanut butter.

   _____ starts by crushing fresh peanuts.

5. The hamburger is a favorite food of Americans.

   _____ has a long history.

B. Write the correct pronoun that follows an action verb.

6. I dodged the ball. Then I threw _____ .

7. The grocer unpacked the bananas. Then he marked _____
   with a price.

8. My mother invited Mrs. German for Thanksgiving dinner.

   Mom asked _____ to bring some cranberry sauce.

9. Please take Arnie and me to the park.

   The team needs _____ to play today.

10. My mother hugged my baby brother. Then she kissed _____ .

11. Mr. Stacy hired Lila and you to shovel the snow.

    After the job was done he paid _____ .

12. I am called Lee. I wish someone would call _____ to play today.

13. The doctor visited Denise. He told _____ to stay in bed all week.

14. Take out the garbage. Put _____ near the curb.

15. The choir sings to the students. The singing pleases _____ .

Possessive Pronouns pages 208–209

A. Underline the possessive pronoun in each sentence.

1. My socks do not match.

2. Does your brother attend college?

3. Our piano is being tuned by the piano tuner.

4. I think that his teacher is out sick today.

5. The boys left their swim fins at the pool.

6. Her aunt and uncle still live in Italy.

7. Marilyn does not like to share her toys.

8. Does my singing bother you?

9. The bird found its nest blown down by the wind.

10. Their friends came to visit last week from Chicago.

B. Read the pairs of sentences. Fill in each blank with the correct possessive pronoun.

11. Do you know Mr. Richards? _____ store is on Main Street.

12. I live on this block. This is _____ house.

13. Nell took a bus downtown. She went to visit _____ mother's office.

14. Which bike belongs to you? Is that red one _____ bike?

15. Jimmy and I have to go inside. _____ lunch is ready.

16. The truck is at the edge of the road. _____ tires are flat.

17. The five children slept outside. _____ sleeping bags were warm.

18. It is a special day for me. It is _____ birthday.

19. This is Brenda's. I borrowed _____ belt.

20. The puppy is lonely. I hear _____ barking outside.

21. I will see you later. _____ phone is ringing.

22. The kitten is limping. _____ paw is sore.

23. Susan's bird is blue. _____ bird is also yellow.

24. Ted is tall. _____ brother is tall too.

Name _____

Using <u>I</u> and <u>Me</u> pages 210-211

A. Use <u>I</u> or <u>me</u> in each sentence.

1. Last summer _____ spent two weeks at Camp Winnepaug.

2. My father drove _____ there in his new van.

3. _____ enjoyed swimming in Lake Winnepaug because the water is clear and cold.

4. One day _____ rowed a boat across the entire lake.

5. _____ liked the camp because we did a lot of hiking.

6. At night _____ sat by the campfire.

7. The other campers and _____ sang songs.

8. The campers asked _____ to play my guitar.

9. _____ had lots of fun there.

10. I will ask my father to bring _____ again next year.

B. Underline the correct noun and pronoun for each sentence. Choose from the words in parentheses ( ).

11. At Camp Winnepaug (Sara and I, Sara and me, me and Sara) went to crafts class every morning.

12. (Sara and I, Sara and me, I and Sara) brought an apple or a banana for a snack.

13. Mr. Sette taught (Sara and I, Sara and me, me and Sara) how to weave a mat.

14. Miss Jenkins helped (Sara and I, Sara and me, me and Sara) put the mat together.

15. Mr. Sette told (Sara and I, Sara and me, I and Sara) that our mat might win a prize.

16. The second week (Pablo and I, Pablo and me, me and Pablo) made a bird feeder.

17. Mr. Sette told (Pablo and I, Pablo and me, I and Pablo) to fill the feeder with bird seed.

18. (Pablo and I, Pablo and me, I and Pablo) hung the feeder on a fir tree.

19. Miss Jenkins gave (Pablo and I, Pablo and me, me and Pablo) a camera.

20. Then (Pablo and I, Pablo and me, me and Pablo) took pictures of the birds.

Using Pronouns That End with <u>self</u> or <u>selves</u>
pages 212–213

A. Add *self* or *selves* to each pronoun. Write the new pronoun.

1. my _____   2. them _____

3. him _____   4. her _____

5. our _____   6. it _____

7. your _____

B. Underline the pronoun that correctly completes each sentence.

8. Larry (himself, he) planned a surprise birthday party for Nick.

9. We did some of the work (themselves, ourselves) to help him.

10. I especially wanted to decorate the cake (herself, myself).

11. Bill and Larry decided on the games (ourselves, themselves).

12. You moved the table (yourself, myself), didn't you?

13. The table was placed in a corner by (itself, myself).

14. Becky (she, herself) blew up the balloons and hung them.

15. Brian swept the floor by (him, himself).

16. Mary set up the chairs by (her, herself).

17. Everyone enjoyed (ourselves, themselves).

C. Write the correct pronoun ending in *self* or *selves.*

18. Bill and Larry went to buy the birthday presents _____.

19. My little brother dressed _____ for the party.

20. I got ready in my room by _____.

21. We baked the cake _____.

22. Becky stirred the flour and eggs together _____.

23. You whipped the creamy frosting _____.

24. Dan put ten candles on the cake _____.

25. The cake sat by _____ in the center of the table.

26. My brother wrote the play by _____.

27. The students enjoyed _____.

28. You can do this by _____.

Making an Outline pages 220–221

Read each set of notes. For each write the title, main topics, and
subtopics in outline form.

1. Title: Crickets
   Main Topics: What crickets look like   How a cricket makes noise
   Subtopics: Male cricket makes noise   Has two wings
            Brown or black   Sound made by rubbing wings together
            Hard, shiny body   Has six legs

_____

_____

_____

_____

_____

_____

_____

_____

2. Title: Raccoons
   Main Topics: What raccoons look like   What raccoons eat
   Subtopics: Faces have black masks   Eat crayfish and fish
          Eat wild fruit   Have long gray fur
          Eat mice and frogs   Ringed tail

_____

_____

_____

_____

_____

_____

_____

Writing Titles page 225
MECHANICS PRACTICE

A. Write these titles correctly. Use capital letters, underlines, and quotation marks where they are needed.

1. the jade eagle (book)

   _____

2. I ride an old paint (song)

   _____

3. the muppet show (TV show)

   _____

4. atoms and molecules (report)

   _____

5. tree at my window (poem)

   _____

6. jack and the bean futures (story)

   _____

7. white water, still water (book)

   _____

8. the amazon river (report)

   _____

9. the flea and the ox (story)

   _____

10. over the rainbow (song)

   _____

B. Write the sentences correctly. Use capital letters, underlines, and quotation marks where they are needed.

11. I like to sing america the beautiful.

   _____

12. Do you know a story called the brother and sister?

   _____

13. The book they are reading is the call of the wild.

   _____

14. We watched nova on television.

   _____

15. She knows the poem the emperor's rhyme by heart.

   _____

16. Do you know the song she'll be coming round the mountain?

   _____

17. My favorite television show is eight is enough.

   _____

18. Have you read the book a wrinkle in time?

   _____

Simple Subjects pages 240–241

A. Draw one line under the complete subject of each sentence.
Circle the simple subject.

1. The sparkling new snow covers the ground.
2. All five children want to go out into the snow.
3. Their father says it is fine.
4. The two boys pull their boots on first.
5. The three girls grab their coats and mittens.
6. Everyone looks ready to go out.
7. Their mother waits at the door.
8. She hands out the hats and mittens.
9. The eager children open the door and race outside.
10. They frolic in the powdery snow.

B. Write the simple subject of each sentence.

_____ 11. The children sorted out their junk collections.

_____ 12. Two boys discovered an old alarm clock.

_____ 13. Ellie found some brightly colored wire.

_____ 14. The best treasure was at the bottom of the pile.

_____ 15. Biff found it.

_____ 16. He carried it to the table.

_____ 17. The children stood around to look at it.

_____ 18. It was a rusty old toolbox.

_____ 19. The box rattled.

_____ 20. Many useful tools were in it.

_____ 21. The hamsters are active.

_____ 22. The team won.

_____ 23. The plants are pretty.

_____ 24. Your coat is warm.

_____ 25. The red hat is lost.

Simple Predicates   pages 242–243

A. Draw two lines under the complete predicate of each sentence.
Circle the simple predicate.

1. Michelle is going to the museum.
2. The actress enters the stage.
3. Pedro sails down the street on his roller skates.
4. That airplane landed on the runway.
5. The window washer has climbed up the ladder.
6. Everyone is quiet in the library.
7. My brother has brought pizza from the pizzeria.
8. Someone is chasing me around the playground.
9. I have sharpened all of my pencils.
10. The parade went down their street.

B. Write the simple predicate of each sentence.

_____ 11. I have waited for Martha.

_____ 12. Bruce and Susan are brother and sister.

_____ 13. The twins posed for a picture.

_____ 14. We saw an anteater at the zoo.

_____ 15. One TV station is having a special movie festival.

_____ 16. Our baseball game was almost over.

_____ 17. Antonio leaped up onto the monkey bars.

_____ 18. The train was rumbling down the track.

_____ 19. Yesterday Paul and Carlo rode on a double-decker bus.

_____ 20. I am so hungry.

_____ 21. My dog likes cottage cheese and apples.

_____ 22. Jackie read a biography of Mickey Mantle.

_____ 23. Joshua is happy.

_____ 24. There are some weeds in the garden.

_____ 25. I will pick a basket of raspberries.

Subject-Verb Agreement pages 244–245

A. Underline the form of the verb that agrees with each subject. Choose from the words in parentheses ( ).

1. My neighbors (enjoy, enjoys) the beautiful summer day.

2. The baby next door (enjoy, enjoys) walking barefoot.

3. Lisa (skate, skates) across her driveway.

4. Tara and Joey (skate, skates) on the sidewalk.

5. Mr. and Mrs. Abeyto (sit, sits) on their front porch.

6. Their new puppy (sit, sits) close by.

7. Melvin (race, races) his ten-speed bike in the street.

8. Yoko and León (race, races) their tricycles in a circle.

B. Change the verbs to agree with each subject. Rewrite each sentence with the correct verb.

9. Kelly's broken kite hang from the maple tree.

_____

10. The gardeners cuts the grass in our school yard.

_____

11. My two sisters practices batting the ball.

_____

12. The twins eats lunch at the picnic table.

_____

13. Miss Lopez polish her new car.

_____

14. Mrs. Hand's cat dash through her rose bushes.

_____

15. On my street the people seems very busy.

_____

16. Angela and I watches the race.

_____

17. Grandfather meet us for a picnic lunch.

_____

18. I walks to the playground after lunch.

_____

Prefixes and Suffixes pages 250-253

A. Write *prefix* if a word contains a prefix. Write *suffix* if a word contains a suffix.

_____	1. replay	_____	2. improper
_____	3. unhappy	_____	4. disprove
_____	5. formless	_____	6. himself
_____	7. sweetly	_____	8. impossible
_____	9. incorrect	_____	10. baseless
_____	11. collector	_____	12. recount
_____	13. friendly	_____	14. prejudge
_____	15. unsaid	_____	16. faithful
_____	17. trader	_____	18. disprove
_____	19. prewar	_____	20. suitable
_____	21. lawless	_____	22. misplace
_____	23. recall	_____	24. lightly
_____	25. impure	_____	26. wireless
_____	27. prefix	_____	28. traceable
_____	29. sickly	_____	30. nonfiction

B. Underline the base word in each word. Circle the prefix or the suffix in the word. Then write the meaning of the word.

31. careless _____   32. disagree _____

33. recount _____   34. misguide _____

35. colorful _____   36. nonsense _____

37. director _____   38. unhappy _____

39. leader _____   40. actor _____

C. On a separate piece of paper write a sentence for each word in Part B.

Compound Words pages 254–255

A. Underline the compound word in each sentence. Then write the two words that form the compound.

1. The detective went over to headquarters. _____

2. High in the treetop a robin sings. _____

3. Write the alphabet on the chalkboard. _____

4. There are 20 students in the classroom _____

5. The basketball rolled into the street. _____

6. Bella's grandfather is a good bowler. _____

7. The hot sunshine feels good on my face. _____

8. Put the candlesticks on the table. _____

9. My job is to clean my bedroom. _____

10. That cabin is where the cowboys sleep. _____

B. Read the first word in each line. Find another word to make a compound word. Write the compound word.

11. butter	a. heart	b. orange	c. fly	_____
12. play	a. ground	b. foot	c. game	_____
13. rail	a. hat	b. road	c. stop	_____
14. cook	a. see	b. fat	c. book	_____
15. saddle	a. bag	b. cat	c. small	_____
16. foot	a. fin	b. ball	c. card	_____
17. air	a. car	b. cloud	c. plane	_____
18. finger	a. hair	b. nine	c. print	_____
19. sail	a. copy	b. boat	c. ship	_____
20. side	a. big	b. boy	c. walk	_____
21. base	a. house	b. street	c. ball	_____
22. book	a. rule	b. case	c. mat	_____

Homophones pages 256–257

A. Underline the correct homophone for each sentence.

1. My cousins are meeting me (their, there, they're) by the clock.
2. (Their, There, They're) names are Bobby and Tricia.
3. (Their, There, They're) coming with Uncle Al at twelve o'clock.
4. (Its, It's) only eleven o'clock now.
5. Would you like to come with us (two, too, to) the football game?
6. I have (two, too, to) extra tickets.
7. Your sister could come (two, too, to).
8. (Your, You're) going to like my cousins.
9. (Your, You're) sister will like them too.
10. Let's ask your parents if (its, it's) all right for you to go.

B. Replace each underlined word with a homophone. Then write the sentences correctly.

11. We had to weight in line a long thyme at the football stadium.

_____

12. We passed threw the ticket gait slowly.

_____

13. Eye no it will be hard to find good seats.

_____

14. I am knot going to sit hear by the exit.

_____

15. The son beets down on my hare.

_____

16. Wood you please come by won o'clock?

_____

17. Whose going to by the hot dogs?

_____

18. Mike eight five hot dogs at the game a weak ago.

_____

19. Do you know if it's supposed to reign?

_____

20. The weather is fare and warm now.

_____

Using Commas page 263
MECHANICS PRACTICE

A. Put commas where they are needed in these sentences.

1. No I did not see her.
2. Yes spring is coming at last.
3. Yes I'll wait for you.
4. Wear jeans sneakers and a jacket.
5. No look in the closet.
6. Let us call Amy Tom and Lou.

B. Write the sentences correctly. Use commas where they are needed.

7. It is a warm clear and sunny day.

_____

8. No this is not a day to be indoors.

_____

9. Gregory Sally and Kate made kites.

_____

10. Yes the wind is strong enough today.

_____

11. Yes I won the kite-flying contest.

_____

12. Never make a kite from wire metal or foil.

_____

13. Yes these materials can be dangerous.

_____

14. Only paper wood and cloth should be used.

_____

15. Watch for trees power lines and other kites.

_____

16. My kite is orange brown and black.

_____

17. Yes I call it my Flying Magician.

_____

18. My kite will fly higher faster and farther than yours.

_____

Making Introductions pages 274–275

A. Write the words of introduction you would say.

1. Introduce your new friend Marcus Simpson to your father. Your friend lives on the next street and is in your class at school.

   _____

   _____

   _____

2. Introduce your sister, Sally, to Mrs. Roberts, the principal of your school. Your sister will be starting kindergarten at your school next year.

   _____

   _____

   _____

3. Introduce your cousins, Pepe and Maria Sanchez, to Miss Tate, your baseball coach.

   _____

   _____

   _____

4. Introduce Mr. Kerrigan, the librarian, to your Uncle Walter, who loves to read mysteries.

   _____

   _____

   _____

B. Complete these introductions.

5. "Grandma, this is my friend Billy Baker."

   _____

6. "Mrs. Gordon, I'd like you to meet my mother. Both of you are

   interested in _____

   _____

7. "Dr. O'Neill, this is my brother, Harry." _____

   _____

Name _____

Following Directions   pages 280–281

A. Complete this school information form.

Please print.

Name _____
            Last   First   Middle Initial

School Name _____

School Address _____
            Number   Street

_____
City or Town   State   Zip Code

Classroom Number _____

Teacher's Name _____

Number of Students in Class _____

B. Complete this form to play baseball.

Town Baseball League (Minors—Ages 9–12)

Please print neatly.

Name _____

Address _____

Circle the part of town you live in.   North   South   East   West

Birth Date _____ Telephone Number _____

School _____ Grade _____

Have you ever played in a baseball league before? _____

Which league? _____ Name of team _____

What position did you play? _____

What position do you want to play? _____

Are you in good health? _____

Do you have your parents' permission to play? _____

The Telephone Directory pages 286–287

White Pages

```
PUE-PYT
Pue Peter 2 Treat Rd. . . . . . . . . . .329-0538      Purvis M 19870 Center St. . . . . . .468-9009
Pugh Thomas 33 Mills Rd. . . . . . .562-3874          Putnam Auto Parts 2 Putnam St. . .933-2511
Puglia A 49 Main St. . . . . . . . . . .461-3388       Putnam Beauty Shop 9 Putnam St. 933-2244
Puglisi Frank 36 Beers Ave. . . . . .224-3456         Puzello Mary 2345 Redwood Ave. 776-5678
Puhalski R Mrs 2 Clark St. . . . . . .577-2308        Pyne Virginia 112 Ferry Rd. . . . . .289-0011
Puklin Francis 10 Laurel Dr. . . . . .687-3872        Pyramid Health Club 34 Maple Rd. 624-7896
Pullman Alfonse 678 Elm St. . . . . .555-7788         Pyszkowski M 675 State St. . . . . .224-1133
Puppy Center 2 Eastern Blvd. . . . .234-0987          Pytlak Ralph 90 Second Ave. . . . .456-2233
```

A. Write the telephone numbers of the people or businesses listed below.
Locate the numbers on the page from a White Pages Directory.

1. Puppy Center _____

2. Pyramid Health Club _____

3. Ralph Pytlak _____

4. Thomas Pugh _____

5. Mrs. R. Puhalski _____

6. Alfonse Pullman _____

7. Putnam Beauty Shop _____

8. Mary Puzello _____

Yellow Pages

```
Ice                                          Ice Cream Cones
ABC Ice                                      Caputo Ice Cream Co.
Cubes-Blocks-Crushed                         45 Oak St. – – – – – – – – – –932-0134
We Deliver Anytime
12 Pond St. – – – – – – – – – –457-3245      Ice Cream Freezers
                                             Taylor Freezer
Dina Ice Co.                                 162 Eagle Rd. – – – – – – – –452-1880
We Rent Machines
Free Delivery Service                        Ice Cream Manufacturers
Blocks-Cubes-Bushel Bags                     Mayfair Farms Dairy
1456 Blonder Ave. – – – – – –342-9087        81 Main St. – – – – – – – – – –301-6552
```

B. Answer the questions using information from the Yellow Pages Directory.

11. What company sells ice by the bushel? _____

12. What company delivers ice anytime? _____

13. From what company can you buy an ice cream freezer? _____

14. Who sells ice cream cones? _____

15. Which dairy manufactures ice cream? _____

16. What is the telephone number of the Dina Ice Company? _____

17. What is the address of Taylor Freezer? _____

18. How many ice cream manufacturers are listed? _____

Writing Quotations page 297
MECHANICS PRACTICE

A. Write the sentences correctly. Use capital letters, quotation marks, and other punctuation marks where they are needed.

1. detective Jill Solvesit said this case is puzzling

   _____

2. a trail of banana peels *is* odd agreed Chauncey

   _____

3. consider who likes bananas said the girl detective

   _____

4. monkeys like bananas cried Chauncey.

   _____

5. we're off to the zoo said Jill.

   _____

6. Chauncey said this case is almost closed now

   _____

B. Write this conversation correctly. Add quotation marks, punctuation marks, and capital letters. Begin a new paragraph for each speaker.

   oh, woe is me sighed the zookeeper sadly. what is
   wrong asked the young detectives. my prize chimp
   has escaped moaned the zookeeper. he continued
   Chatty the Chimp was my dearest friend. I think
   we can help you find Chatty said Jill. Chauncey added bring along
   some bananas, and come with us!

   _____

   _____

   _____

   _____

   _____

   _____

ANSWER KEY FOR EXTRA PRACTICE MASTERS

UNIT 1

Extra Practice Master 1
A. 1. are lined with people. 2. are filled with shoppers. 3. pick up people. 4. have hundreds of workers. 5. cook meals for the people. 6. has some trees and a place to rest.
B. Items 9, 12, 13, and 15 are complete sentences.
C. 16.–20. Answers will vary.

Extra Practice Master 2
A. 1. imperative 2. interrogative 3. interrogative 4. exclamatory 5. declarative 6. imperative
B. 7. b 8. c 9. a 10. b 11. a 12. a 13. c 14. b 15. a 16. a 17. a 18. b
C. 19. period 20. question mark 21. period 22. exclamation point

Extra Practice Master 3
A. 1. Mr. Clemson took our class on a hike. 2. We saw a lot of traffic. 3. José pointed to an unusual building. 4. Three girls stopped at an old fountain. 5. The warm sun shone brightly. 6. We grew hotter and hotter. 7. Mary and Tish told Mr. Clemson. 8. He turned into a building. 9. We shrieked for joy. 10. A sign said "City Swimming Pool."
B. 11. picked up riders at the stop. 12. returned to his ship. 13. went downtown together. 14. yapped at the mail carrier. 15. soaked the garden.
C. 16.–20. Answers will vary.

Extra Practice Master 4
A. 1. fiction 2. biography 3. reference 4. nonfiction 5. fiction 6. biography 7. nonfiction 8. nonfiction 9. reference 10. fiction
B. author card, title card, subject card 11. A Very Young Rider 12. Jill Krementz 13. Show Riding
C. 14. subject card 15. title card 16. author card

Extra Practice Master 5
A. 1. (?) 2. (.) 3. (!) 4. (.) 5. (?) 6. (.) 7. (.) 8. (?) 9. (.) 10. (!)
B. 11. I play first base and left field. 12. My friend Susan is our star pitcher. 13. How fast she can pitch! 14. Who hit a home run in the first inning? 15. Richie plays on another team in the summer. 16. Please buy me a drink. 17. What a great catch that was! 18. Where is the refreshment stand? 19. It is near the children's playground. 20. Is our team up at bat now? 21. Do not forget to take pictures today. 22. Do you think we'll win the game?

UNIT 2

Extra Practice Master 6
A. 1. heart 3. pumpkin 5. library 6. Maple Avenue 9. snowball 10. Mr. Don 12. hat 13. pencil 14. calendar 15. Tuesday
B. 16. Marta, book 17. story, gnomes, giants 18. tale, elf 19. librarian, Harold, paper 20. list, stories, class
C. 21.–30. Answers will vary.

Extra Practice Master 7
A. 1. machines 2. cities 3. matches 4. glasses 5. quizzes 6. doctors 7. lullabies 8. monkeys 9. radios 10. rashes
B. 11. batches 12. cookies 13. classes 14. bowls 15. nuts 16. dairies 17. chips 18. dishes 19. boxes 20. parties 21. cherries 22. plates

Extra Practice Master 8
A. 1. grandchildren 2. mice 3. gentlemen 4. deer 5. feet 6. moose 7. women 8. sheep 9. geese 10. oxen
B. 11. scissors 12. Englishmen 13. elk 14. glasses 15. children 16. men 17. teeth 18. deer 19. pants 20. saleswomen
C. 21.–28. Answers will vary.

Extra Practice Master 9
A. 1.–10. Answers will vary.
B. 11. My uncle lives in a country called Italy. 12. It is on the continent of Europe. 13. He speaks a language called Italian. 14. A sea called the Adriatic Sea is on the coast. 15. My uncle takes trips by car to the town of Rimini. 16. Then he drives through a tunnel called the Apennine Tunnel. 17. He arrives in the town of Pisa. 18. He sees a famous tower called the Tower of Pisa.

Extra Practice Master 10
A. 1. Rev. T. G. Hoyt 2. Ms. Linda B. Kaplan 3. Gov. Morris S. Ferguson 4. Mr. Chan Tung Lee
B. 5. Did Miss Ellen Powers come to Career Day? 6. She and Dr. L. W. Atkins train animals for television. 7. They own Zeke, a beagle, and Miss Daisy, a spaniel. 8. Miss Janet Sun spoke about art and music. 9. Mr. and Mrs. Ray helped with Career Day. 10. My teacher, Mrs. Conroy, met with R. P. Ives. 11. Did you enjoy the slide show given by Gov. Scott? 12. My friend, Mr. Quincy M. Summers, writes her speeches. 13. What did Dr. Mae Stewart and Mr. Ed Black talk about? 14. Were Jimmy Mercer and Kathy Turner there? 15. Mrs. Rosa Hernandez talked about careers in science.

Extra Practice Master 11

A. 1. Benton Harbor, Michigan   2. Windsor, Ontario
3. Tremain St.   4. Fisher Rd.   5. Cleveland,
Ohio   6. Kansas City, Kansas   7. Grand Ave.
8. Acapulco, Mexico   9. Rome, Italy   10. Holmes
Road   11. Buffalo, New York   12. Ferry Street
13. Baltimore, Maryland   14. Paris, France

B. 15. Philadelphia, Pennsylvania   16. East River
Drive, West River Drive   17. Watts Street
18. Chestnut Street, Walnut Street   19. Ardmore,
Lansdowne, Philadelphia   20. Camden, New
Jersey   21. We, Lincoln Center   22. My, Hudson
River.

Extra Practice Master 12

A. 1. king's   2. Roger's   3. ravens'   4. children's
5. magician's

B. 6. goblins'   7. women's   8. baby's   9. Queen
Bess's   10. men's   11. riders'   12. family's
13. King Edward's   14. children's   15. Horse's

C. 16. the queen's jewels   17. the elves' magic
18. the knights' horses   19. the dragons' cave
20. the princess's hand   21. the duke's castle
22. the witches' spell   23. Prince Charles's
bravery   24. Queen Hilda's kindness   25. the
wizards' wands

Extra Practice Master 13

A. 1. opinion   2. fact   3. fact   4. opinion   5. fact
6. opinion   7. opinion   8. fact   9. fact
10. opinion   11. fact   12. opinion   13. fact
14. opinion   15. fact   16. opinion   17. opinion
18. fact   19. fact   20. opinion

B. 21.–22. Answers will vary.

Extra Practice Master 14

A. 1. Mr. Ron Cummings   2. Sen. Ann Dempsey
3. Thunder   4. Mrs. L. S. Lorenz   5. Gov. Pat A.
Landau   6. Miss Kathy Kinski   7. Vincent
Reynolds   8. Dr. Ruth Blair   9. Chuckles
10. Sen. Bill Greenman   11. Ms. Sally Anderson
12. Mr. S. M. Marchard

B. 13. Gov. P. B. Armstrong   14. Ms. Kathy Warren
Smith   15. Rev. Chris B. Cahill   16. Dr. Sandra
Marsilio

C. 17. On Monday Mrs. Kahn's class is going to the
zoo.   18. Will you talk to Dr. Leslie Jonas about his
work?   19. His favorite zoo animal is a snake
named Slim.   20. His assistant is Miss Laura
Knowlton.

UNIT 3

Extra Practice Master 15

A. 1. glowed   2. toasted   3. trotted   4. rests
5. glided   6. yawn   7. speed   8. ties
9. crush   10. practice   11. swim   12. fasten
13. looked   14. wrote   15. packed   16. blinks,
sighs   17. Chew, swallow, leave   18. roll,
knead   19. trained, taught   20. slides, turns.

B. 21.–26. Answers will vary.

Extra Practice Master 16

A. 1. are   2. is   3. were   4. were   5. are   6. is
7. are   8. is   9. was   10. was

B. 11. am   12. is   13. am   14. are   15. are

C. 16. was   17. was   18. were   19. was
20. were

D. 21. travel, action verb   22. are, linking verb
23. were, linking verb   24. is, linking verb
25. are, linking verb

Extra Practice Master 17

A. 1. The girl on the horse will ride around the ring.
2. Kenny is hanging upside down on the monkey
bars.   3. The little dog has jumped through the
hoop.   4. I have gone to the circus every year.
5. My grandmother will come next week.   6. The
girls have taken the bus into town.   7. We were
sailing last week at the lake.   8. The truck is
collecting newspapers today.   9. We will return the
lawn mower this afternoon.   10. Marla had spent all
her savings on a tiny radio.   11. Freddy is
vacuuming the living room.   12. May had ridden in
the ambulance to the hospital.   13. We were sliding
down the snowy hill on a sled.   14. I am wandering
down the path.   15. Jack and Missy were going to
the pizza shop.   16. They will meet you there.
17. He is working hard on the reading lesson.
18. The sun is shining brightly through the
window.   19. I had spoken to my friend on the
telephone just yesterday.   20. I was checking for
some books at the library.

B. 21.–28. Answers will vary.

Extra Practice Master 18

1. mowed, past   2. watched, past
3. join, present   4. will meet, future
5. will fix, future   6. will swim, future
7. started, past   8. collected, past
9. will take, future   10. comes, present
11. raised, past   12. looks, present
13. will buy, future   14. earned, past
15. mends, present   16. dig, present
17. will watch, future   18. reads, present
19. will throw, future   20. tie, present
21. dribbled, past   22. lick, present
23. will show, future   24. watches, present

Extra Practice Master 19

A. 1. <u>Didn't</u>, did not   2. <u>doesn't</u>, does not   3. <u>isn't</u>, is not   4. <u>Won't</u>, will not   5. <u>wasn't</u>, was not   6. <u>can't</u>, cannot   7. <u>Aren't</u>, are not   8. <u>haven't</u>, have not   9. <u>Don't</u>, do not   10. <u>hasn't</u>, has not

B. 11. aren't   12. wasn't   13. won't   14. didn't   15. haven't   16. can't

C. 17.–20. Answers will vary.

D. 21. contraction   22. apostrophe

Extra Practice Master 20

A. 1. stirred   2. hurried   3. spotted   4. dried   5. hopped   6. scrapped   7. emptied   8. strummed   9. flopped   10. tried

B. 11. pried   12. slapped   13. trapped   14. lapped   15. denied   16. jammed   17. planned   18. fanned   19. canned   20. tried   21. trimmed   22. dried

Extra Practice Master 21

A. 1. rung   2. went   3. began   4. given   5. grown   6. taken   7. written   8. did   9. rang   10. ran   11. begun   12. did   13. took   14. gave   15. came   16. sang   17. come   18. taken   19. wrote   20. grew   21. done   22. come   23. grown   24. went   25. done   26. sang   27. sung   28. ran   29. taken   30. grown   31. sang, grew   32. begun   33. rang   34. took, gave   35. began

Extra Practice Master 22

A. 1. arbor, arc, arena, arrow, art   2. olive, onion, ostrich, otter, oyster   3. sleep, sleigh, slicker, slide, slim   4. zipper, zodiac, zone, zoo, zoom   5. excavate, exchange, exercise, explain, explode

B. 6. joiner, joker, jolly, Jordan, josh, journal   7. pilot, pimple, pincers, pinch, pineapple, pinfeather   8. river, roach, roadside, roaring, roaster, rob

C. compare, comma, complain, computer, community

Extra Practice Master 23

A. 1. pronunciation, part of speech, entry word, entry, definition, example

B. 7. before   8. after   9. 2   10. a verb   11. 2   12. He frightened us into agreeing; to frighten a thief away

C. 13. a verb   14. 2   15. 2   16. He inquired the way. to inquire into the causes of heart disease

Extra Practice Master 24

A. 1. 20 Cedar Mill Lane; Seaford, New York 11783   2. 114 Barron Avenue; Ashland, Pennsylvania 17921   3. 407 Buckler Drive; Cody, Wyoming 82414   4. 7743 Dela Cruz St.; Kaneohe, Hawaii 96744   5. 88 Larchmont Way; Chamblee, Georgia 30341   6. 555 Estes Lake Drive; Rancho Mirage, California 92270   7. 118 Wright St.; Salem, Oregon 97310   8. 2074 North Elbe Blvd.; Belleville, Illinois 62223

B. 9. People at my school in Carbondale, Colorado, came from all over the world.   10. One girl was from Mexico City, Mexico.   11. Twin boys were from San Juan, Puerto Rico.   12. One day we visited the museum on High Stone Drive.

UNIT 4

Extra Practice Master 25

Items 1, 3, 5, 6 and 7 are good paragraphs. The main ideas of these paragraphs are as follows: 1. the oldest living tree;   3. the first telephone book;   5. how a snake hears;   6. a short history of hats;   7. Marie's birthday party.

Extra Practice Master 26

Answers will vary. Possible answers include: 1. My family enjoys camping together every summer.   2. Sara bought several things.   3. Volleyball is an interesting sport.   4. Casey loves to ride his bike.   5. People enjoy music in many ways.   6. Children watch a lot of television.   7. Gerbils need care.

Extra Practice Master 27

A. 1. The correct order is: 1, 4, 2, 3, 5.   2. The correct order is: 3, 1, 5, 2, 4.
Then, First, and Finally show time order.

B. 3. She worried that she would miss her play.   4. Instead she hailed a taxi.   5. The driver parked at the back of the theater.   6. The director of the play was waiting there.

Extra Practice Master 28

A. 1. in the front   2. All About Spiders   3. Arlene Silver   4. Greene Book Company   5. New York and Chicago   6. yes, it's all about spiders

B. 7. 8   8. 50   9. yes   10. no   11. no   12. yes, there is a chapter on spider relatives   13. Chapter 5   14. Chapter 8   15. the index

Extra Practice Master 29

1. the science of the stars, planets, and other heavenly bodies, page 12   2. a giant ball of gas that gives off heat and light, pages 22–48   3. a body that moves in a path around a sun, pages 48–59   4. the total of everything that exists including the Earth, the stars, the planets, and outer space, page 83   5. a sun with all that moves in orbit around it, pages 28–30   6. the galaxy of which our Earth and sun are a part, pages 32–35   7. a shooting star, page 20

Extra Practice Master 30

A. 1. 2   2. 7   3. 21   4. 2   5. 3   6. 4   7. 1   8. 9   9. 15   10. 21   11. 11   12. 15   13. 5   14. 19

B. 15. Ruth   16. Tree   17. Brain   18. Planets   19. Money   20. Pasteur   21. Whales   22. China   23. Indiana   24. Volcano   25. Peanut   26. Eskimo

C. 27. information, encyclopedia   28. volumes, alphabetical   29. number   30. subjects

Extra Practice Master 31

A. 1. Saturday 2. Valentine's Day 3. Tues.
   4. October 5. Thanksgiving 6. Feb.
   7. Father's Day 8. Nov. 9. Thurs. 10. June
   11. Halloween 12. Mon. 13. Dec. 14. Wed.
   15. New Year's Day

B. 16. On Friday, January 27 we leave for a ski trip.
   17. People celebrate Labor Day in September.
   18. Is Halloween on a Tuesday or a Wednesday?
   19. The first Tuesday in November is Election
   Day. 20. I help my parents cook on
   Thanksgiving. 21. The month of February is full of
   holidays. 22. Valentine's Day, Lincoln's Birthday,
   and Washington's Birthday are all in February.

UNIT 5

Extra Practice Master 32

A. 1. small 2. tall 3. red 4. speedy, sharp
   5. deep 6. sleepy 7. murky 8. dripping, tiny
   9. delicious 10. yellow

B. Answers will vary. Possible answers include:
   11. unhappy, little 12. big 13. open, many
   14. loud, ferocious 15. chattering
   16. wonderful 17. cheerful 18. helpful, wet
   19. open, high 20. happy, own
   21.–25. Answers will vary.

Extra Practice Master 33

A. 1. the, the, the 2. the, a, an, the 3. A, the, the
   4. the, the, the 5. a, an 6. The 7. the 8. the

B. 9. a 10. an 11. a 12. a 13. an 14. an
   15. a 16. a 17. a 18. an 19. an 20. a
   21. an 22. a 23. a 24. a

C. 25. a 26. a, the 27. a, a 28. a, the 29. a
   30. The, a 31. a 32. an

Extra Practice Master 34

A. 1. neatly 2. politely 3. Later 4. usually
   5. Sometimes 6. there 7. cheaply
   8. always 9. Later 10. snugly

B. 11. often, when 12. Today, when 13. quietly,
   how 14. wearily, how 15. Finally, when
   16. outside, where

C. 17.–20. Answers will vary.

Extra Practice Master 35

1. good 2. well 3. neat 4. neatly 5. sad
6. sadly 7. soft 8. softly 9. blank
10. blankly 11. briskly 12. slowly 13. good
14. Suddenly 15. beautiful 16. well
17. easy 18. smoothly 19. fair 20. Quickly
21. gladly 22. clear 23. slow 24. wildly
25. quietly

Extra Practice Master 36

bridge 1. 1 2. 2, fly 3. 3 4. 4, well 5. 6
6. 5, bank 7. 7 8. 8, date 9. 10 10. 9,
curry 11. 12 12. 11, cricket 13. 14 14. 13,
bay 15. 16 16. 15, tip 17. 18 18. 17

Extra Practice Master 37

A. 1. antonyms 2. synonyms 3. synonyms
   4. antonyms 5. synonyms 6. synonyms
   7. antonyms 8. antonyms 9. synonyms
   10. antonyms 11. antonyms 12. synonyms
   13. synonyms 14. synonyms 15. antonyms
   16. antonyms 17. antonyms 18. synonyms
   19. antonyms 20. antonyms

B. Answers will vary. Possible answers include:
   21. slow 22. sun 23. clean 24. thin
   25. deep 26. sweet 27. sad 28. absent
   29. wide 30. caught 31. crowded 32. heavy

Extra Practice Master 38

A. 1. March 7, 1940 2. February 14, 1876 3. May
   21, 1939 4. July 1, 1963 5. January 4, 1801
   6. September 12, 1917 7. May 5, 1922
   8. November 24, 1889 9. August 9, 1981
   10. April 23, 1950

B. 11. 7:25 A.M. 12. 4:33 P.M. 13. 1:09 P.M.
   14. 12:45 P.M. 15. 2:22 A.M. 16. 11:15 P.M.
   17. 3:55 P.M. 18. 7:48 A.M. 19. 6:00 A.M.

C. 20. I kept a special diary from March 1 to March
   15. 21. Most school days I woke up at 7:15 A.M.
   22. We ate breakfast from 7:40 A.M. to 8:00 A.M.
   23. School began at 8:20 A.M. 24. On March 11,
   1981 my diary was different. 25. That day I had a
   doctor's appointment at 10:15 A.M. 26. I read a
   page of a diary written on May 1, 1899. 27. The
   writer woke up at 6:00 A.M. to walk to school.
   28. She did not return home until 5:00 P.M.

UNIT 6

Extra Practice Master 39

A. 1. she 2. She, her 3. her 4. he, her
   5. they 6. They, me 7. you 8. we, them
   9. I 10. We, us

B. 11. *They*—days 12. *She*—Tanya,
   them—rabbits 13. *They*—Tanya and Grandfather,
   it—cage 14. *He*—grandfather, *it*—hay
   15. *They*—pussy willows, *her*—Juanita
   16. *She*—Annie 17. *She*—Paula,
   them—flowers 18. *They*—Paula and Annie

Extra Practice Master 40

A. 1. We 2. He 3. They 4. He 5. It
B. 6. it 7. them 8. her 9. us 10. him
   11. you 12. me 13. her 14. it 15. them

Extra Practice Master 41

A. 1. My 2. your 3. Our 4. his 5. their
   6. Her 7. her 8. my 9. its 10. Their

B. 11. His 12. my 13. her 14. your 15. Our
   16. Its 17. Their 18. my 19. her 20. its
   21. My 22. Its 23. Her 24. His

Answer Key for Extra Practice Masters

Extra Practice Master 42

A. 1. I 2. me 3. I 4. I 5. I 6. I 7. I
8. me 9. I 10. me

B. 11. Sara and I 12. Sara and I 13. Sara and
me 14. Sara and me 15. Sara and me
16. Pablo and I 17. Pablo and me 18. Pablo
and I 19. Pable and me 20. Pablo and I

Extra Practice Master 43

A. 1. myself 2. themselves 3. himself
4. herself 5. ourselves 6. itself
7. yourself(selves)

B. 8. himself 9. ourselves 10. myself
11. themselves 12. yourself 13. itself
14. herself 15. himself 16. herself
17. themselves

C. 18. themselves 19. himself 20. myself
21. ourselves 22. herself 23. yourself
24. himself 25. itself 26. himself
27. themselves 28. yourself

Extra Practice Master 44

Accept alternative orders for topics and subtopics.
1. Crickets I. What crickets look like A. Brown or
black B. Hard, shiny body C. Has two wings
D. Has six legs II.How a cricket makes noise
A. Male cricket makes noise B. Sound made by
rubbing wings together 2. Raccoons I. What
raccoons look like. A. Faces have black masks
B. Have long, gray fur C. Ringed tail II. What
raccoons eat A. Eat wild fruit B. Eat mice and
frogs C. Eat crayfish and fish

Extra Practice Master 45

A. 1. The Jade Eagle 2. "I Ride an Old Paint"
3. "The Muppet Show" 4. Atoms and Molecules
5. "Tree at My Window" 6. "Jack and the Bean
Futures" 7. White Water, Still Water 8. The
Amazon River 9. "The Flea and the Ox"
10. "Over the Rainbow"

B. 11. I like to sing "America the Beautiful." 12. Do
you know a story called "The Brother and Sister?"
13. The book they are reading is The Call of the
Wild. 14. We watched "Nova" on television.
15. She knows the poem "The Emperor's Rhyme"
by heart. 16. Do you know the song "She'll be
Coming Round the Mountain?" 17. My favorite
television show is "Eight is Enough." 18. Have you
read the book A Wrinkle in Time?

UNIT 7

Extra Practice Master 46

A. 1. The sparkling new snow covers the ground.
2. All five children want to go out into the snow.
3. Their father says it is fine. 4. The two boys pull
their boots on first. 5. The three girls grab their
coats and mittens. 6. Everyone looks ready to go
out. 7. Their mother waits at the door. 8. She
hands out the hats and mittens. 9. The eager
children open the door and race outside. 10. They
frolic in the powdery snow.

B. 11. children 12. boys 13. Ellie 14. treasure
15. Biff 16. He 17. children 18. It 19. box
20. tools 21. hamsters 22. team 23. plants
24. coat 25. hat

Extra Practice Master 47

A. 1. Michelle is going to the museum. 2. The
actress enters the stage. 3. Pedro sails down the
street on his roller skates. 4. That airplane landed
on the runway. 5. The window washer has climbed
up the ladder. 6. Everyone is quiet in the library.
7. My brother has brought pizza from the pizzeria.
8. Someone is chasing me around the
playground. 9. I have sharpened all of my
pencils. 10. The parade went down their street.

B. 11. have waited 12. are 13. posed 14. saw
15. is having 16. was 17. leaped 18. was
rumbling 19. rode 20. am 21. likes
22. read 23. is 24. are 25. will pick

Extra Practice Master 48

A. 1. enjoy 2. enjoys 3. skates 4. skate
5. sit 6. sits 7. races 8. race

B. 9. Kelly's broken kite hangs from the maple tree.
10. The gardeners cut the grass in our
school yard. 11. My two sisters practice batting
the ball. 12. The twins eat lunch at the picnic
table. 13. Miss Lopez polishes her new car.
14. Mrs. Hand's cat dashes through her rose
bushes. 15. On my street the people seem very
busy. 16. Angela and I watch the race.
17. Grandfather meets us for a picnic lunch.
18. I walk to the playground after lunch.

Answer Key for Extra Practice Masters

Extra Practice Master 49

A. 1. prefix   2. prefix   3. prefix   4. prefix
5. suffix   6. suffix   7. suffix   8. prefix
9. prefix   10. suffix   11. suffix   12. prefix
13. suffix   14. prefix   15. prefix   16. suffix
17. suffix   18. prefix   19. prefix   20. suffix
21. suffix   22. prefix   23. prefix   24. suffix
25. prefix   26. suffix   27. prefix   28. suffix
29. suffix   30. prefix

B. 31. careless, without care   32. disagree, not
agree   33. recount, count again   34. misguide,
not guide correctly   35. colorful, full of color
36. nonsense, not sensible   37. director, one who
directs   38. unhappy, not happy   39. leader, one
who leads   40. actor, one who acts
C. Answers will vary.

Extra Practice Master 50

A. 1. headquarters—head/quarters
2. treetop—tree/top
3. chalkboard—chalk/board
4. classroom—class/room
5. basketball—basket/ball
6. grandfather—grand/father
7. sunshine—sun/shine
8. candlesticks—candle/sticks
9. bedroom—bed/room
10. cowboys—cow/boys
B. 11. butterfly   12. playground   13. railroad
14. cookbook   15. saddlebag   16. football
17. airplane   18. fingerprint   19. sailboat
20. sidewalk   21. baseball   22. bookcase

Extra Practice Master 51

A. 1. there   2. Their   3. They're   4. It's   5. to
6. two   7. too   8. You're   9. Your   10. it's
B. 11. wait, time   12. through, gate   13. I, know
14. not, here   15. sun, beats, hair   16. Would,
one   17. Who's, buy   18. ate, week
19. whether, rain   20. weather, fair

Extra Practice Master 52

A. 1. No, I did not see her.   2. Yes, spring is coming at
last.   3. Yes, I'll wait for you.   4. Wear jeans,
sneakers, and a jacket.   5. No, look in the closet.
6. Let us call Amy, Tom, and Lou.
B. 7. It is a warm, clear, and sunny day.   8. No, this is
not a day to be indoors.   9. Gregory, Sally, and
Kate made kites.   10. Yes, the wind is strong
enough today.   11. Yes, I won the kite-flying
contest.   12. Never make a kite from wire, metal, or
foil.   13. Yes, these materials can be dangerous.

14. Only paper, wood, and cloth should be used.
15. Watch for trees, power lines, and other kites.
16. My kite is orange, brown, and black.   17. Yes, I
call it my Flying Magician.   18. My kite will fly
higher, faster, and farther than yours.

UNIT 8

Extra Practice Master 53

A. Answers will vary. Possible answers include:
1. Dad, this is my friend Marcus Simpson. Marcus
lives on the next street. He's in my class at school.
2. Mrs. Roberts, this is my sister Sally. She will be
starting kindergarten here next year.   3. Miss Tate,
I'd like you to meet Pepe and Maria Sanchez. They
are my cousins.   4. Uncle Walter, this is Mr.
Kerrigan our librarian. Mr. Kerrigan, Uncle Walter
loves to read mysteries.
B. Answers will vary. Possible answers are given.
5. We play softball on the same team.
6. gardening. Mom belongs to the Garden Club,
Mrs. Gordon.   7. Harry is nervous because he has
to get a shot today.

Extra Practice Master 54

A. Answers will vary.
B. Answers will vary.

Extra Practice Master 55

A. 1. 234-0987   2. 624-7896   3. 456-2233
4. 562-3874   5. 577-2308   6. 555-7788
7. 933-2244   8. 776-5678
B. 11. Dina Ice Company   12. ABC Ice   13. Taylor
Freezer   14. Caputo Ice Cream Company
15. Mayfair Farms Dairy   16. 342-9087   17. 162
Eagle Road   18. 1

Extra Practice Master 56

A. 1. Detective Jill Solvesit said, "This case is
puzzling."   2. "A trail of banana peels is odd,"
agreed Chauncey.   3. "Consider who likes
bananas," said the girl detective.   4. "Monkeys like
bananas," cried Chauncey.   5. "We're off to the
zoo," said Jill.   6. Chauncey said, "This case is
almost closed now."
B.   "Oh woe is me," sighed the zookeeper sadly.
   "What is wrong?" asked the young detectives.
   "My prize chimp has escaped," moaned the
zookeeper. He continued, "Chatty the Chimp was my
dearest friend."
   "I think we can help you find Chatty," said Jill.
   Chauncey added, "Bring along some bananas,
and come with us!"

TESTS

The tests that accompany this level of *Language for Daily Use*, *Phoenix Edition* appear on the following pages. Included in the tests are pretests and posttests for each unit, a midyear test, and an end-of-year test, all in standardized-test format.

Pretests: Each pretest contains 35 items measuring objectives taught in all four strands of the unit. The pretest appears in reduced form after the Unit Opener page in the Teacher's Edition. There you will also find an answer key, the measurement objectives with an item analysis, and a scoring key.

Posttests: The posttest for each unit measures the identical objectives as the pretest, and in the same sequence. Each posttest contains 35 items. The posttest appears in reduced form after the Unit Test page in the Teacher's Edition. There you will also find an answer key, the measurement objectives with an item analysis, and a scoring key.

Midyear Test: The midyear test evaluates skills and concepts covered in Units 1–4 of this level. It contains 60 items. The midyear test appears in the Teacher's Edition in reduced form following the posttest for Unit 4. There you will also find an answer key, the measurement objectives with an item analysis, and a scoring key. Assign the midyear test when students have completed work through Unit 4.

End-of-Year Test: The end-of-year test is a comprehensive test of skills and concepts taught and developed in this level. It contains 100 items. The end-of-year test appears in the Teacher's Edition in reduced form following the posttest for Unit 8. Included with the end-of-year test are an answer key, the measurement objectives with an item analysis, and a scoring key.

An answer key for these tests follows the test pages in this Teacher's Resource Book. Answer forms for the tests are provided in the Teaching Aids section of this book.

(The Tests are also available as separate consumable pads.)

Name _____

Unit 1: Pretest

1. Which group of words is a complete sentence?
   - **A.** A dog on the sidewalk.
   - **B.** When the grass and pretty flowers.
   - **C.** The snake slept on a log.
   - **D.** Took off fast over the water.

2. Which sentence is a declarative sentence?
   - **A.** How tall Tim is!
   - **B.** Have some ice cream.
   - **C.** When did the rain start?
   - **D.** Liza finished her chores.

3. Which sentence is an imperative sentence?
   - **A.** Carry the chairs inside.
   - **B.** What a big cat is on the roof!
   - **C.** Where is Hilley's Pond?
   - **D.** My coat is on the hook.

4. Which is the best answer to this question?
   Where was Eddie Brown born?
   - **A.** In San Diego.
   - **B.** He lives in San Diego.
   - **C.** He was born in San Diego.
   - **D.** Born in San Diego.

5. What is the complete subject of this sentence?
   My mother rides a bus to work.
   - **A.** My mother rides
   - **B.** My mother
   - **C.** to work
   - **D.** rides a bus

6. Which group of words is *not* a sentence?
   - **A.** Tossed the toy up and down.
   - **B.** Please close the door.
   - **C.** Do you like cats?
   - **D.** Carl asked me to his house.

7. Which sentence is a declarative sentence?
   - **A.** This is unbelievable!
   - **B.** Did Barb find her glasses?
   - **C.** Frank painted a big picture.
   - **D.** Find out when the shop opens.

8. Which sentence is an exclamatory sentence?
   - **A.** Those records are scratched.
   - **B.** Don't forget your lunch.
   - **C.** When is the party?
   - **D.** What a mean dog!

9. Which is the best answer to this question?
   How often do you have music class?
   - **A.** Music class every day.
   - **B.** Every day.
   - **C.** I practice from one until two.
   - **D.** I have music class every day.

10. What is the complete subject of this sentence?
    Adam's grandparents sent him a postcard.
    - **A.** Adam's
    - **B.** Adam's grandparents
    - **C.** sent him
    - **D.** sent him a postcard

Go on to the next page.

11. Which group of words is a complete sentence?

    A. Crossed the street slowly.
    B. With all her friends.
    C. When will the game start?
    D. Not enough rain this year.

12. Which sentence is an interrogative sentence?

    A. What a lot of packages Anne has!
    B. Who scored the winning run?
    C. October is my favorite month.
    D. Tod, take Al's bike.

13. Which sentence is an imperative sentence?

    A. Bring me those keys.
    B. Which day is Paul coming?
    C. What a birthday surprise this is!
    D. Lily got a haircut.

14. Which is this best answer to this question?

    Why did the dog bark?
    A. Stranger at the door.
    B. The dog barked because it saw a stranger.
    C. Wagged its tail at the same time.
    D. Saw a stranger.

15. What is the complete predicate of this sentence?

    Cindy nailed the boards together.
    A. nailed
    B. the boards together
    C. Cindy
    D. nailed the boards together

16. Which is the best answer to this question?

    Who painted the picture?
    A. My sister Georgia painted the picture.
    B. My sister Georgia bought it.
    C. My sister Georgia.
    D. Georgia.

17. In which section of the library would you look for a book about the history of tennis?

    A. biography
    B. reference
    C. nonfiction
    D. fiction

18. Which of these books would you find in the *biography* section of the library?

    A. *How a Newspaper Is Printed*
    B. *All About Courts and the Law*
    C. *Larousse Encyclopedia of Music*
    D. *Clara Barton: A Life of Service*

19. What is the complete subject of this sentence?

    A baby kangaroo lives in its mother's pouch.
    A. A baby kangaroo
    B. A baby
    C. lives in
    D. A baby kangaroo lives in its mother's pouch

Go on to the next page.

Use this card from a library card catalog to answer questions 20–22.

```
C 771      DISCOVERIES AND EXPLORATIONS
  S
           Sperry, Armstrong

              Captain Cook explores the South Seas.
           Written and illus. by Armstrong Sperry.
           Random House c. 1955
```

20. What is this type of card called?
   A. a magazine card
   B. an author card
   C. a subject card
   D. a title card

21. Who is the author of the book listed on the card?
   A. Random House
   B. James Cook
   C. Discoveries and Explorations
   D. Armstrong Sperry

22. What is the title of the book?
   A. *James Cook, 1728–1779*
   B. *Captain Cook Explores the South Seas*
   C. *Discoveries and Explorations*
   D. *Sperry Armstrong*

23. What is the correct way to combine these sentences with *but*?
   Daisies are usually white.
   One kind is pink.
   A. Daisies are usually white or pink.
   B. Daisies are usually white, But one kind is pink.
   C. Daisies are usually white but one kind is pink.
   D. Daisies are usually white, but one kind is pink.

24. What must be done to correct this sentence?
   Found a baby bird.
   A. Add a predicate.
   B. Add punctuation at the end.
   C. Add a subject.
   D. Capitalize the first letter.

25. What does the editing mark in this sentence tell the writer to do?

our house has been torn down.

   A. Make a capital letter.
   B. Take out a word.
   C. Add a word.
   D. Add a comma.

26. Which of these books would you find in the *fiction* section of the library?
   A. *Fun with Your Camera*
   B. *Southwest Ghost Stories of Old*
   C. *Dictionary of American History*
   D. *Space Science and You*

Go on to the next page.

27. What is the correct way to combine these sentences with *and*?

Mary loves pizza.
She also likes spaghetti.

A. Mary loves pizza, And she also likes spaghetti.

B. Mary loves pizza, and she also likes spaghetti.

C. Mary loves pizza, and, she also likes spaghetti.

D. Mary loves pizza but not hamburger.

28. What must be done to correct this sentence?

Television for young children.

A. Capitalize the first letter.

B. Add a subject.

C. Add punctuation at the end.

D. Add a predicate.

29. What does the editing mark in this sentence tell the writer to do?

We live next to Mr⊙ Gonzales.

A. Make a capital letter.

B. Add a period.

C. Add a word.

D. Take out a word.

30. What is the correct way to combine these sentences with *or*?

Tie your shoes.
You'll trip on the laces.

A. Tie your shoes, or, you'll trip on the laces.

B. Tie your shoes or you'll trip on the laces.

C. Tie your shoes, or you'll trip on the laces.

D. Tie your shoes or your laces.

31. What must be done to correct this sentence?

the books are on the table.

A. Add a predicate.

B. Add a subject.

C. Capitalize the first letter.

D. Add punctuation at the end.

32. What does the editing mark in this sentence tell the writer to do?

That is the johnsons' house.

A. Take out a word.

B. Add a period.

C. Add a word.

D. Make a capital letter.

Read this poem to answer questions 33–35.

(1) Little Louie Landon loved lemonade.
(2) He poured twenty glasses, icy and tall,
(3) And lined them up on the grass in the shade.
(4) Then, slurp, glug, blurp, he drank them all!

33. Which line in the poem contains words that name sounds?

A. 4 **B.** 2 **C.** 3 **D.** 1

34. Which are lines in the poem that rhyme?

A. 1,2 **B.** 2,4 **C.** 3,4 **D.** 1,4

35. Which line in the poem contains alliteration?

A. 1 **B.** 2 **C.** 3 **D.** 4

Writing Sample Write five complete sentences about a pet. Include two declarative, one interrogative, one imperative, and one exclamatory sentence.

Stop!

Name _____

Unit 1: Posttest

1. Which group of words is a complete sentence?
   A. The lion's large paw.
   B. Crashed into the fence.
   C. Jack needed help.
   D. The first ride to try.

2. Which sentence is a declarative sentence?
   A. Drive by Greg's house, please.
   B. How strange that animal looks!
   C. Have you found your pen yet?
   D. Carrots have vitamin A.

3. Which sentence is an imperative sentence?
   A. Put your name on your paper.
   B. What a perfect day for our picnic!
   C. Sara's model is the best.
   D. Who invented the typewriter?

4. Which is the best answer to this question?
   How many sisters does Tyler have?
   A. He has no brothers.
   B. Three of them.
   C. He has three sisters.
   D. Has three sisters.

5. What is the complete subject of this sentence?
   My brother Rocky drove me home.
   A. Rocky
   B. My brother Rocky
   C. My brother
   D. drove me home

6. Which group of words is *not* a sentence?
   A. The highest jump.
   B. Write clearly.
   C. Anne put it away.
   D. His bike is new.

7. Which sentence is an interrogative sentence?
   A. Take us to the museum.
   B. The movie starts at seven.
   C. Are giraffes shy?
   D. What a mess this room is!

8. Which sentence is an exclamatory sentence?
   A. Have you ever gone camping?
   B. Ice cubes are good for burns.
   C. Be careful with your milk.
   D. What a large bear that is behind us!

9. Which is the best answer to this question?
   Where was the movie made?
   A. Chicago.
   B. In the city of Chicago.
   C. It was based on a book.
   D. The movie was made in Chicago.

10. What is the complete predicate of this sentence?
    All the campers toasted marshmallows in the fire.
    A. campers toasted
    B. toasted marshmallows in the fire
    C. All the campers
    D. toasted

Go on to the next page.

11. Which group of words is a complete sentence?
   A. The strong west wind.
   B. A strange surprise.
   C. Do you like peas?
   D. Rolled over and played dead.

12. Which sentence is a declarative sentence?
   A. Is anyone home?
   B. William swims well.
   C. Call us on Thanksgiving Day.
   D. What a good meal this is!

13. Which sentence is an imperative sentence?
   A. Fasten your seat belt.
   B. Una comes from New York.
   C. Which program is your favorite?
   D. What a big tiger that is!

14. Which is the best answer to this question?
   Who planned the surprise party?
   A. Crystal.
   B. Crystal planned the party.
   C. Lots of people came.
   D. Crystal planned.

15. What is the complete subject of this sentence?
   Most lions live in Africa.
   A. in Africa
   B. lions
   C. live in Africa
   D. Most lions

16. Which is the best answer to this question?
   Why did the cowboys sing to their cattle?
   A. The cowboys sang to keep the cattle calm.
   B. To calm them down.
   C. They made the songs up.
   D. Kept them calm.

17. In which section of the library would you find the book *Amerigo Vespucci: Scientist and Sailor*?
   A. reference
   B. nonfiction
   C. biography
   D. fiction

18. Which of these books would you find in the *reference* section of the library?
   A. *The Three Wishes and Other Tales*
   B. *Ben Franklin, the Statesman from Phildelphia*
   C. *American Women in the Space Program*
   D. *Encyclopedia of Natural Sciences*

19. What is the complete subject of this sentence?
   The small green snake slid across the yard.
   A. The small green snake
   B. green snake
   C. The small
   D. slid across the yard

Go on to the next page.

Use this card from a library card catalog to answer questions 20–22.

```
        The boy who could fly
  N
        Newman, Robert, 1909
        The boy who could fly. Illus. by
        Paul Sagsoorian. Atheneum
        Publishers. 1967
```

20. What is this type of card called?
 A. a subject card
 B. an author card
 C. a title card
 D. a magazine card

21. Who is the author of the book listed on this card?
 A. Atheneum Publishers
 B. Paul Sagsoorian
 C. a boy who could fly
 D. Robert Newman

22. What is the title of this book?
 A. *Robert Newman*
 B. *The Boy Who Could Fly*
 C. *Atheneum Publishers*
 D. *Paul Sagsoorian*

23. What is the correct way to combine these sentences with *but*?
    Sally knocked on the door.
    Nobody answered.
 A. Nobody answered Sally at the door.
 B. Sally knocked on the door but, nobody answered.
 C. Sally knocked on the door, But nobody answered.
 D. Sally knocked on the door, but nobody answered.

24. What must be done to correct this sentence?
    Was lost in the desert.
 A. Add punctuation at the end.
 B. Add a predicate.
 C. Add a subject.
 D. Capitalize the first letter.

25. What does the editing mark in this sentence tell the writer to do?
    I saw mr. Lee yesterday.
 A. Make a capital letter.
 B. Add a word.
 C. Take out a word.
 D. Add a period.

26. Which of these books would you find in the *nonfiction* section of the library?
 A. *Rand McNally Road Atlas*
 B. *Origami: Japanese Paper Folding Made Easy*
 C. *Favorite Fairytales from Around the World*
 D. *Pepper Adams Visits Mars*

Go on to the next page.

27. What is the correct way to combine these sentences with *or*?

       Turn down the radio.
       You'll wake up Grandma.

  A. Turn down the radio, or, you'll wake up Grandma.
  B. Turn down the radio, or you'll wake up Grandma.
  C. Turn down the radio Or you'll wake up Grandma.
  D. Grandma will wake up from the radio.

28. What must be done to correct this sentence?

       these puppies are for sale.

  A. Add a predicate.
  B. Add punctuation at the end.
  C. Add a subject.
  D. Capitalize the first letter.

29. What does the editing mark in this sentence tell the writer to do?

      Have you seen Mrs. Lazo's dog?

  A. Add a word.
  B. Add a period.
  C. Take out a word.
  D. Make a capital letter.

30. What is the correct way to combine these sentences with *and*?

       The rain stopped.
       The sun came out.

  A. The rain, stopped and the sun, came out.
  B. The rain stopped, and, the sun came out.
  C. The rain stopped, and the sun came out.
  D. The rain and the sun stopped and came out.

31. What must be done to correct this sentence?

       I have a new coat

  A. Add a subject.
  B. Capitalize the first letter.
  C. Add punctuation at the end.
  D. Add a predicate.

32. What does the editing mark in this sentence tell the writer to do?

      tomorrow is my birthday.

  A. Add a period.
  B. Add a word.
  C. Take out a word.
  D. Make a capital letter.

Read this poem to answer questions 33–35.

  (1) Clumsy Clyde Cleaver couldn't catch.
  (2) He never could get that ball.
  (3) One day he really met his match.
  (4) When bang, crash, smash, he caught the wall!

33. Which line of the poem contains words that name sounds?

  A. 4 **B.** 3 **C.** 2 **D.** 1

34. Which are lines in the poem that rhyme?

  A. 1,2 **B.** 2,4 **C.** 3,4 **D.** 1,4

35. Which line in the poem contains alliteration?

  A. 1 **B.** 2 **C.** 3 **D.** 4

Writing Sample Write five complete sentences about your school. Include two declarative, one interrogative, one imperative, and one exclamatory sentence.

                              Stop!

Name _____

Unit 2: Pretest

1. Which word in this sentence is a noun?
   Their rusty old car finally broke
   down completely.
   A. rusty   **B.** car
   C. broke   **D.** completely

2. Which word is a plural noun?
   A. hour   **B.** balloon
   C. kiss   **D.** windows

3. Which word is a plural noun?
   A. thinks   **B.** one
   C. feet   **D.** guess

4. Which word in this sentence is a
   common noun?
   Bill's favorite book is by Ed Bly.
   A. favorite   **B.** book
   C. Bill's   **D.** Ed

5. Complete this sentence correctly.
   Tomorrow ____ will speak.
   A. Mr. Arno Smitt
   B. Mr. arno Smitt
   C. Mr Arno Smitt
   D. mr arno Smitt

6. Complete this sentence correctly.
   The Hoyts live at 234 ____ .
   A. File rd.   **B.** File rd
   C. file rd   **D.** File Rd.

7. Complete this sentence correctly.
   My ____ husband enjoys cooking.
   A. sisters'   **B.** sisters
   C. sister's   **D.** sisteres'

8. Which word in the sentence is a
   noun?
   These young animals always like
   to play.
   A. animals   **B.** young
   C. like   **D.** play

9. Which word is the plural of *box*?
   A. boxen   **B.** boxs
   C. boxies   **D.** boxes

10. Which word is the plural of *sheep*?
    A. sheeps   **B.** sheep
    C. ships   **D.** sheepies

11. Which word in this sentence is a
    proper noun?
    Washington is the only state
    named for a president.
    A. only   **B.** Washington
    C. state   **D.** president

12. Complete this sentence correctly.
    This important message was
    written to ____ .
    A. gov. Adams
    B. governor Adams
    C. Gov.Adams
    D. Gov adams

13. Complete this sentence correctly.
    The world's largest flowering plant
    is in ____ .
    A. Sierra Madre, California
    B. Sierra madre, California
    C. sierra madre, California
    D. sierra madre, california

Go on to the next page.

14. Complete this sentence correctly.
Both ____ names were hard to say.
A. men's   B. mans'
C. mens'   D. mens

15. Which word in this sentence is a noun?
Her magic trick fooled us.
A. us   B. magic
C. fooled   D. trick

16. Which word is the plural of *bunch*?
A. bunchs   B. bunches
C. bunch   D. bunchies

17. Which word is the plural of *mouse*?
A. mices   B. mouses
C. mice   D. mouse

18. Which word in this sentence is a common noun?
Columbus searched for a route to the Indies.
A. route   B. Columbus
C. searched   D. Indies

19. Complete this sentence correctly.
Our school is named after ____ .
A. dr Charles drew
B. Dr. Charles drew
C. Dr. Charles Drew
D. Dr Charles Drew

20. Complete this sentence correctly.
On this map, find the ____ .
A. United states of america
B. United States Of America
C. united states of America
D. United States of America

21. Complete this sentence correctly.
That ____ whiskers are six inches long.
A. cats'   B. cats
C. cat's   D. cates'

Read this paragraph and answer questions 22–24.

The red piranha fish is found in the waters around South America. At 14 inches (35 cm) long, it is not a very big fish. It is known for its strong jaws full of very sharp teeth. Piranhas find their food through their sense of smell. They are especially attracted to blood coming from wounds. When they travel in large groups, or schools, they are very dangerous. They attack larger fish and swimming land animals, even humans.

22. What is the main idea of the paragraph?
A. Most land animals can swim.
B. South America has dangerous waters.
C. The piranha is a small but dangerous fish.
D. Fish travel in schools.

23. Which fact is *not* stated in the paragraph?
A. Piranhas find food through their sense of smell.
B. Piranhas are caught for their meat.
C. Piranhas are 35 centimeters long.
D. Piranhas are found in waters around South America.

Go on to the next page.

10 UNIT 2:   Pretest

Name _____

24. Which of these ideas from the paragraph is a statement of opinion?
- **A.** The piranha has very sharp teeth.
- **B.** Piranhas have a good sense of smell.
- **C.** The piranha is the most dangerous fish in the world.
- **D.** Piranhas sometimes attack humans.

Read this paragraph and answer questions 25–27.

The banana is a sweet, creamy fruit. It is germ-proof and dirt-proof since the skin of the banana keeps out all bacteria. It is a healthful food that is rich in fruit sugars and other important vitamins and minerals. Whether eaten cooked or raw, the banana is delicious and healthful.

25. What is the main idea of the paragraph?
- **A.** Banana skins keep out dirt.
- **B.** Bananas are ripe all year.
- **C.** The banana is a sweet, wholesome fruit.
- **D.** Bananas have vitamins and minerals.

26. Which fact is stated in the paragraph?
- **A.** Banana skins are easy to peel.
- **B.** Bananas are sometimes cooked.
- **C.** Bananas have no particular season.
- **D.** Some bananas have red skins.

27. Which of these ideas from the paragraph is a statement of opinion?
- **A.** Banana skins keep out bacteria.
- **B.** Bananas are sweet and creamy.
- **C.** Bananas are rich in fruit sugars.
- **D.** Bananas are a delicious fruit.

Read this paragraph and answer questions 28–29.

Baseball is one of America's most popular sports. No other sport in America is more exciting or interesting. It is played all over the country, from small villages to large cities. Every year Americans enjoy watching baseball in local parks and giant stadiums. Millions of fans also follow their favorite teams on radio and television. They read about this sport in newspapers and magazines. People like to study the standings of the professional teams and the records of the players.

28. What is the main idea of the paragraph?
- **A.** Americans enjoy baseball.
- **B.** Baseball is played in large and small cities.
- **C.** Baseball is fun to play.
- **D.** People watch baseball on TV.

29. Which of these ideas from the paragraph is a statement of opinion?
- **A.** People read about baseball in newspapers.
- **B.** Millions of fans follow baseball on TV and radio.
- **C.** No other sport in America is more exciting than baseball.
- **D.** Americans watch baseball in parks and stadiums.

Go on to the next page.

Read this paragraph and answer questions 30–31.

Sequoya was born and grew up in the Cherokee village of Tuskegee, Tennessee, around 1770. As a young man he saw many white men who could read and write letters. He became fascinated with their "talking leaves." He decided to invent a system of writing for his own people. In 1821, after 21 years of work, he finally succeeded. Thanks to Sequoya the Cherokee Indians were able to publish books and newspapers in their own language.

30. What is the main idea of the paragraph?
   A. Sequoya was an Indian.
   B. Sequoya created a system of writing.
   C. Sequoya was fascinated with "talking leaves."
   D. The Cherokee published books and newspapers.

31. Which fact is stated in the paragraph?
   A. Sequoya died in 1843.
   B. Giant sequoia trees are named after Sequoya.
   C. It took Sequoya 21 years to complete his writing system.
   D. Sequoya was interested in the betterment of all Indians.

Read this book report and answer questions 32–34.

TITLE *Child of the silent night*
AUTHOR *Edith Fisher Hunter*
SUMMARY *This is the story of Laura Bridgman. She was* (This book tells about the special school she attended.) *deaf, blind, and mute.* ∧ *She learned to read and write.*

32. What is the correct way to write the title of the book?
   A. Child of the silent night
   B. Child of the Silent Night
   C. Child of The Silent Night
   D. Child of the silent Night

33. What does the mark ∧ between the last two sentences tell the writer to do?
   A. Add something.
   B. Take something out.
   C. Make a new paragraph.
   D. Correct a spelling mistake.

34. What part of a book report did the writer forget to include?
   A. whom the story was about
   B. the name of the author of the book
   C. the writer's opinion of the book
   D. facts about the main character

35. What do we call the story of a real person's life, written by someone else?
   A. a biography   **B.** a play
   C. a fable   **D.** a short story

Writing Sample Write a book report about a book you have read recently. Write a summary of the book, including the main idea and some interesting details. Tell your opinion of the book.

Stop!

Unit 2: Posttest

1. Which word is this sentence is a noun?
   The bird looked at me and flew away.
   - **A.** me
   - **B.** bird
   - **C.** looked
   - **D.** away

2. Which word is a plural noun?
   - **A.** juice
   - **B.** dish
   - **C.** sweet
   - **D.** cups

3. Which word is a plural noun?
   - **A.** goes
   - **B.** dress
   - **C.** children
   - **D.** tear

4. Which word in this sentence is a common noun?
   China is almost 6,000 miles west of California.
   - **A.** China
   - **B.** miles
   - **C.** west
   - **D.** California

5. Complete this sentence correctly.
   There was a program about ___ on television.
   - **A.** Dr. Emily Black
   - **B.** dr emily Black
   - **C.** Dr Emily black
   - **D.** dr. emily black

6. Complete this sentence correctly.
   My grandfather has visited our house on ___ .
   - **A.** curtis st
   - **B.** Curtis st.
   - **C.** curtis St
   - **D.** Curtis St.

7. Complete this sentence correctly.
   Tamina won first prize in the ___ art contest.
   - **A.** childrenses'
   - **B.** childrens'
   - **C.** children's
   - **D.** childrens

8. Which word in this sentence is a noun?
   Her left shoe is too tight.
   - **A.** shoe
   - **B.** her
   - **C.** left
   - **D.** tight

9. Which word is the plural of *pony*?
   - **A.** pony
   - **B.** ponyes
   - **C.** ponys
   - **D.** ponies

10. Which word is the plural of *tooth*?
    - **A.** teeths
    - **B.** teeth
    - **C.** tooths
    - **D.** teethes

11. Which word in this sentence is a proper noun?
    My class visited a museum in Atlanta.
    - **A.** my
    - **B.** Atlanta
    - **C.** class
    - **D.** museum

12. Complete this sentence correctly.
    My father is ___ .
    - **A.** sen. robert romano
    - **B.** Sen Robert Romano
    - **C.** Sen. Robert Romano
    - **D.** sen robert romano

13. Complete this sentence correctly.
    Lisa was born near ___ in 1972.
    - **A.** Lake Placid
    - **B.** lake Placid
    - **C.** lake placid
    - **D.** Lake placid

Go on to the next page.

14. Complete this sentence correctly.
    The star ____ fans clapped for him.
    A. player's   **B.** playeres'
    C. players'   **D.** players

15. Which word in this sentence is a noun?
    We walked to the library together.
    A. We   **B.** together
    C. walked   **D.** library

16. Which word is the plural of *sandwich*?
    A. sandwichies **B.** sandwiches
    C. sandwichs   **D.** sandswichs

17. Which word is the plural of *moose*?
    A. mooses   **B.** meeses
    C. moose   **D.** mice

18. Which word in this sentence is a common noun?
    Neil's cats are named Cloudy and Sunny.
    A. cats   **B.** Cloudy
    C. Neil's   **D.** Sunny

19. Complete this sentence correctly.
    The first American cookbook was written by ____ .
    A. miss. Amelia Simmons
    B. Miss. Amelia Simmons
    C. Miss Amelia Simmons
    D. miss amelia simmons

20. Complete this sentence correctly.
    The old house on ____ is haunted.
    A. walker Rd   **B.** walker rd.
    C. Walker rd   **D.** Walker Rd.

21. Complete this sentence correctly.
    The ____ thick coats keep them warm.
    A. sheepes'   **B.** sheeps
    C. sheep's   **D.** sheeps'

Read this paragraph and answer questions 22–24.

    The sun sends out enormous amounts of energy. This energy from the sun is called solar energy. Solar energy makes all life on earth possible. Without the sun's heat and light, our earth would be a wasteland. The sun's energy is needed to grow the food we eat. It shapes the weather. It gives us beautiful sunsets to watch. We also use solar energy stored in coal, oil, and gas.

22. What is the main idea of the paragraph?
    A. The sun's energy shapes the weather.
    B. We need the sun for light.
    C. The sun's energy is important to life on earth.
    D. Solar energy is stored in coal, oil, and gas.

23. Which fact is stated in the paragraph?
    A. The sun is a mass of hot gases.
    B. We need the sun's energy to help grow our food.
    C. You can become blind if you look directly at the sun.
    D. The sun lights up half of the earth at a time.

Go on to the next page.

24. Which of these ideas from the paragraph is a statement of opinion?
 - **A.** Energy from the sun is called solar energy.
 - **B.** The sun helps our crops to grow.
 - **C.** Sunsets are beautiful to watch.
 - **D.** Coal, oil, and gas provide us with energy.

Read this paragraph and answer questions 25–27.

A trip to Colorado is not complete without a visit to Pike's Peak. Yet, not many people know anything about the man for whom it was named. Zebulon Pike (1779–1813) was an American soldier, general, and explorer. He explored the Mississippi, Red, and Arkansas Rivers. His explorations helped to open up the American Southwest to settlement. Pike never climbed the peak he discovered. In fact, he gave it the name "Great Peak." No one knows how or when its name was changed to Pike's Peak.

25. What is the main idea of the paragraph?
 - **A.** Pike's Peak was first called "Great Peak."
 - **B.** Pike opened up the American Southwest.
 - **C.** Pike's Peak was named after an American explorer.
 - **D.** Pike's Peak is a good place to visit.

26. Which fact is *not* stated in the paragraph?
 - **A.** Pike's Peak is located in Colorado.
 - **B.** Pike wrote a book about his explorations.
 - **C.** Pike never climbed Pike's Peak.
 - **D.** Pike was a general.

27. Which of these ideas from the paragraph is a statement of opinion?
 - **A.** No one knows how or why the peak's name was changed.
 - **B.** Pike traveled along the Mississippi, Red, and Arkansas Rivers.
 - **C.** Not many people know anything about Zebulon Pike.
 - **D.** A trip to Colorado is not complete without a visit to Pike's Peak.

Read this paragraph and answer question 28.

The South American rain forest is the home of the sloth. This slow-moving mammal spends its entire life hanging upside down from a tree branch. It does everything from this curious position. It eats, sleeps, and does most other things upside down.

28. What is the main idea of the paragraph?
 - **A.** The sloth is an unusual animal.
 - **B.** Sloths eat upside down.
 - **C.** Sloths are slow-moving.
 - **D.** Sloths hang from trees.

Go on to the next page.

Read this paragraph and answer questions 29–31.

  Everyone in the neighborhood was afraid of the man with the house full of cats. The kids would only pass in front of his house if they had to. There were always cats on his front porch or in the trees nearby. Mrs. Calley said he was really quite harmless, even friendly. None of the kids believed this, of course. Anyone with that many cats had to be crazy.

29. Which of these ideas from the paragraph is a statement of opinion?
 A. The children ran past the man's house.
 B. The man had a house full of cats.
 C. Anyone with that many cats had to be crazy.
 D. The kids didn't believe Mrs. Calley.

30. What is the main idea of the paragraph?
 A. Every neighborhood has cats.
 B. Children were afraid of the man with the cats.
 C. The mail carrier liked the man.
 D. The man had 30 cats.

31. Which fact is *not* stated in the paragraph?
 A. There were always cats on the man's porch.
 B. Mrs. Calley said the man was harmless.
 C. The owner of the cats was old.
 D. There were cats in the trees.

Read this book report and answer questions 32–34.

TITLE *The house of dies drear*
AUTHOR *Virginia Hamilton*
SUMMARY *Thomas Small's new house had been a way station on the Underground Railroad. It was a strange house with ^hidden passages. Thomas thought it was haunted.*

32. What is the correct way to write the title of the book?
 A. The house of Dies Drear
 B. The House of Dies Drear
 C. The House Of Dies Drear
 D. The house of dies drear

33. What does the mark ∧ in the second sentence tell the writer to do?
 A. Add something.
 B. Take something out.
 C. Make a new paragraph.
 D. Correct a spelling mistake.

34. Who is Virginia Hamilton?
 A. the author of the book report
 B. the owner of the house
 C. the author of the book
 D. one of the slaves who fled on the Underground Railroad

35. A biography is a story about
 A. a real person's life
 B. imaginary people and places
 C. life in the future
 D. animals that act like people

Writing Sample   Write a book report about a book you have read recently.

Stop!

Unit 3: Pretest

1. Which word in this sentence is an action verb?

   Water dripped from the faucet all night.

   A. night   B. faucet
   C. Water   D. dripped

2. Which word in this sentence is a helping verb?

   Two frogs were stranded on a rock.

   A. on   B. stranded
   C. were   D. Two

3. Which sentence has a verb in the present tense?

   A. We will play in the park.
   B. Sandy walked the dog.
   C. Ted knows how to swim.
   D. The bird chased a worm.

4. What is the contraction for *did not*?

   A. didnt   B. didn't
   C. diddn't   D. did'nt

5. What is the past tense of the verb *bury*?

   A. buryd   B. burried
   C. buryed   D. buried

6. Complete this sentence correctly.

   Dixie has ____ to visit her aunt.

   A. goes   B. gone
   C. go   D. went

7. Which word in this sentence is an action verb?

   Sarah fills the bird feeder every morning.

   A. fills   B. bird
   C. feeder   D. morning

8. Which word in this sentence is a helping verb?

   Jeff is learning to climb mountains.

   A. climb   B. learning
   C. is   D. mountains

9. Which sentence has a verb in the future tense?

   A. Pat wants us to help her.
   B. Liz planted some pea seeds.
   C. Jake showed me his new rocket.
   D. Peter will stay home tomorrow.

10. What is the contraction for *were not*?

    A. weren't   B. werent
    C. were'nt   D. weren'

11. What is the past tense of the verb *pop*?

    A. poped   B. popped
    C. popd   D. popied

12. Complete this sentence correctly.

    Gil ____ 2 inches taller last year.

    A. grow   B. grows
    C. grown   D. grew

Go on to the next page.

13. Which word in this sentence is a linking verb?

      Frieda's party was lots of fun.
- **A.** fun
- **B.** lots
- **C.** party
- **D.** was

14. Which word in this sentence is a helping verb?

      I have seen that program before.
- **A.** seen
- **B.** have
- **C.** program
- **D.** before

15. Which sentence has a verb in the past tense?
- **A.** The raisins spilled all over.
- **B.** My mother is teaching my sister to drive.
- **C.** Dave's family will go camping soon.
- **D.** It always rains a lot in the spring.

16. What is the contraction for *have not*?
- **A.** havn't
- **B.** have'nt
- **C.** havent
- **D.** haven't

17. What is the past tense of the verb *try*?
- **A.** tryd
- **B.** tryed
- **C.** tried
- **D.** treed

18. Complete this sentence correctly.

      Alison has ____ the math problems already.
- **A.** done
- **B.** did
- **C.** do
- **D.** does

19. *Feud* would come between which pair of guide words in the dictionary?
- **A.** few–fig
- **B.** feeler–fender
- **C.** fern–fever
- **D.** fuel–gag

20. Which word would come between the guide words *aria—armory* in the dictionary?
- **A.** army
- **B.** argue
- **C.** area
- **D.** arise

21. *Pizza* would come between which pair of guide words in the dictionary?
- **A.** plane–plastic
- **B.** pivotal–plan
- **C.** plate–play
- **D.** pit–pivot

Use this dictionary entry to answer questions 22-24.

cheat [chēt] **1** *v.* To act in a dishonest way: to cheat on the test. **2** *v.* To get away from; escape. **3** *n.* A person who cheats. **4** *n.* A cheating act; swindle. —**cheat′er** *n.*

22. How many meanings does the word *cheat* have?
- **A.** 2
- **B.** 4
- **C.** 3
- **D.** 1

23. What does the part you see marked with a circle tell you?
- **A.** a definition of *cheat*
- **B.** what part of speech *cheat* is
- **C.** how to pronounce *cheat*
- **D.** how to use *cheat*

24. *Cheat* can be used as a verb or as
- **A.** an adjective
- **B.** a verb
- **C.** a noun
- **D.** an adverb

25. What part of speech is *apple*?
- **A.** adjective
- **B.** verb
- **C.** noun
- **D.** adverb

Go on to the next page.

Look at the symbols in this pronunciation key from the dictionary. Use them to find the correct spellings for the words in questions 26–28.

add, āce, câre, pälm; end, ēqual; it, īce; odd, ōpen, ôr-
der; tŏŏk, pōōl; up, bûrn; ə = a in *above*, e in *sicken*, i in
possible, o in *melon*, u in *circus*; yōō = u in *fuse*; oil;
pout; check; ring; thin; this; zh in *vision*.

26. kat′el
   A. kilter   **B.** cater
   C. cattail   **D.** cattle

27. hā′lō
   A. hollow   **B.** hall
   C. halo   **D.** holly

28. mēt
   A. meet   **B.** met
   C. mate   **D.** mat

Use this invitation to answer questions 29–34.

(1)   21 Lee Street
       Denver, Colorado 80231
       November 8, 19—
(2) Dear Joy
       Would you like to go to a dog
     show next saturday? It's
     especially for small dogs like
(3) ours. My father and I can pick
     you up at nine o'clock in the
     morning. Please come.
            (4) your friend
            (5)

29. What is the name for part 1?
   A. return address
   B. greeting
   C. heading
   D. body

Go on to the next page.

30. What editing mark will show how to make part 2 completely correct?

    A. Dear Joy ⌐ﬤ   **B.** Dear Joy /

    C. Dear Joy ⊙   **D.** Dear Joy ⋏

31. What information is missing from part 3?

    A. what the invitation is for

    B. who is going

    C. where Jack is inviting Joy

    D. when the activity will be finished

32. What editing mark will show how to make the underlined word in part 3 correct?

    A. (saturday)   **B.** ʂaturday

    C. saturday   **D.** Ⓢaturday

33. What is the correct way to write part 4?

    A. Your Friend,

    B. Your friend,

    C. "your friend"

    D. Your friend'

34. What is the name for part 5?

    A. closing   **B.** greeting

    C. signature   **D.** body

35. A story that is written to be acted out is called

    A. a play   **B.** a tale

    C. a poem   **D.** a report

Writing Sample: Write a friendly letter to a classmate who is sick. Tell your classmate what your class has been doing.

                             Stop!

Unit 3: Posttest

1. Which word in this sentence is a linking verb?

    Peaches are my favorite fruit.
- **A.** favorite
- **B.** fruit
- **C.** Peaches
- **D.** are

2. Which word in this sentence is a helping verb?

    I am teaching my pet mouse a new trick.
- **A.** trick
- **B.** teaching
- **C.** am
- **D.** pet

3. Which sentence has a verb in the present tense?
- **A.** Ron finished the book.
- **B.** The cow called her calf.
- **C.** My uncle drives a truck.
- **D.** The plane will land soon.

4. What is the contraction for *do not*?
- **A.** dont
- **B.** don't
- **C.** do'nt
- **D.** don'

5. What is the past tense of the verb *hurry*?
- **A.** huryd
- **B.** hurred
- **C.** hurryed
- **D.** hurried

6. Complete this sentence correctly.

    Mary Lou has ____ in two races.
- **A.** ran
- **B.** run
- **C.** runs
- **D.** ranned

7. Which word in this sentence is an action verb?

    Lena dives happily into the icy water.
- **A.** dives
- **B.** happily
- **C.** icy
- **D.** water

8. Which word in this sentence is a helping verb?

    Tina will cook some popcorn.
- **A.** cook
- **B.** popcorn
- **C.** will
- **D.** some

9. Which sentence has a verb in the future tense?
- **A.** Betty lifted the heavy rock.
- **B.** José knocked at the door.
- **C.** Stan turns the chair over.
- **D.** Snow will fall tomorrow.

10. What is the contraction for *is not*?
- **A.** isn't
- **B.** isnt
- **C.** is'nt
- **D.** isen'

11. What is the past tense of the verb *clap*?
- **A.** clapied
- **B.** clapped
- **C.** claped
- **D.** clapt

12. Complete this sentence correctly.

    Mother ____ me my allowance yesterday.
- **A.** give
- **B.** given
- **C.** gives
- **D.** gave

Go on to the next page.

13. Which word in this sentence is a linking verb?

> The park is full of people.

    A. people   **B.** park
    C. full   **D.** is

14. Which word in this sentence is a helping verb?

> An old car was stuck in the mud.

    A. old   **B.** was
    C. stuck   **D.** mud

15. Which sentence has a verb in the past tense?

    A. Everyone laughed at the joke.
    B. The package will arrive next week.
    C. The sun helps plants grow.
    D. The bus will come any minute.

16. What is the contraction for *has not*?

    A. hasnt   **B.** has'nt
    C. hasen'   **D.** hasn't

17. What is the past tense of the verb *study*?

    A. studyed   **B.** studyd
    C. studied   **D.** studdied

18. Complete this sentence correctly.

> Francis has ____ music lessons
> for two years.

    A. taken   **B.** took
    C. takes   **D.** take

19. *Mirth* would come between which pair of guide words in the dictionary?

    A. mingle–minute
    B. miserable–mission
    C. minute–miser
    D. missionary–mix

20. Which word would come between the guide words *severity–shadow* in the dictionary?

    A. shady   **B.** science
    C. shriek   **D.** shabby

21. Which word would come between the guide words *wedding–well* in the dictionary?

    A. weasel   **B.** weird
    C. webbed   **D.** west

Use this dictionary entry to answer questions 22 – 24.

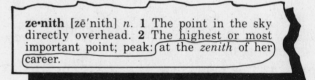

ze•nith [zē′nith] *n.* **1** The point in the sky directly overhead. **2** The highest or most important point; peak: at the *zenith* of her career.

22. The part of this entry you see marked with a circle tells

    A. how to pronounce *zenith*
    B. how to use *zenith*
    C. what part of speech *zenith* is
    D. a definition of *zenith*

23. How many meanings does the word *zenith* have?

    A. 3   **B.** 4
    C. 1   **D.** 2

24. What part of speech is *zenith*?

    A. adjective   **B.** adverb
    C. noun   **D.** verb

25. The respelling for *zenith* is

    A. point   **B.** overhead
    C. zē′nith   **D.** peak

Go on to the next page.

Look at the symbols in this pronunciation key from a dictionary. Use them to find the correct spellings for the words in questions 26–28.

add, āce, câre, pälm; end, ēqual; it, īce; odd, ōpen, ôr-der; tŏŏk, pōōl; up, bûrn; ə = a in *above*, e in *sicken*, i in *possible*, o in *melon*, u in *circus*; yōō = u in *fuse*; oil; pout; check; ring; thin; this; zh in *vision*.

26. nīte
   A. net   **B.** neat
   C. knit   **D.** night

27. dā′ zē
   A. days   **B.** dose
   C. daisy   **D.** dizzy

28. ped′ əl
   A. pedal   **B.** paddle
   C. petal   **D.** puddle

Use this thank you note to answer questions 29–34.

(1) 55 Cable Drive
    Rye, New York 10580
    July 7, 19—
(2) Dear Jeff,
       I had a wonderful time in portland meeting all your new friends was great. The picnic and fireworks were the most fun I've had all summer. The
(3) food at the picnic was delicious. Let's go skiing this winter. Your old friends in New York say "hi!" Please visit in August.
                    (4) your cousin
                    (5) Lisa

29. What is the name for part 2?
   A. greeting   **B.** return address
   C. heading   **D.** body

Go on to the next page.

30. What editing mark will show how to make part 2 completely correct?
- **A.** Dear jeff,
- **B.** Dear jeff,
- **C.** Dear jeff,
- **D.** Dear jeff,

31. What is the name for part 1?
- **A.** greeting
- **B.** body
- **C.** closing
- **D.** heading

32. What editing marks will make the underlined section in part 3 correct?
- **A.** Portland⊙ meeting
- **B.** Portland∧ meeting
- **C.** Portland⌿ meeting
- **D.** Portland∧ meeting

33. What is the correct way to write part 4?
- **A.** Your cousin
- **B.** Your cousin,
- **C.** Your Cousin,
- **D.** "Your cousin"

34. What is the name for part 3?
- **A.** heading
- **B.** closing
- **C.** body
- **D.** greeting

35. In a play the conversation the actors speak is called the
- **A.** dialog
- **B.** setting
- **C.** scenery
- **D.** characters

Writing Sample   Write a friendly letter to a real or a make-believe friend who has moved away. Tell your friend what you are doing in school.

Stop!

Name _____

Unit 4: Pretest

Read this paragraph and answer questions 1–3.

    Most of Wanda's mornings are very busy. When she wakes up, she gets dressed right away. Then she takes her dog for a walk. After that she makes her bed and eats breakfast. Sometimes she helps pack lunch for herself and her brothers. Then she catches the bus for school.

1. What is the main idea of the paragraph?
  A. Wanda takes good care of her dog.
  B. Wanda has a lot to do in the mornings.
  C. Wanda takes her lunch to school.
  D. Wanda has two brothers.

2. What is the topic sentence of the paragraph?
  A. Most of Wanda's mornings are very busy.
  B. When she gets up, she gets dressed right away.
  C. Then she takes her dog for a walk.
  D. Then she catches the bus for school.

3. Which sentence would add a detail that also tells about the topic?
  A. Wanda's favorite sport is soccer.
  B. Wanda's best friend is Sally Linn.
  C. Wanda does the breakfast dishes.
  D. Wanda's brothers are twins.

Read this paragraph and answer question 4.

    My parakeet Trump is a very smart bird. He can say five words. His favorite word is "Trump." He understands some words I say too. When I say "Jump, Trump," he jumps up on my finger.

4. What is the topic sentence of the paragraph?
  A. His favorite word is "Trump."
  B. He can say five words.
  C. My parakeet Trump is a very smart bird.
  D. He understands some words I say too.

Read this paragraph and answer questions 5–6.

    Borrowing a book from the school library is easy. Then you take it to the desk and sign the card. First you choose the book you want to take out. The librarian stamps a date on the card. You have to bring the book back by that date. My favorite book is *Big Red*.

5. Which sentence should be the *second* sentence in the paragraph?
  A. The librarian stamps a date on the card.
  B. Borrowing a book from the school library is easy.
  C. You have to bring the book back by that date.
  D. First you choose the book you want to take out.

Go on to the next page.

6. Which sentence does *not* tell about the topic?

    A. My favorite book is *Big Red*.

    B. First you choose the book you want to take out.

    C. The librarian stamps a date on the card.

    D. Then you take it to the desk and sign the card.

Read this paragraph and answer questions 7–9.

       The buffalo was very important to the Plains Indians. Buffalo meat was their main food. The Indians made clothes and teepees from buffalo skins. Their rope was made of buffalo hair and their glue of buffalo hooves. They made cooking pots from the buffalo's stomach and spoons from its horns. They even used parts of the buffalo to make the children's toys.

7. What is the main idea of the paragraph?

    A. The Plains Indians were great hunters.

    B. The Plains Indians used the buffalo in many ways.

    C. The Plains Indians ate a lot of buffalo meat.

    D. The Plains Indians made toys to give to their children.

8. What is the topic sentence of the paragraph?

    A. They even used parts of the buffalo to make children's toys.

    B. Their rope was made from buffalo hair, and their glue from buffalo hooves.

    C. They made clothes and teepees from buffalo skins.

    D. The buffalo was very important to the Plains Indians.

9. Which sentence would add a detail that also tells about the topic?

    A. The average buffalo weighs 2,500 pounds.

    B. Today there are very few buffalo left.

    C. They made scraping tools from buffalo bones.

    D. The Plains Indians also ate many kinds of berries, and they searched for roots and seeds.

Read this paragraph and answer questions 10–11.

       After dinner my family has jobs to do. My little brother clears the table. My sister Joan dries them. I wash the dishes. Mom and Dad put the dishes away together. Tod likes to go outside to play.

Go on to the next page.

10. Which sentence should be the *third* sentence in the paragraph?

    A. Mom and Dad put the dishes away together.

    B. I wash the dishes.

    C. Tod likes to go outside to play.

    D. My sister Joan dries them.

11. Which sentence does *not* tell about the topic?

    A. Tod likes to go outside to play.

    B. My sister Joan dries them.

    C. Mom and Dad put the dishes away together.

    D. I wash the dishes.

Read this paragraph and answer questions 12–14.

    Last Monday Joel rode his sled to school. He lives at the top of Braintree Hill. His school is at the bottom. Two feet of snow had fallen Sunday night. Cars couldn't go, but Joel could. He whizzed down the hill. There was only one problem. School was called off because of the snow.

12. What is the main idea of the paragraph?

    A. The snow that fell Sunday night was too deep for Joel.

    B. Joel could not get to school on time.

    C. Joel's house is up the hill from his school.

    D. Joel used his sled to get to school on a snowy day.

13. What is the topic sentence of this paragraph?

    A. Two feet of snow had fallen Sunday night.

    B. Cars couldn't go, but Joel could.

    C. Last Monday Joel rode his sled to school.

    D. School was called off because of the snow.

14. Which sentence would add a detail that also tells about the topic?

    A. Joel got to school in record time.

    B. Braintree Hill has a lot of trees.

    C. Joel is a very good iceskater.

    D. Joel's sled was a birthday present.

Read this paragraph and answer questions 15–16.

    Sunflower seeds are an easy snack to grow. Plant the seeds in the late spring. During the summer, the plants grow very tall. Peanuts are easy to grow too. In the fall, cut off the flower head. Leave it in a dry place for a few weeks. Store the dried seeds in a can or jar. Then rub the seeds from the flower head.

15. Which sentence should be the *last* sentence in the paragraph?

    A. In the fall, cut off the flower head.

    B. Leave it in a dry place for a few weeks.

    C. During the summer, the plants grow very tall.

    D. Store the dried seeds in a can or jar.

Go on to the next page.

16. Which sentence does *not* tell about the topic?

    A. Plant the seeds in the late spring.

    B. Peanuts are easy to grow too.

    C. Leave it in a dry place for a few weeks.

    D. Sunflower seeds are an easy snack to grow.

Use this table of contents from a book to answer questions 17–20.

TABLE OF CONTENTS

17. Which information is found in the table of contents?

    A. who wrote the book

    B. the page on which each chapter begins

    C. the meanings of unfamiliar words in the book

    D. what company publishes the book

18. On which page does Chapter 3 begin?

    A. 4   **B.** 3

    C. 23   **D.** 44

19. Which chapter tells about life on a farm?

    A. 7   **B.** 4

    C. 1   **D.** 3

20. Which chapter begins on page 44?

    A. The Long Journey

    B. Good News

    C. Life on the Farm

    D. New Friends

Use this index from a book to answer questions 21–24.

21. On which page(s) would you find information about Sputnik II?

    A. 11–13   **B.** 18

    C. 51,53   **D.** 13

22. On how many pages would you find information about the effects of space travel on humans?

    A. 6   **B.** 21

    C. 2   **D.** 25

Go on to the next page.

23. On which page(s) can information about weather control be found?
    A. 104–105, 172
    B. 74–75, 97–99, 127
    C. See Meteorology
    D. 50, 51, 53

24. Under which main topic can information about the Apollo spaceship be found?
    A. Space travel
    B. Spacecraft
    C. Telstar
    D. Sputnik

25. You would like to read about the American painter Mary Cassatt. In which volume of the encyclopedia would you look first?
    A. M   **B.** D
    C. C   **D.** A

26. You would like some information about the life of Dr. Martin Luther King, Jr. In which volume of the encyclopedia would you look first?
    A. K   **B.** L
    C. M   **D.** D

27. You would like to know about the climate and location of the British Isles. In which volume of the encyclopedia would you look first?
    A. L   **B.** I
    C. C   **D.** B

28. You want to read about music and dance in ancient Greece. In which volume of the encyclopedia would you look first?
    A. M   **B.** A
    C. G   **D.** D

To answer questions 29–31, read these directions for preparing rice. The missing steps are below.
    A. Measure 1 cup rice, 1 tsp. salt, 1 tbsp. butter.
    B. Boil 2 1/2 cups of water.
    C. Lower heat to "simmer" and cover pan tightly.
    D. Let cooked rice stand for 5 minutes before serving.

29. Where does the following step belong?
    Mix rice, salt, and butter into boiling water.
    A. before step A
    B. after step B
    C. after step C
    D. after step D

30. Where does the following step belong?
    Cook at low heat for twenty minutes.
    A. before step A
    B. after step C
    C. after step B
    D. after step D

Go on to the next page.

31. Where does the following step belong?

      Serve with butter.

    A. before step B
    B. after step C
    C. after step A
    D. after step D

Read these directions for polishing shoes and answer questions 32–34.

It's easy to polish leather shoes. All you need is polish and some rags. ^First^ Wipe off any dust and loose dirt from the shoes. Next put a light coat of polish on each shoe with a rag. The polish may smell ~~bad~~ funny. Then let it dry for a few minutes. Rub the shoes with a soft rag until they shine.

32. Which sentence in these directions is unnecessary?

    A. It's easy to polish leather shoes.
    B. All you need is polish and some rags.
    C. Let it dry for a few minutes.
    D. The polish may smell funny.

33. Which editing mark should be used to take out the unnecessary sentence?

    A. ꟼ
    B. ⌐
    C. ℛ
    D. ∿

34. The writer has added the word *first* to the third sentence. What does the editing mark on *wipe* mean?

    A. Spell the word correctly.
    B. Take the word out of the sentence.
    C. Make the first letter lowercase.
    D. Move the word to another place.

35. You are most likely to read about people who do unusual or exciting things in

    A. science fiction
    B. fables
    C. poems
    D. adventure stories

Writing Sample Write a paragraph giving directions. Tell how to make a simple object such as a pinwheel or a paper boat. Use time words to show correct order.

Stop!

Name _____

Unit 4: Posttest

Read this paragraph and answer questions 1–3.

Many kinds of animals make nests for their babies. Birds make nests of grass, straw, and twigs. Rabbits line their grass nests with their own soft fur. One kind of fish makes a nest out of bubbles.

1. What is the main idea of the paragraph?
    A. Rabbits' nests are the softest of all.
    B. There are many kinds of nests.
    C. Bubble nests break very easily.
    D. Birds use straw to make their nests.

2. What is the topic sentence of this paragraph?
    A. Many kinds of animals make nests for their babies.
    B. Birds make nests of grass, straw, and twigs.
    C. Rabbits line their grass nests with their own soft fur.
    D. One kind of fish makes a nest out of bubbles.

3. Which sentence would add a detail that also tells about the topic?
    A. Don't ever get too close to a wasp nest.
    B. Baby birds leave their nests when they learn to fly.
    C. Deer push branches to the ground to make nests.
    D. Once a bird built a nest near my window.

Read this paragraph and answer question 4.

This is how to decorate an egg. First poke a hole about the size of a pencil point in one end. Then make a smaller hole in the other end. Once the holes are made, hold the egg over a bowl. Blow gently into the smaller end. When all the egg is out, wash the shell. Let it dry and then paint it.

4. What is the topic sentence of this paragraph?
    A. When all the egg is out, wash the shell.
    B. Let it dry and then paint it.
    C. This is how to decorate an egg.
    D. Blow gently into the smaller end.

Read this paragraph and answer questions 5–6.

I had a trading-post party. My birthday is in October. Everybody brought something to trade. When the trading was done, we had ice cream and cake. We put all the things on the table. Then everybody chose one thing to keep.

5. Which sentence should be the last sentence of the paragraph?
    A. I had a trading-post party for my birthday.
    B. We put all the things on the table.
    C. Everybody brought something to trade.
    D. When the trading was done, we had ice cream and cake.

Go on to the next page.

6. Which sentence does *not* tell about the topic?

   A. My birthday is in October.
   B. I had a trading-post party.
   C. Everybody brought something to trade.
   D. We put all the things on the table.

Read this paragraph and answer questions 7–9.

     Judy makes money by walking her neighbor's dogs. Every morning she takes Buff and Mac to the park. She plays with them there for fifteen minutes. After school she takes them out again. She has more time in the afternoon, and so she plays with them for an hour. Judy saves the money she earns.

7. What is the main idea of this paragraph?

   A. Judy loves dogs.
   B. To earn extra money, Judy takes her neighbor's dogs out twice a day.
   C. The names of the neighbor's dogs are Buff and Mac.
   D. Buff and Mac like to go to the park.

8. What is the topic sentence of the paragraph?

   A. She has more time in the afternoon, and so she plays with them for an hour.
   B. Every morning she takes Buff and Mac to the park.
   C. After school she takes them out again.
   D. Judy makes money by walking her neighbor's dogs.

9. Which sentence would add a detail that also tells about the topic?

   A. Judy has a cat named Jerry.
   B. Next year Judy will be old enough to babysit.
   C. Judy's neighbor pays her five dollars every week.
   D. Judy's neighbor works in a big office building.

Read this paragraph and answer questions 10–11.

     In the summer and fall bears eat and eat to get ready for winter. In late fall they go to sleep in their dens. They sleep almost all winter. Then they go back to sleep until spring arrives. Most bears are really very shy. If there is a warm winter day, they get up for a little while.

10. Which sentence should be the *last* sentence of the paragraph?

   A. In the summer and fall bears eat and eat to get ready for winter.
   B. Then they go back to sleep until spring arrives.
   C. In late fall they go to sleep in their dens.
   D. They sleep almost all winter.

11. Which sentence does *not* tell about the topic?

   A. Most bears are really very shy.
   B. In late fall they go to sleep in their dens.
   C. They sleep almost all winter.
   D. Then they go back to sleep until spring arrives.

Go on to the next page.

Read this paragraph and answer questions 12–14.

Mr. Suarez's class wanted to raise money to help the school library. They collected aluminum cans. They collected almost a ton of cans. Then they sold them to a metal dealer. The class gave the money to the school library for new books.

12. What is the main idea of the paragraph?
   A. Mr. Suarez's class gave some money to the school library.
   B. Pop-tops can cut people's feet at the beach.
   C. Mr. Suarez's class learned to count to a million.
   D. Mr. Suarez's students collected aluminum cans to raise money for the school library.

13. What is the topic sentence of the paragraph?
   A. The class gave the money to the school library for new books.
   B. They collected almost a ton of cans.
   C. Mr. Suarez's class wanted to raise money to help the school library.
   D. Then they sold them to a metal dealer.

14. Which sentence would add a detail that also tells about the topic?
   A. It took three months to collect the cans.
   B. You can make a necklace from soda can pop-tops.
   C. Mr. Suarez's class likes arithmetic.
   D. The library is down the hall.

Read this paragraph and answer questions 15–16.

Last week Jason built a tree house. On Monday he got some wood, some nails, and a hammer. On Wednesday he fixed the roof and walls. On Tuesday he made the floor. He painted the house on Thursday. On Friday he finished the house. Jason likes to build models too.

15. Which sentence should be the *third* sentence of the paragraph?
   A. On Friday he finished the house.
   B. On Monday he got some wood, some nails, and a hammer.
   C. He painted the house on Thursday.
   D. On Tuesday he made the floor.

16. Which sentence does *not* tell about the topic?
   A. On Wednesday he fixed the roof and walls.
   B. Jason likes to build models too.
   C. Last week Jason built a tree house.
   D. On Friday he finished the house.

Go on to the next page.

Use this table of contents from a book to answer questions 17–20.

Use this index from a book to answer questions 21–24.

Table of Contents

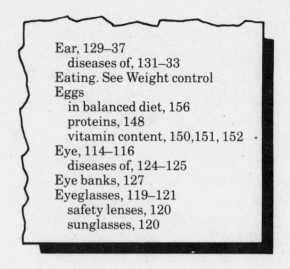

17. Which information is found in the table of contents?
  A. the title of the book
  B. the title of each chapter
  C. what company published the book
  D. who wrote the book

18. What would be the best chapter to read to find out which is the smallest planet?
  A. The Earth   **B.** The Moon
  C. The Planets **D.** The Sun

19. Which chapter begins on page 5?
  A. The Sun
  B. The Stars
  C. The Air or Atmosphere
  D. The Earth

20. On which page does Chapter 3 begin?
  A. 3   **B.** 24
  C. 37   **D.** 25

21. On what page(s) would you find information about diseases of the eye?
  A. 119–120   **B.** 114–116
  C. 131–133   **D.** 124–125

22. On how many pages would you find information about eyeglasses?
  A. 4   **B.** 2
  C. 3   **D.** 1

23. On what page(s) can information about eggs in a balanced diet be found?
  A. 156
  B. 148–156
  C. See Weight control
  D. 6

24. Under what main topic can information about safety lenses be found?
  A. Eye   **B.** Eyeglasses
  C. Eye banks   **D.** Sunglasses

Go on to the next page.

25. You would like some information about farming in New York State. In which volume of the encyclopedia would you look first?

A. S   **B.** Y
C. N   **D.** F

26. You would like to know some facts about the life of President William McKinley. In which volume of the encyclopedia would you look first?

A. M   **B.** L
C. P   **D.** W

27. You would like to learn about the discoverers and explorers of the Mississippi River. In which volume of the encyclopedia would you look first?

A. R   **B.** D
C. E   **D.** M

28. You would like some information about the religious beliefs of the Navajo Indians. In which volume of the encyclopedia would you look first?

A. R   **B.** I
C. N   **D.** B

To answer questions 29–31, read these directions for making a paper snowflake. The missing steps are below.

A. Place the piece of paper on the table.
B. Fold it in half, making a triangle.
C. Then fold your triangle in half.
D. Open the "snowflake" and paste it onto colored paper.

29. Where does the following step belong?

Cut out a design along all three edges.

A. after step D
B. after step C
C. before step A
D. after step B

30. Where does the following step belong?

Hang the snowflake on the bulletin board.

A. after step C
B. after step D
C. after step B
D. after step A

31. Where does the following step belong?

First find a square piece of white paper.

A. after step D
B. before step C
C. after step B
D. before step A

Go on to the next page.

Read these directions for popping
popcorn and answer questions 32–34.

*To make popcorn, you will
need popping corn and oil.
First pour three tablespoons of
oil into a pan. Spread about 3/4
cup of popcorn over the oil.
Then cover the pan with a lid.
Popcorn is good for you. Heat
the popcorn over a medium
flame. Move the pan back and
forth over the burner. Do not lift
the lid while the corn is popping.
Finally
⌄Pour in butter and salt.*

32. Which sentence in these directions
is unnecessary?
   A. Do not lift the lid while the corn is
   popping.
   B. Heat the popcorn over a medium
   flame.
   C. Move the pan back and forth over
   the burner.
   D. Popcorn is good for you.

33. What editing mark should be used to
take out the unnecessary sentence?
   A. ∧
   B. ⍲
   C. ℋ
   D. 𝒩

34. What is the best "time order" word to
put at the beginning of the third sentence?
   A. Fourth
   B. Third
   C. Next
   D. Last

35. An adventure story is about
   A. animals that teach a lesson.
   B. how machines work.
   C. someone who lived a long time
   ago.
   D. people who do exciting things.

Writing Sample   Write a paragraph
giving directions. Tell how to make a kind
of food such as tuna fish sandwiches, hot
oatmeal, or cheeseburgers. Use time
words to show correct order.

Stop!

Midyear Test

1. Which group of words is a sentence?
   A. Hopped like a rabbit.
   B. Rose skated down the sidewalk.
   C. After the thunder and lightning.
   D. Pitcher at the first game of the year.

2. Which sentence is a declarative sentence?
   A. Our house is on fire!
   B. Don knows a card trick.
   C. Be on time, Polly.
   D. Does May have a ponytail?

3. Which sentence is an imperative sentence?
   A. We just saw the astronauts!
   B. Did you hear the fire engine?
   C. Don't play with matches.
   D. Donna Mae has a tree house.

4. What is the best answer to this question?
   What are the smallest birds?
   A. Hummingbirds are the smallest birds.
   B. Hummingbirds.
   C. Hummingbirds are smallest.
   D. Hummingbirds are very beautiful birds.

5. What is the complete subject of this sentence?
   Roger's brother is a lifeguard.
   A. brother is
   B. is a lifeguard
   C. lifeguard
   D. Roger's brother

6. Which word in this sentence is a noun?
   Joy loves to sing and dance.
   A. sing   B. loves
   C. Joy   D. dance

7. Which word is a plural noun?
   A. tooth   B. princess
   C. puppies   D. glass

8. Which word is a plural noun?
   A. ox   B. women
   C. goes   D. class

9. Which word in this sentence is a common noun?
   Susan's brother raced Neil.
   A. raced   B. Susan's
   C. Neil   D. brother

10. Complete this sentence correctly.
    Did ____ give a speech?
    A. Sen. June p. Ross
    B. Sen. June P. Ross
    C. Sen June P Ross
    D. sen. june p. ross

11. Complete this sentence correctly.
    On ____ the flowers are blooming.
    A. Moonbeam Blvd.
    B. Moonbeam blvd.
    C. Moonbeam Blvd
    D. moonbeam blvd

12. Complete this sentence correctly.
    This ____ cow won a prize.
    A. farmers'   B. farmers
    C. farmer's   D. farmeres

Go on to the next page.

13. Which word in this sentence is an action verb?

> The clown juggled three eggs and three oranges.

A. clown   **B.** three
C. eggs   **D.** juggled

14. Which word in this sentence is a helping verb?

> Sherry was rocking the boat.

A. was   **B.** Sherry
C. rocking   **D.** the

15. Which sentence has a verb in the present tense?

A. Cindy and Jan stopped for a soda.
B. The moon shines brightly.
C. We laughed at his joke.
D. Greg will pitch in the game.

16. What is the contraction for *are not*?

A. ar'nt   **B.** are'nt
C. arent   **D.** aren't

17. What is the past tense of the verb *worry*?

A. worreed   **B.** worryed
C. worried   **D.** worreyed

18. Complete this sentence correctly.

> The snow _____ to fall last night.

A. begun   **B.** began
C. begin   **D.** beginned

Read this paragraph and answer questions 19–21.

> Wearers of blue jeans the world over can thank Levi Strauss. Strauss went west during the great gold rush around 1849. But he did not find gold. He saw that miners needed strong work pants that did not wear out easily. He had brought some heavy brown material to make tents. He used the material to make pants instead. Later he changed to blue material.

19. What is the main idea of the paragraph?

A. Levi Strauss developed the first blue jeans.
B. Levi Strauss didn't find gold.
C. Levi Strauss was a tentmaker.
D. Levi Strauss used brown and blue tent material.

20. What is the topic sentence of the paragraph?

A. But he did not find gold.
B. He used the material to make pants instead.
C. He saw that miners needed strong work pants that did not wear out easily.
D. Wearers of blue jeans the world over can thank Levi Strauss.

Go on to the next page.

21. Which sentence would add a detail that also tells about the topic?
   A. Many gold searchers came to California.
   B. Many gold searchers had no success in finding gold.
   C. The blue dye was easier to use than the brown.
   D. Prices of food were high during the gold rush.

Read this paragraph and answer questions 22 and 23.

Pam looked out her window. She saw a pair of robins. Two weeks later the little birds were flying. They were building their nest in the oak tree. Soon Pam saw three blue eggs in the nest. A blue jay flew by one day. Twelve days later she heard the baby birds.

22. Which sentence should be the *last* sentence of the paragraph?
   A. Two weeks later the baby birds were flying.
   B. Pam looked out her window.
   C. Twelve days later she heard the baby birds.
   D. A blue jay flew by one day.

23. Which sentence does *not* tell about the topic?
   A. Soon Pam saw three blue eggs in the nest.
   B. She saw a pair of robins.
   C. They were building their nest in the oak tree.
   D. A blue jay flew by one day.

24. Which sentence is an interrogative sentence?
   A. Take your jacket.
   B. Can your canary talk?
   C. Milly tooted her horn.
   D. Wow, Jeff won the prize!

25. Which sentence is an exclamatory sentence?
   A. Go get the pizza.
   B. What is that noise?
   C. Help, the bathtub is flooding!
   D. Mike fed the ducks.

26. What is the best answer to this question?
      When was the telephone invented?
   A. The telephone was invented in 1876.
   B. In 1876.
   C. Alexander Graham Bell invented it.
   D. Invented in 1876.

27. What is the complete predicate of this sentence?
      Mary and Sally jumped rope all afternoon.
   A. jumped rope all afternoon
   B. Mary and Sally
   C. Sally jumped
   D. rope

28. Which word in this sentence is a proper noun?
      Asia is the largest continent in the world.
   A. Asia   B. continent
   C. largest   D. world

Go on to the next page.

29. Complete this sentence correctly.

Both _____ bikes need repairs.

A. childrens'
B. childrens
C. children's
D. childrenes

30. Which word in this sentence is a linking verb?

I am a princess in the play.

A. play
B. a
C. in
D. am

31. Which of these books would you find in the *nonfiction* section of the library?

A. *Irish Fairy Tales*
B. *Tales of Ghosts, Goblins, and Gremlins*
C. *The Story of the Washington Monument*
D. *Martha Mouse Finds a Home*

Use this card from a library card catalog to answer questions 32–33.

```
j 523        The ancient Maya
As 42h       Burland, Cottie Arthur, 1905-
             The ancient Maya, Drawings by
             Elizabeth Hammond, New York,
             John Day Co.      1967
```

32. The card is called

A. a magazine card
B. an author card
C. a subject card
D. a title card

33. Who is the author of the book listed on the card?

A. John Day
B. Elizabeth Hammond
C. Cottie Arthur Burland
D. The ancient Maya

Read this paragraph and answer questions 34–36.

The walking stick has an unusual way of protecting itself. It looks like a twig. During the day it may sit for hours, just as still as a twig. In fact, walking sticks rarely move at all, except slowly. They do not do much walking. Sitting on a tree branch, a walking stick cannot be seen easily. This helps protect it from other creatures. The walking stick is the strangest insect of all.

34. What is the main idea of the paragraph?

A. The walking stick should have another name.
B. The walking stick's looks and slow speed protect it.
C. A walking stick cannot be seen easily on a tree branch.
D. Walking sticks move slowly.

35. Which fact is *not* stated in the paragraph?

A. Walking sticks look like twigs.
B. Some walking sticks are over fifteen inches long.
C. Walking sticks are not easily seen on tree branches.
D. Walking sticks do not walk much.

Go on to the next page.

36. Which of these ideas from the paragraph is a statement of opinion?
- **A.** Walking sticks cannot be seen easily on a tree branch.
- **B.** Walking sticks rarely move, except slowly.
- **C.** The walking stick is the strangest insect of all.
- **D.** Walking sticks sit still during the day.

Read this paragraph and answer questions 37–39.

      The Taj Mahal in India is one of the world's great wonders. This beautiful building is made of white marble and semiprecious stones. Gardens and pools line its entrance. Shah Jahan, who ruled in the 1600's, had it built in memory of his wife. It took 22 years to complete. Today, the Taj Mahal is a tourist attraction. Everyone dreams of seeing the Taj Mahal by moonlight.

37. What is the main idea of the paragraph?
- **A.** The Taj Mahal is a very special building.
- **B.** The Taj Mahal is a memorial to Shah Jahan's wife.
- **C.** The Taj Mahal was built over many years.
- **D.** Everyone dreams of seeing the Taj Mahal by moonlight.

38. Which fact is *not* stated in the paragraph?
- **A.** White marble and semiprecious stones decorate the Taj Mahal.
- **B.** The Taj Mahal is a tourist attraction in India.
- **C.** The Taj Mahal was built by Shah Jahan, who ruled in the 1600's.
- **D.** Twenty thousand workers built the Taj Mahal.

39. Which of these ideas from the paragraph is a statement of opinion?
- **A.** The Taj Mahal took 22 years to complete.
- **B.** Today the Taj Mahal is a tourist attraction.
- **C.** Everyone dreams of seeing the Taj Mahal by moonlight.
- **D.** Its entrance is lined with gardens and pools.

40. *Harp* would come between which pair of guide words in the dictionary?
- **A.** Hartford–haul
- **B.** hangout–hardy
- **C.** hare–hart
- **D.** haunch–hay fever

Go on to the next page.

Use this dictionary entry to answer questions 41–42.

sear (sir) **1** *v.* To wither; dry up: Sun and drought *seared* the lawn. **2** *adj.* Withered; dried up: used mostly in poems. **3** *v.* To burn the surface of; scorch: The heat *seared* his skin. **4.** *v.* To make hard or insensitive: War had *seared* his feelings.

41. The part you see marked with a circle tells you

   A. what part of speech *sear* is

   B. how to use *sear*

   C. a definition of *sear*

   D. how to pronounce *sear*

42. How many meanings does *sear* have?

   A. 7   **B.** 4

   C. 1   **D.** 2

Look at the symbols in this pronunciation key from the dictionary. Use them to find the correct spellings for the words in questions 43–44.

add, āce, câre, pälm; end, ēqual; it, īce; odd, ōpen, ôr-der; tŏŏk, pōol; up, bûrn; ə = a in *above*, e in *sicken*, i in *possible*, o in *mèlon*, u in *circus*; yōo = u in *fuse*; oil; pout; check; ring; thin; this; zh in *vision*.

43. mus′ əl

   A. muscle   **B.** muzzle

   C. missile   **D.** musical

44. sēl

   A. sole   **B.** sell

   C. seal   **D.** sale

Use this table of contents from a book to answer questions 45 and 46.

CONTENTS

		Page
Chapter **1**	Early Viking Explorers	6
Chapter **2**	Columbus Discovers America	12
Chapter **3**	DeSoto and the Mississippi	18
Chapter **4**	Jamestown: An English Colony	28
Chapter **5**	The French in Canada	30
Chapter **6**	The Pilgrims	36

45. What would be the best chapter to read to find out about the Pilgrims' first Thanksgiving?

   A. Chapter 2   **B.** Chapter 1

   C. Chapter 5   **D.** Chapter 6

46. What is the title of the chapter that begins on page 18?

   A. DeSoto and the Mississippi

   B. The French in Canada

   C. Columbus Discovers America

   D. Jamestown: An English Colony

Go on to the next page.

Use this index from a book to answer questions 47–48.

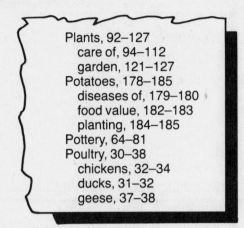

Plants, 92–127
  care of, 94–112
  garden, 121–127
Potatoes, 178–185
  diseases of, 179–180
  food value, 182–183
  planting, 184–185
Pottery, 64–81
Poultry, 30–38
  chickens, 32–34
  ducks, 31–32
  geese, 37–38

47. On what pages might you find information on what to feed ducks?
  A. 37–38   **B.** 31–32
  C. 182–183   **D.** 184–185

48. Under what main topic can information on planting potatoes be found?
  A. Pottery
  B. Plants
  C. Garden
  D. Potatoes

49. You would like some information about the customs of the mountain people of Bolivia. In which volume of the encyclopedia would you look first?
  A. P
  B. M
  C. B
  D. C

50. You would like to learn about training dogs for farm work. In which volume of the encyclopedia would you look first?
  A. T   **B.** D
  C. F   **D.** W

51. What is the correct way to combine these sentences with *but*?
    The water was rough.
    We went boating anyway
  A. The water was rough, but we went boating anyway.
  B. The water was rough, But we went boating anyway.
  C. The water was rough, but, we went boating anyway.
  D. The water was rough and not good for boating.

52. What must be done to correct this sentence?
    Went to the store.
  A. Add a predicate.
  B. Add punctuation at the end.
  C. Capitalize the first letter.
  D. Add a subject.

53. What is the correct way to write this title of a book?
  A. Deep in the Forest
  B. Deep in the forest
  C. Deep In The Forest
  D. deep in The Forest

54. What is the name for this letter part?
    Dear Miguel
  A. signature   **B.** heading
  C. body   **D.** greeting

55. Which editing mark will make this letter part completely correct?
  A. Dear Miguel⊙
  B. Dear Miguel⋀
  C. Dear Miguel⊙
  D. Dear Miguel‗

Go on to the next page.

Read these directions for planting lettuce.
  A. Plant lettuce in early spring or late summer.
  B. Spread seeds thinly in each row.
  C. Cover the seeds with dirt.
  D. Thin out small plants as they grow.

56. Where does this sentence belong?
    Make rows 8 inches apart.
  A. before A   **B.** after A
  C. after C   **D.** after D

57. Which line in this poem contains words that name sounds?
    (1) A polka-dotted clown
    (2) Beats a big bass drum.
    (3) Sha . . . boom! Ta . . . boom!
    (4) The circus has come!
  A. 3   **B.** 2
  C. 1   **D.** 4

58. Which story is most likely a biography?
  A. the story of tennis star Andrea Jaeger, written by her coach
  B. Pearl Bailey's life, written by Pearl Bailey
  C. a race between a rabbit and a turtle, by Aesop
  D. the childhood of Zia, Queen of Mars, by Luna–125

59. In a play the setting is shown on the stage by means of
  A. dialog
  B. characters
  C. stage directions
  D. scenery

60. Which topic would make a good true adventure story?
  A. Duties of the Mayor of Smithtown
  B. Two Teenagers Climb Mt. Everest
  C. Looking at Plants Under the Microscope
  D. Daydreaming About the Future

Writing Sample   Choose one of the writing assignments below. On a separate sheet of paper, complete the assignment you choose.
• Write a paragraph explaining how to set a table for a holiday dinner.
• Write a friendly letter to a make-believe pen pal who lives in another state. Include any information that might be of interest to your pen pal.

Stop!

Name _____

Unit 5: Pretest

1. Which word in this sentence is an adjective?

A dish fell to the floor with a loud crash.

A. loud   **B.** fell
C. crash   **D.** with

2. Complete this sentence correctly.

Linda is one inch _____ than Jane.

A. tall   **B.** taller
C. more tall   **D.** tallest

3. Which word in this sentence is an article?

Tina got a new pair of shoes yesterday.

A. new   **B.** got
C. of   **D.** a

4. Which word in this sentence is an adverb?

When I opened the door, the dog ran outside.

A. the   **B.** opened
C. outside   **D.** ran

5. Which word in this sentence tells *how*?

Maria carefully cleaned the machine yesterday.

A. yesterday   **B.** cleaned
C. machine   **D.** carefully

6. Complete this sentence correctly.

Chris _____ helped Bill with his homework.

A. glad   **B.** happy
C. gladly   **D.** eager

7. Which word in this sentence is an adjective?

The brave soldier happily accepted his medal.

A. brave   **B.** happily
C. medal   **D.** accepted

8. Complete this sentence correctly.

Your bicycle is _____ than mine is.

A. more clean   **B.** cleanest
C. cleaner   **D.** clean

9. Which word in this sentence is an article?

He ran like the wind over that racecourse.

A. ran   **B.** the
C. He   **D.** like

10. Which word in this sentence is an adverb?

Theodore instantly dropped the hot pan.

A. hot   **B.** instantly
C. pan   **D.** dropped

11. Which word in this sentence tells *when*?

Troy usually does his homework slowly.

A. slowly   **B.** usually
C. homework   **D.** his

12. Complete this sentence correctly.

Marge told her story _____.

A. well   **B.** good
C. quick   **D.** beautiful

Go on to the next page.

13. Which word in this sentence is an adjective?

      Roses are my favorite flowers.

    A. flowers   **B.** roses

    C. favorite   **D.** are

14. Complete the sentence correctly.

      This is the _____ problem in the book.

    A. most hard

    B. hardest

    C. most hardest

    D. more hard

15. Which word in this sentence is an article?

      On Sunday the sky was cloudy.

    A. On   **B.** the

    C. cloudy   **D.** Sunday

16. Which word in this sentence is an adverb?

      The crowd cheered wildly when Bea caught the ball.

    A. ball   **B.** cheered

    C. caught   **D.** wildly

17. Which word in this sentence tells *where*?

      The skier glided swiftly down.

    A. down   **B.** slope

    C. swiftly   **D.** glided

18. Complete this sentence correctly.

      My dad is more _____ than my mother.

    A. patiently   **B.** proudly

    C. patient   **D.** carefully

19. Complete this sentence correctly.

      The children sang very _____ .

    A. sweet   **B.** good

    C. nice   **D.** sweetly

Use this section from a dictionary to answer questions 20–21.

> **pool**[1] [pool] *n.* **1** A small body of still water. **2** A deep place in a stream. **3** A puddle: a *pool* of blood. **4** A swimming pool.
> **pool**[2] [pool] **1** *n.* A game whose object is to use a cue to make a ball hit others into the pockets of a special table. **2** *n.* A sum of money put together by a group of people for use in a common venture or as the stakes in a contest or race. **3** *n.* A number of persons or things used or available for use by a particular group: a *pool* of typists. **4** *v.* To combine (money, things, efforts, etc.) for common benefit.

20. Look at these homographs from the dictionary. Which sentence goes with the first entry for *pool*?

    A. They had to *pool* their marbles for the game.

    B. Let's *pool* our money to buy Mom a present.

    C. Sharon likes to play *pool* with her son.

    D. He can swim across the *pool* under water.

21. Which definition of *pool* is meant in this sentence?

      The baby played with the *pool* of milk on her tray.

    A. a puddle

    B. a small body of still water

    C. a deep place in a stream

    D. a number of things used by a particular group

Go on to the next page.

Use this section from a dictionary to answer questions 22–23.

> **bound¹** [bound] **1** *v.* To strike and spring back from a surface; bounce. **2** *v.* To move by a series of leaps. **3** *n.* A bounce, leap, or spring.
> **bound²** [bound] **1** Past tense and past participle of BIND. **2** *adj.* Having a cover or binding: a *bound* book. **3** *adj.* Certain; sure: It's *bound* to rain. **4** *adj. informal* Resolved; determined: I'm *bound* on finishing this.
> **bound³** [bound] *adj.* On the way; headed; going: *bound* for home.
> **bound⁴** [bound] **1** *n. (usually pl.* A boundary, edge, or limit: the *bounds* of space; Keep within the *bounds* of reason. **2** *v.* To form the boundary of; enclose: The jungle *bounds* the village. **3** *v.* To name the boundaries of (a state, country, etc.).

22. Look at these homographs from the dictionary. Which entry for *bound* goes with this sentence?

He was *bound* for the beach when it began to rain.

A. bound¹   **B.** bound⁴
C. bound³   **D.** bound²

23. Which entry for *bound* goes with this sentence?

The soda was *bound* to spill.

A. bound¹   **B.** bound²
C. bound³   **D.** bound⁴

24. Which pair of words are antonyms?
A. doubt, question
B. dull, bright
C. simple, plain
D. first, second

25. Which pair of words are synonyms?
A. down, stairs
B. bitter, sweet
C. search, hunt
D. sale, sail

26. Which pair of words are synonyms?
A. knight, night
B. brave, fearful
C. growing, up
D. honest, truthful

27. Which pair of words are antonyms?
A. pain, comfort
b. stop, finish
C. breaking, apart
D. late, latest

Use the information given below to answer questions 28–31.

> **like**, v., approve, enjoy, esteem, fancy, love, relish.
> *Antonyms*, despise, detest, dislike, hate, loathe, scorn, shun.

28. This kind of information would be found in
A. a dictionary
B. the glossary of a book
C. a thesaurus
D. the index of a book

29. What part of speech is *like*?
A. noun   **B.** verb
C. adjective **D.** adverb

30. What is a synonym for *like*?
A. fancy   **B.** dislike
C. shun   **D.** despise

31. What is an antonym for *like*?
A. approve   **B.** esteem
C. detest   **D.** relish

Go on to the next page.

Name _____

Read this paragraph and answer questions 32–34.

     (1) The best thing about Old Home Day is the wonderful parade. (2) Beautiful floats are decorated with real flowers. (3) Marching bands fill the air with∧music. (4) Horses and riders ride gaily through the town. (5) The parade is colorful. (6) The parade is noisy. (7) The parade is long.

32. What is the most colorful word to add to sentence 3 at the∧?
  A. nice   **B.** band
  C. good   **D.** stirring

33. What is a more colorful verb to use in place of *ride* in sentence 4?
  A. walk   **B.** prance
  C. travel   **D.** go

34. What is the best way for the writer to combine sentences 5 through 7?
  A. The parade is colorful, noisy and long.
  B. The parade is colorful and noisy and long.
  C. The parade is colorful, noisy, and long.
  D. The parade is colorful and noisy, and long.

35. Stories that exaggerate or stretch the truth are called
  A. biographies   **B.** tall tales
  C. fables   **D.** short stories

Writing Sample   Write a descriptive paragraph telling about a place you have visited. Use colorful and exact words.

                           Stop!

Name _____

1. Which word in this sentence is an adjective?

    The championship game will be played on Sunday.

    A. championship B. played
    C. game   D. Sunday

2. Complete this sentence correctly.

    This package is ____ than that one.

    A. most heavy   B. heavier
    C. more heavy   D. heaviest

3. Which word in this sentence is an article?

    Jessica lives on a farm.

    A. on   B. farm
    C. lives   D. a

4. Which word in this sentence is an adverb?

    Jim picked those flowers today.

    A. those   B. picked
    C. today   D. flowers

5. Which word in this sentence tells *how*?

    The horse leaped gracefully over the fence.

    A. leaped   B. fence
    C. over   D. gracefully

6. Complete this sentence correctly.

    How ____ do you know your piano lesson?

    A. good   B. nice
    C. well   D. fast

7. Which word in this sentence is an adjective?

    The magician did an amazing trick.

    A. amazing   B. trick
    C. did   D. magician

8. Complete this sentence correctly.

    Of the six apples, this one is the ____ .

    A. most tastier   B. tasty
    C. tastiest   D. most tastiest

9. Which word in this sentence is an article?

    The school bus was late today.

    A. late   B. The
    C. bus   D. was

10. Which word in this sentence is an adverb?

    We looked up at the hot air balloon.

    A. hot   B. up
    C. looked   D. air

11. Which word in this sentence tells *when*?

    Our Aunt Ellen always happily whistles the same tune.

    A. happily   B. always
    C. whistles D. same

12. Complete this sentence correctly.

    The old man ____ sat down.

    A. slowly   B. tired
    C. sleepy   D. slow

Go on to the next page.

13. Which word in this sentence is an adjective?

Victor carelessly stepped on a rusty nail.

A. stepped   **B.** nail
C. rusty   **D.** carelessly

14. Complete this sentence correctly.

On the ____ day of winter, Sheila forgot her gloves.

A. most coldest **B.** coldest
C. more cold   **D.** more colder

15. Which word in this sentence is an article?

An increase in oil prices is expected.

A. oil   **B.** An
C. in   **D.** expected

16. Which word in this sentence is an adverb?

Joan has finally finished her book report.

A. report   **B.** finished
C. book   **D.** finally

17. Which word in this sentence tells *where*?

"Go inside," Father said sternly.

A. inside   **B.** Go
C. sternly **D.** said

18. Complete this sentence correctly.

Please do a ____ job on this room.

A. somewhere **B.** excellently
C. neat   **D.** neatly

19. Complete this sentence correctly.

I ____ remembered to feed the cat.

A. smart   **B.** quick
C. sudden   **D.** suddenly

Use this section from a dictionary to answer questions 20–21.

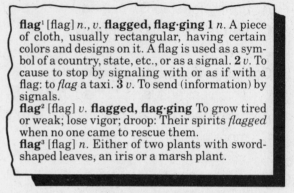

flag[1] [flag] *n., v.* **flagged, flag·ging 1** *n.* A piece of cloth, usually rectangular, having certain colors and designs on it. A flag is used as a symbol of a country, state, etc., or as a signal. **2** *v.* To cause to stop by signaling with or as if with a flag: to *flag* a taxi. **3** *v.* To send (information) by signals.
flag[2] [flag] *v.* **flagged, flag·ging** To grow tired or weak; lose vigor; droop: Their spirits *flagged* when no one came to rescue them.
flag[3] [flag] *n.* Either of two plants with sword-shaped leaves, an iris or a marsh plant.

20. Look at these homographs from the dictionary. Which sentence goes with the second entry for *flag*?

A. The *flag* waved in the breeze.
B. Everyone was quiet as the *flag* was raised.
C. They had to *flag* down a passing car.
D. The plant began to *flag* from lack of water.

21. Which definition of *flag* is meant in this sentence?

The spirited crowd cheered when they saw the *flag*.

A. a piece of cloth, having colors or designs on it
B. to send by signals
C. to grow weak
D. a plant with sword-shaped leaves

Go on to the next page.

Use this section from a dictionary to answer questions 22–23.

> **duck**[1] [duk] *n.* **1** A swimming bird either wild or tame, having short legs, webbed feet, and a broad bill. **2** The female of this bird. The male is called a drake. **3** The flesh of the duck used as food.
> **duck**[2] [duk] **1** *v.* To thrust or plunge under water suddenly and briefly: to *duck* someone in a swimming pool. **2** *v.* To lower the head or stoop down quickly. **3** *v.* The act of ducking. **4** *v.* To dodge, as by lowering the head or bending the body: to *duck* a punch.
> **duck**[3] [duk] *n.* A strong, tightly woven liner or cotton cloth similar to canvas but of a lighter weight: slacks made of *duck*.
> **duck**[4] [duk] *n.* A military truck which can travel on land and on water.

22. Look at these homographs from the dictionary. Which entry for *duck* goes with this sentence?

> They all had to *duck* under the umbrella.

A. duck[4]   **B.** duck[3]
C. duck[2]   **D.** duck[1]

23. Which entry for *duck* goes with this sentence?

> The sailors wore white *duck* uniforms.

A. duck[1]   **B.** duck[3]
C. duck[2]   **D.** duck[4]

24. Which pair of words are synonyms?
  A. come, in
  B. start, begin
  C. dirty, clean
  D. wait, weight

25. Which pair of words are synonyms?
  A. fined, find
  B. half, time
  C. discover, find
  D. open, close

26. Which pair of words are antonyms?
  A. pack, age
  B. our, hour
  C. sad, unhappy
  D. follow, lead

27. Which pair of words are antonyms?
  A. short, tall
  B. flour, flower
  C. strong, powerful
  D. good, better

Use the information given below to answer questions 28–31.

> **new,** adj., fresh, inventive, modern, novel, original, recent, unfamiliar, young. *Antonyms,* decrepit, aged, ancient, gray, elderly, old, time-honored, time-worn.

28. This kind of information would be found in
  A. the index of a book
  B. the glossary of a book
  C. a thesaurus
  D. a dictionary

29. What part of speech is *new*?
  A. noun   **B.** adjective
  C. adverb   **D.** verb

30. What is a synonym for *new*?
  A. novel   **B.** ancient
  C. decrepit   **D.** gray

31. What is an antonym for *new*?
  A. original
  B. modern
  C. time-honored
  D. unfamiliar

Go on to the next page.

Read this paragraph and answer questions 32–34.

(1) The state fair opens soon. (2) Farmers from all over Texas show their livestock. (3) Day and night,∧ crowds mill through the grounds. (4) Game stands of all kinds offer prizes to lucky winners. (5) The Ferris wheel moves through the air. (6) Booths are filled with hot popcorn. (7) Booths are filled with buttery popcorn. (8) Booths are filled with delicious popcorn.

32. What is the most colorful word to add to sentence 3 at the∧ mark?
   A. some   **B.** good
   C. the   **D.** huge

33. What is a more colorful verb to use in place of *moves* in sentence 5?
   A. travels   **B.** spins
   C. rides   **D.** goes

34. What is the best way for the writer to combine sentences 6 through 8?
   A. Booths are filled with hot popcorn, buttery popcorn and delicious popcorn.
   B. Booths are filled with hot popcorn, and buttery popcorn, and delicious popcorn.
   C. Booths are filled with hot, buttery, and delicious popcorn.
   D. Booths are filled with hot popcorn and buttery and delicious popcorn.

35. Which sentence contains a simile?
   A. The flower was large and pretty.
   B. The flower looked like a butterfly.
   C. The flower was orange and black.
   D. A butterfly landed on the flower.

Writing Sample   Write a descriptive paragraph telling about a person you know well. Use colorful and exact words.

Stop!

Name _____

Unit 6: Pretest

1. Which word in this sentence is a pronoun?

      Dotty and I are making a kite.

  A. Dotty   **B.** a

  C. I   **D.** are

2. Which word can take the place of the underlined words in this sentence?

      Tomorrow the girls will visit Grandpa.

  A. her   **B.** me

  C. us   **D.** they

3. Which word can take the place of the underlined word in this sentence?

      Rocky and Lila gave mother that present.

  A. her   **B.** I

  C. he   **D.** we

4. Which word can take the place of the underlined words in this sentence?

      We saw the boy's dog at school.

  A. its   **B.** his

  C. her   **D.** their

5. Complete this sentence correctly.

      Jefferson took his sister and ____ to the show.

  A. I   **B.** we

  C. they   **D.** me

6. Complete this sentence correctly.

      Last night we made dinner ____ .

  A. yourself   **B.** ourself

  C. ourselves   **D.** themselves

7. Which word in this sentence is a pronoun?

      We listened to the speech given by Dr. Roth.

  A. the   **B.** We

  C. speech   **D.** by

8. Which word can take the place of the underlined word in this sentence?

      Rick and Jim left the party early.

  A. he   **B.** him

  C. they   **D.** us

9. Which word can take the place of the underlined words in this sentence?

      Rona gave George and Arthur some cake.

  A. they   **B.** him

  C. we   **D.** them

10. Which word can take the place of the underlined words in this sentence?

      The prize is Ned's and Sam's.

  A. his   **B.** its

  C. theirs   **D.** them

11. Complete this sentence correctly.

      Last week ____ drove from Nevada to Arizona.

  A. I   **B.** us

  C. me   **D.** them

12. Complete this sentence correctly.

      I made this kite all by ____ .

  A. themselves **B.** himself

  C. ourselves   **D.** myself

Go on to the next page.

13. Which word in this sentence is a pronoun?

> The child watched her build a fire.

A. fire   B. her

C. child   D. build

14. Which word can take the place of the underlined word in this sentence?

> Didn't <u>Barbara</u> model in the fashion show?

A. we   B. she

C. her   D. me

15. Which word can take the place of the underlined words in this sentence?

> Bob said, "Let's not let Jill hear <u>you and me.</u>"

A. I   B. we

C. us   D. her

16. Which word can take the place of the underlined word in this sentence?

> Did you find <u>Monica's</u> pen yet?

A. her   B. theirs

C. its   D. our

17. Complete this sentence correctly.

> Both Ben and ____ enjoyed the book.

A. I   B. her

C. him   D. me

18. Complete this sentence correctly.

> Nina, can you do these chores by ____?

A. itself   B. myself

C. yourselves D. yourself

19. Complete this sentence correctly.

> The boys treated ____ to some milk.

A. ourselves

B. himself

C. themselves

D. yourself

20. Which topic is the best choice for a short report?

A. My Dog's Best Trick

B. Sheep Dogs

C. Performing Animals

D. How to Train Your Dog

21. Which topic is the best choice for a short report?

A. Climates of the World

B. What Causes Thunder

C. History of South America

D. How We Forecast Weather

22. Which topic is the best choice for a short report?

A. The Pacific Ocean

B. Spanish Explorers

C. Ponce de Leon's Exploration of Florida

D. The Life of Christopher Columbus

23. Which topic is the best choice for a short report?

A. Why I Like to Play Basketball

B. Winter Sports

C. Outdoor Games for Children

D. The History of Baseball and Softball

Go on to the next page.

Name _____

24. You are taking notes for a report on the building of the Great Pyramid of Egypt. Which idea should *not* go into your report?
- **A.** It was built about 2500 B.C.
- **B.** Pharaoh Khufu planned the Great Pyramid.
- **C.** Several million tons of stone were used.
- **D.** Many people visited the Great Pyramid last year.

25. You are taking notes for a report on farming in Iowa. Which fact should go into your report?
- **A.** There are eight state parks and ten state forests in Iowa.
- **B.** The capital city of Iowa is Des Moines.
- **C.** Corn, hay, soybeans, wheat, and potatoes are grown in Iowa.
- **D.** The state flower of Iowa is the wild rose.

26. You are taking notes for a report on how glass is made. Which fact should go into your report?
- **A.** Almost all ancient glass is colored.
- **B.** All glass is made with sand.
- **C.** There are many uses of glass.
- **D.** Cloth made from glass is fireproof.

27. You are taking notes for a report on the music of Frederick Chopin. Which fact should *not* go into your report?
- **A.** He used folk dance themes in his music.
- **B.** His father was a school teacher.
- **C.** His works include concertos, preludes, and mazurkas.
- **D.** He wrote music especially for the piano.

Use this outline to answer questions 28–31.

Living in a Big City

I. Good things about city life
- A. Many different people to meet
- B. Many museums and libraries to visit
- C. _____

II. Bad things about city life
- A. Problems of noise and dirt
- B. People are too crowded
- C. Things cost more money
- D. _____

28. What is the title of the outline?
- **A.** Bad Things About City Life
- **B.** Good Things About City Life
- **C.** Living in a Big City
- **D.** Good and Bad Things About City Life

29. Which is a subtopic?
- **A.** People are too crowded
- **B.** Living in a big city
- **C.** Good things about city life
- **D.** Bad things about city life

30. Which would best fit in the blank next to I.C.?
- **A.** A car is needed
- **B.** Air is dirty
- **C.** Food costs more
- **D.** Many interesting jobs

31. Which would best fit in the blank next to II.D.?
- **A.** Many places to shop
- **B.** Good hospitals and medical care
- **C.** Streets can be dangerous
- **D.** Beautiful scenery

Go on to the next page.

Name _____

Read this part of a research report to answer questions 32–34.

Seeds travel in many different ways. The wind takes seeds near and far. The seeds of ~~(mapel)~~ maple *trees have wings. Each seed of the maple tree* ~~and orchid~~ *has silky hairs that catch the wind like parachutes. The seeds of orchids are as fine as dust they travel thousands of miles. ¶Animals carry seeds from place to place, too. Wading birds...*

32. Why are the words ~~*and orchid*~~ marked this way?

  A. A new paragraph should start here.
  B. They are not the correct words for this sentence.
  C. They are spelled incorrectly.
  D. They should be capitalized.

33. Look at the underlined words in the report. What editing mark(s) must the writer use in this place?

  A. dust₀ they
  B. dust∧ they
  C. dust∧ ⱦhey
  D. dustℕ they

34. What does the editing mark ¶ in the report tell the writer to do?

  A. Add a topic sentence.
  B. Take something out.
  C. Start a new paragraph.
  D. Change the sentence order.

35. Factual information for reports is most likely to be found in

  A. magazine articles
  B. short stories
  C. tall tales
  D. plays

Writing Sample   Look up information about an animal that interests you. Write a two-paragraph report.

Stop!

Unit 6: Posttest

1. Which word in this sentence is a pronoun?

　　Please return the tools to me soon.
- **A.** to
- **B.** Please
- **C.** me
- **D.** return

2. Which word can take the place of the underlined words in this sentence?

　　Nancy and Dan gave an interesting report.
- **A.** them
- **B.** he
- **C.** we
- **D.** they

3. Which word can take the place of the underlined words in this sentence?

　　Grandmother gave Ann and me tropical fish.
- **A.** us
- **B.** we
- **C.** her
- **D.** them

4. Which word can take the place of the underlined words in this sentence?

　　We'll meet at Mr. and Mrs. Gold's house.
- **A.** his
- **B.** their
- **C.** our
- **D.** them

5. Complete this sentence correctly.

　　Sally and ____ brought doughnuts to the party.
- **A.** them
- **B.** me
- **C.** her
- **D.** I

6. Complete this sentence correctly.

　　Can the little girl feed ____ yet?
- **A.** myself
- **B.** himself
- **C.** herself
- **D.** ourselves

7. Which word in this sentence is a pronoun?

　　They raced across the field.
- **A.** across
- **B.** They
- **C.** field
- **D.** raced

8. Which word can take the place of the underlined word in this sentence?

　　Last night Mike showed me his coin collection.
- **A.** he
- **B.** we
- **C.** him
- **D.** they

9. Which word can take the place of the underlined word in this sentence?

　　The librarian helped James locate a book.
- **A.** his
- **B.** he
- **C.** she
- **D.** him

10. Which word can take the place of the underlined word in this sentence?

　　Dad said, "Put the hammer in Dad's toolbox."
- **A.** our
- **B.** his
- **C.** my
- **D.** mine

11. Complete this sentence correctly.

　　Teresa gave ____ a gift.
- **A.** me
- **B.** she
- **C.** we
- **D.** I

12. Complete this sentence correctly.

　　Earl and Randy put up the tent ____.
- **A.** ourselves
- **B.** himself
- **C.** yourselves
- **D.** themselves

Go on to the next page.

13. Which word in this sentence is a pronoun?

 After the rain stopped, we played outside.

 A. rain **B.** we
 C. After **D.** stopped

14. Which word can take the place of the underlined word in this sentence?

 Angela is friendly and funny.

 A. Her **B.** She
 C. Me **D.** You

15. Which word can take the place of the underlined words in this sentence?

 We watched the girls play basketball.

 A. her **B.** him
 C. them **D.** they

16. Which word can take the place of the underlined words in this sentence?

 My sister's hair is very long.

 A. Her **B.** She
 C. Their **D.** His

17. Complete this sentence correctly.

 After dinner ___ often watch TV.

 A. I **B.** us
 C. me **D.** her

18. Complete this sentence correctly.

 He is teaching ___ to roller skate.

 A. herself **B.** ourselves
 C. myself **D.** himself

19. Complete this sentence correctly.

 Did you build this canoe by ___ ?

 A. herself **B.** himself
 C. yourself **D.** itself

20. Which topic is the best choice for a short report?

 A. How to Start a Shell Collection
 B. Plant Life in the Ocean
 C. Life on the Ocean Floor
 D. A Study of the Pacific Ocean

21. Which topic is the best choice for a short report?

 A. American Artists
 B. Picasso's First Painting
 C. The Metropolitan Museum of Art
 D. The Paintings of Georgia O'Keeffe

22. Which topic is the best choice for a short report?

 A. The Peoples of Africa
 B. The History of Egypt
 C. The Dunes of the Sahara Desert
 D. Education in Africa

23. Which topic is the best choice for a short report?

 A. Raising Sheep
 B. Foods of the World
 C. How to Raise Farm Animals
 D. Farming in the United States

24. You are taking notes for a report on how cheese is made. Which of these facts should go into your report?

 A. It is sold in supermarkets.
 B. It is a very healthful food.
 C. Cream cheese is one of the most popular kinds of cheese.
 D. It can be made from either curds or whey.

Go on to the next page.

58 UNIT 6: Posttest

25. You are taking notes for a report on the history of ballet dancing. Which of these ideas should go into your report?

    A. Dancers practice every day.

    B. Most dancers begin dancing as children.

    C. The eighteenth-century center of ballet was Russia.

    D. Two ballet companies are coming to our town.

26. You are writing a report on the childhood of John F. Kennedy. Which of these notes should *not* go into your report?

    A. He was born in Brookline, Massachusetts.

    B. He was the youngest man to be elected President.

    C. He was the second child of Joseph and Rose Kennedy.

    D. He studied at private schools in Brookline and New York City.

27. You are writing a report on the proper food for cats. Which of these notes should *not* go into your report?

    A. Some cats eat vegetables and certain fruit.

    B. Cats see well in the dark and like to prowl at night.

    C. Chicken is better for cats than tuna.

    D. Cats may eat more than they need.

Use this outline to answer questions 28–31.

Diamonds Around You

  I. Kinds of diamonds

    A. Gemstone diamonds

    B. _____

  II. Uses for diamonds

    A. Phonograph needles

    B. Cutting tools

    C. _____

28. What is the title of the outline?

    A. Uses for Diamonds

    B. Kinds of Diamonds

    C. Diamonds Around You

    D. Kinds and Uses of Diamonds

29. Which is a subtopic?

    A. Gemstone diamonds

    B. Uses for diamonds

    C. Kinds of diamonds

    D. Diamonds around you

30. Which would best fit in the blank next to I.B.?

    A. Earliest diamonds came from India

    B. Diamond mines

    C. Diamonds are hard and smooth

    D. Industrial diamonds

31. Which would best fit in the blank next to II.C.?

    A. Heat does not melt diamonds

    B. Famous diamonds

    C. Jewelry

    D. How a diamond is formed

Go on to the next page.

Name _____

Read this part of a research report to answer questions 32–34.

The Mayan Indians lived in Mexico 2,000 years ago. They were the first people who smoked. Many other American Indian tribes used tobacco in their ceremonies. European explorers ~~and people~~ *learned about tobacco from the Indians they took to it quickly. Doctors in europe believed it was a magic cure. They encouraged people to smoke. By 1800 these ideas were proved false. Scientists began to study the effects of smoking. They soon learned the damage smoking can cause to the smoker's heart and lungs...*

32. Why are the words ~~and people~~ marked this way?
   A. A new paragraph should start here.
   B. They should be capitalized.
   C. They are spelled incorrectly.
   D. They should be taken out of this sentence.

33. Look at the underlined words in the report. What editing mark(s) must the writer use in this place?
   A. Indians‸they
   B. Indians⊙ they
   C. Indians⋌they
   D. Indiansₙthey

34. What does the editing mark ¶ in the report tell the writer to do?
   A. Add a topic sentence.
   B. Take something out.
   C. Start a new paragraph.
   D. Change the sentence order.

35. Magazine articles are a good source for reports because they often contain
   A. factual information
   B. authors' names
   C. interesting titles
   D. jokes and riddles

Writing Sample   Look up information about a president, author, or sports star who interests you. Write a two-paragraph report.

Stop!

Unit 7: Pretest

1. What is the simple subject of this sentence?

   Dinosaurs roamed the earth long ago.

   A. roamed   **B.** Dinosaurs
   C. earth   **D.** long

2. What is the simple predicate of this sentence?

   Our plants are growing beautifully.

   A. are   **B.** Our plants
   C. are growing   **D.** are growing beautifully

3. Complete this sentence correctly.

   That man ____ too fast.

   A. drives   **B.** run
   C. ride   **D.** talk

4. What is the best answer to this question?

   Did he see that movie?

   A. Yes, he saw that movie.
   B. Yes, he saw it.
   C. Yes.
   D. Yes, that movie.

5. Complete this sentence correctly.

   My sister and I ____ together.

   A. plays   **B.** study
   C. skates   **D.** works

6. What is the simple subject of this sentence?

   After dinner we usually take a walk.

   A. usually   **B.** dinner
   C. walk   **D.** we

7. What is the simple predicate of this sentence?

   Tomorrow they will visit a museum.

   A. will   **B.** will visit
   C. they will   **D.** visit a museum

8. Complete this sentence correctly.

   Most young animals ____ quickly.

   A. runs   **B.** eats
   C. learn   **D.** grows

9. What is the best answer to this question?

   Is your mother sick?

   A. Yes, she is sick.
   B. Yes my mother is.
   C. Yes she is.
   D. Yes.

10. What is the simple subject of this sentence?

    Tina wants a drink also.

    A. drink   **B.** wants
    C. Tina   **D.** also

11. What is the simple predicate of this sentence?

    Alice likes mystery stories.

    A. mystery stories
    B. likes mystery
    C. Alice
    D. likes

12. Complete this sentence correctly.

    Our rooster always ____ at sunrise.

    A. eat   **B.** crow
    C. awakes   **D.** sleep

Go on to the next page.

13. What is the best answer to this question?

       Did Lara eat eggs?

  A. No, no eggs.

  B. No she didn't eat an egg.

  C. No she didn't.

  D. No, she didn't eat eggs.

14. Which word has a *prefix*?

  A. uniform   **B.** movable

  C. uncover   **D.** painless

15. Which word correctly completes this sentence?

       Do you have _____ bicycles?

  A. to   **B.** their

  C. they're   **D.** too

16. Which word is a compound word?

  A. morning   **B.** drugstore

  C. surprise   **D.** frighten

17. Which word has a *suffix*?

  A. power   **B.** remove

  C. teacher   **D.** reason

18. Which word correctly completes this sentence?

       My dog ate _____ flowers.

  A. two   **B.** too

  C. there   **D.** they're

19. Which word is a compound word?

  A. telephone   **B.** garden

  C. parade   **D.** lighthouse

20. To which word can you add *im* to form a new word?

  A. old   **B.** sure

  C. possible   **D.** please

21. Which word correctly completes this sentence?

       She likes _____ play.

  A. there   **B.** too

  C. to   **D.** they're

22. Which word is a compound word?

  A. blanket   **B.** workmen

  C. captain   **D.** closely

23. To which word can you add *ness* to form a new word?

  A. song   **B.** eat

  C. fun   **D.** dark

24. Which word correctly completes this sentence?

       They wanted to go _____ .

  A. their   **B.** there

  C. to   **D.** two

25. Which word is a compound word?

  A. snowstorm   **B.** reward

  C. courage   **D.** invent

Go on to the next page.

26. What is the best way to combine the subjects of these sentences.?

   Mia's shoes are lost.
   Mia's socks are lost.

   A. Mia's shoes are and Mia's socks are lost.
   B. Mia's shoes are lost and Mia's socks are lost.
   C. Mia's shoes and socks are lost.
   D. Mia's shoes are lost and her socks too.

27. Which sentence has a detail that tells *why*?

   A. The picnic at Lake Wing was called off.
   B. Yesterday the picnic was called off.
   C. The picnic was called off by the principal.
   D. The picnic was called off because of rain.

28. What is the best way to combine the predicates of these sentences?

   The baby laughed.
   The baby cried.

   A. The baby laughed and cried.
   B. The baby laughed and the baby cried.
   C. The baby laughed. Cried too.
   D. The baby and the baby laughed and cried.

29. Which sentence has a detail that tells *when*?

   A. The television set broke in the store.
   B. This week the television set broke.
   C. Because of the storm, the television set broke.
   D. The television set broke in three pieces.

30. What is the best way to combine the predicates of these sentences?

   Mike washed his hair.
   Mike combed his hair.

   A. Mike washed his hair. He combed it also.
   B. Mike washed his hair and Mike combed his hair.
   C. Mike and Mike washed and combed their hair.
   D. Mike washed and combed his hair.

31. Which sentence has a detail that tells *where*?

   A. We saw Mrs.Roth and Mrs. Lyons.
   B. Three days ago we saw Mrs. Roth.
   C. We saw Mrs. Roth at the library.
   D. This morning we saw Mrs. Roth.

Read this paragraph and answer questions 32–34.

> ∧Claudia and Chip decided to have a puppet show. They made puppets. They built a stage∧. Claudia wrote the script. Chip thought up sound effects. (By Friday) the show was ready.

32. Which words can the writer add to the first sentence at the ∧ to tell *when*?

   A. For some friends
   B. To do something different
   C. At school
   D. On Monday

Go on to the next page.

33. Which word(s) can the writer add to the third sentence at the ∧ to tell *where*?
    A. with Dad's help
    B. from wood
    C. in the garage
    D. quickly

34. What will the last sentence be when the editing changes are made?
    A. By Friday The show was ready.
    B. The show by Friday was ready.
    C. The show was ready By Friday.
    D. The show was ready by Friday.

35. In a fable the characters are usually
    A. children
    B. animals
    C. witches
    D. tiny people

Writing Sample   Write five sentences about a favorite place. Add words to the beginning or end of each sentence to tell *how*, *when*, *where*, or *why*.

Stop!

Unit 7: Posttest

Name _____

1. What is the simple subject of this sentence?

Two little mice peeked out of the hole.

A. peeked   **B.** little

C. mice   **D.** Two

2. What is the simple predicate of this sentence?

Tillie is spending the night here.

A. spending the night here.

B. is

C. is spending

D. here

3. Complete this sentence correctly.

Every Monday Roy ____ dinner for the family.

A. makes   **B.** fix

C. cook   **D.** prepare

4. What is the best answer to this question?

Did she read that book?

A. Yes, she read it.

B. Yes she did.

C. Yes.

D. Yes, that book.

5. Complete this sentence correctly.

The hot fire ____ up the room.

A. light   **B.** heats

C. warm   **D.** smoke

6. What is the simple subject of this sentence?

After lunch the baby took a nap.

A. took   **B.** nap

C. lunch   **D.** baby

7. What is the simple predicate of this sentence?

The cars have stopped at the corner.

A. stopped   **B.** have stopped

C. at the corner   **D.** cars have

8. Complete this sentence correctly.

Both Mr. and Mrs. Miranda ____ horses.

A. has   **B.** trains

C. ride   **D.** likes

9. What is the best answer to this question?

Is your father home?

A. Yes, he is home.

B. Yes my father is.

C. Yes he is.

D. Yes.

10. What is the simple subject of this sentence?

Our cabin is far out in the woods.

A. woods   **B.** Our

C. cabin   **D.** is

Go on to the next page.

11. What is the simple predicate of this sentence?

   A fishing boat nearly hit the reef.

   A. nearly hit
   B. hit the reef
   C. boat hit
   D. hit

12. Complete this sentence correctly.

   She ____ her violin every day.

   A. practice   B. take
   C. tunes   D. play

13. What is the best answer to this question?

   Did Sam see a fish?

   A. No, he didn't.
   B. No he never saw a fish at all.
   C. No, no fish.
   D. No, he didn't see a fish.

14. Which word has a *prefix*?

   A. only   B. believable
   C. unhurt   D. real

15. Which word correctly completes the sentence?

   Can I go ____ ?

   A. they're   B. too
   C. to   D. their

16. Which word is a compound word?

   A. movement   B. steamship
   C. pleasant   D. reason

17. Which word has a *suffix*?

   A. under   B. improve
   C. sailor   D. remark

18. Which word correctly completes this sentence?

   I hope ____ much better.

   A. they're   B. to
   C. there   D. too

19. Which word is a compound word?

   A. country   B. neighbor
   C. awful   D. bookmark

20. To which word can you add *re* to form a new word?

   A. cat   B. clue
   C. place   D. fool

21. Which word correctly completes this sentence?

   They need ____ rest.

   A. two   B. there
   C. to   D. they're

22. Which word is a compound word?

   A. kingdom   B. bedroom
   C. contest   D. farming

23. To which word can you add *ness* to form a new word?

   A. glow   B. note
   C. choke   D. good

24. Which word correctly completes this sentence?

   They want ____ hammer.

   A. two   B. their
   C. there   D. too

25. Which word is a compound word?

   A. barnyard   B. family
   C. person   D. mountain

Go on to the next page.

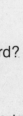

Name _____

26. What is the best way to combine the subjects of these sentences?

      Tomatoes are easy to grow.
      Beans are easy to grow.

  A. Tomatoes are easy and beans are easy to grow.
  B. Tomatoes are easy to grow and beans are easy to grow.
  C. Tomatoes and beans are easy to grow.
  D. Tomatoes are easy to grow and beans too.

27. Which sentence has a detail that tells *when*?

  A. Jack practices the piano for his recital.
  B. Jack practices the piano at school.
  C. Quickly Jack practices the piano.
  D. After supper Jack practices the piano.

28. What is the best way to combine the subjects of these sentences?

      The puzzles are on the shelf.
      The books are on the shelf.

  A. The puzzles and the books are on the shelf.
  B. The puzzles and the books, are on the shelf.
  C. The puzzles are on the shelf and the books are on the shelf.
  D. The puzzles are and the books are on the shelf.

29. Which sentence has a detail that tells *where*?

  A. Last night Patsy found her bike.
  B. Patsy found her bike in the garage.
  C. Right away Patsy found her bike.
  D. Patsy never found her bike.

30. What is the best way to combine the predicates of these sentences?

      Luis floated in the pool.
      Luis swam in the pool.

  A. Luis floated in the pool and Luis swam in the pool.
  B. Luis floated and Luis swam in the pool.
  C. Luis floated, and, swam in the pool.
  D. Luis floated and swam in the pool.

31. Which sentence has a detail that tells *how*?

  A. All morning the puppies slept.
  B. The puppies slept in a box.
  C. The puppies slept peacefully.
  D. The puppies slept because they were tired.

Read this paragraph and answer questions 32–34.

    Lisa likes to paint pictures of flowers. She works in the park. She is painting the daffodils. She will paint tulips next week.

32. Which word(s) can the writer add to the second sentence at the ∧ to tell *when*?

  A. happily
  B. because it is close by
  C. across the street
  D. in the afternoon

Go on to the next page.

33. Which word(s) can the writer add to the third sentence at the∧to tell *how*?
  A. next to the fence
  B. today
  C. with watercolors
  D. around the fountain

34. What will the last sentence be when the editing changes are made?
  A. She will paint tulips Next week.
  B. Next week tulips she will paint.
  C. Next week She will paint tulips.
  D. Next week she will paint tulips.

35. A very short story that teaches a lesson is called a
  A. riddle   **B.** fable
  C. tall tale   **D.** dialog

Writing Sample   Write five sentences about a favorite sport. Add words at the beginning or end of each sentence to tell *how*, *when*, *where*, or *why*.

Stop!

Unit 8: Pretest

1. Tim will introduce his friend Mary to his father. What is the best introduction?
   A. Dad, meet Mary.
   B. Dad, this is Mary. She just moved here from Florida.
   C. Mary, I'd like you to meet my father.
   D. Mary, this is my father.

2. What important detail is missing from this telephone message?

   > To: Bill   From: Yvonne
   > Laura called. Please call her back.

   A. who wrote the message
   B. the name of the caller
   C. whom the message is for
   D. when the call was made

3. What important detail is missing from this emergency message?

   > Hello? This is Rona Glenning. This is an emergency. There's a car on fire here. Please come quickly!

   A. what the emergency is
   B. the name of the caller
   C. the location of the emergency
   D. that there is an emergency

4. Officer Grumbach has come to talk to your school about safety. Which of these would *not* be a good question to ask her?
   A. In which direction should you ride a bike on the street?
   B. What should fourth graders study?
   C. Where can you get a bike license?
   D. What kind of accidents happen most in our town?

5. Lena Files is filling out a form at school. What should she write on the line that says AGE?
   A. 9 years
   B. 53 pounds
   C. May 10, 1976
   D. fourth grade

6. Which of these statements is a fact?
   A. "Skydivers" is the best show on Tuesday nights.
   B. "Skydivers" is a show your whole family will enjoy.
   C. You'll love the action in "Skydivers."
   D. Todd Fetter plays Captain Abe on "Skydivers."

7. Leslie will introduce her friends to her parents. What is the best introduction?
   A. Scott and Tina, meet my Mom and Dad.
   B. Scott and Tina, meet my parents.
   C. Mom and Dad, meet Scott and Tina. They're on my ski team.
   D. Mom and Dad, meet my friends.

8. What important detail is missing from this telephone message?

   > Tuesday, 4:00 P.M.
   > To: Mr. Butteri
   > Your dentist called to remind you to come to his office at 6:15 P.M.

   A. who wrote the message
   B. whom the message is for
   C. when the call was made
   D. what the message is

Go on to the next page.

Name _____

9. What important detail is missing from this emergency message?

> This is an emergency. A boy has fallen through the ice at Eddy Pond on Maple Street. Please come quickly.

A. that the situation needs immediate attention
B. what the problem is
C. the location of the emergency
D. the name of the caller

10. Mr. Lopez is speaking at the state fair about raising goats. Which of these would *not* be a good question to ask him?

A. What kind of shelter does a goat need?
B. Is raising cows expensive?
C. Are goats friendly animals?
D. Is goat's milk as nutritious as cow's milk?

11. George Sanchez is filling out a form to join the Boy Scouts. What should he write on the line that says CITY AND STATE?

A. 1726 Juneway Terrace
B. Evanston, Illinois
C. (312) 794-2031
D. March 9, 1971

12. Which of these statements is a fact?

A. Fairmont Auto Sales is a friendly place to do business.
B. Smart shoppers go to Fairmont Auto Sales.
C. You can buy used cars at Fairmont Auto Sales.
D. The best car buys are at Fairmont Auto Sales.

13. Nicole will introduce her friend to her aunt. What is the best introduction?

A. Aunt Loretta, meet Carlos. He is in my class.
B. Carlos, my aunt is a teacher.
C. Carlos, this is my Aunt Loretta.
D. Aunt Loretta, meet Carlos.

14. What important detail is missing from this telephone message?

> Anita called at noon on Monday. Please call her back as soon as possible. Love, Holly.

A. whom the message is for
B. the name of the caller
C. when the call was made
D. who wrote the message

15. What important detail is missing from this emergency message?

> This is Steve Dunn. This is an emergency. We need help at 6 Mountaindale Road. Please send a doctor at once.

A. the location of the emergency
B. the name of the caller
C. that there is an emergency
D. what the emergency is

16. Miss Samet is visiting your class to talk about good eating habits. Which of these would *not* be a good question to ask her?

A. Is eating too much of the same food unhealthy?
B. Why do some people bite their nails?
C. Why are some foods considered "junk" foods?
D. Which is the most important meal of the day?

Go on to the next page.

17. Elaine Toppel is filling out a form at the library. What should she write on the line that says NAME OF TEACHER?

A. Fourth Grade   B. Elaine Toppel
C. Mrs. Albertson   D. Toppel, Elaine

18. Which of these statements is an opinion?

A. Sunny Orange Drink is delicious.
B. There is no sugar in Sunny Orange Drink.
C. You can buy Sunny Orange Drink at most supermarkets.
D. Sunny Orange Drink comes in bottles or cans.

Use this part of a telephone directory page to answer questions 19–22

```
Nickol Mary 5 Pine Cone Drive .......... 772-8913
Nickol Paul 132 Main Street ............ 233-6542
Nickol Sam 136 Main Street ............. 233-7820
Nickola Sam 43-A Jefferson St ......... 754-1348
Nickola Thos 2 Pinewood Ave .......... 579-6431
Nickols Exercise Spa
  1361 Central Blvd ................. 527-6543
Nick's Auto Parts
  52 McLean Ave ................... 296-6051
Nick's Auto Repair Shop
  1225 Wilson Ave .................. 628-3131
Nick's Fishing Sta & Marina
  North Point Place ................ 555-1301
Nickson M A 23 Farragut Rd ........... 635-1121
Nickson Mary 4 Elmyra Lane .......... 628-8901
Nickson Samuel 2 Sone Rd ........... 235-4985
```

19. What is Mary Nickson's telephone number?

A. 628-8901   B. 235-4985
C. 635-1121   D. 772-8913

20. What is the address of Nick's Auto Repair Shop?

A. 52 McLean Ave.
B. 1361 Central Blvd.
C. North Point Place
D. 1225 Wilson Ave.

21. How many listings are there for the name Nickola?

A. 5   B. 4
C. 2   D. 3

22. What is Sam Nickol's telephone number?

A. 233-6542   B. 233-7820
C. 754-1348   D. 235-4985

Use this map and legend to answer questions 23–26.

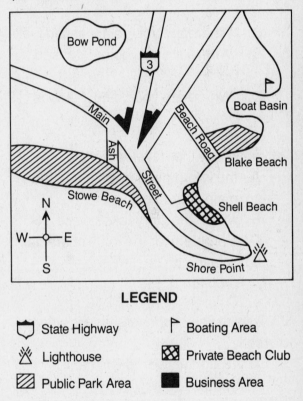

LEGEND

⬡ State Highway   ⚑ Boating Area
☼ Lighthouse   ▨ Private Beach Club
▨ Public Park Area   ■ Business Area

23. Where is the lighthouse located?

A. at the boat basin
B. at Shore Point
C. near Bow Pond
D. on Beach Road

24. How many public parks are shown?

A. 3   B. 1
C. 2   D. 4

Go on to the next page.

Name _____

25. You are at Bow Pond. In which direction should you travel to reach Stowe Beach?
    A. South   **B.** North
    C. East   **D.** West

26. What is the symbol for boating area?
    A. ☖   **B.** ⚑
    C. ■   **D.** ⛉

27. Which line of conversation is written correctly?
    A. "Where are you going?," asked Delia.
    B. "Where are you going, asked Delia?"
    C. "Where are you going?" asked Delia.
    D. "Where are you going"? Asked Delia.

28. In a story the *development* is
    A. the information given about the main characters
    B. where the story takes place
    C. a problem for the main characters
    D. how the characters solve a problem

29. Which line of conversation is written correctly?
    A. "Barry answered you can fix it yourself."
    B. Barry answered, "You can fix it yourself."
    C. Barry answered "You can fix it yourself."
    D. Barry answered, "you can fix it yourself".

30. In a story the *conclusion* comes at the
    A. middle   **B.** beginning or end
    C. beginning   **D.** end

31. Which line of conversation is written correctly?
    A. "I'm not staying" Chris replied.
    B. "I'm not staying," Chris replied.
    C. "I'm not staying, Chris replied."
    D. "I'm not staying", Chris replied.

32. The *setting* of a story is
    A. where the story takes place
    B. the problems the characters have
    C. the main characters
    D. the person telling the story

33. Which line of conversation is written correctly?
    A. Kip said "Let's try it."
    B. Kip said, "let's try it."
    C. Kip said, "Let's try it."
    D. Kip said, "Let's try it".

34. The *introduction* of a story comes at the
    A. middle   **B.** end
    C. middle or end   **D.** beginning

35. Which of the following is an example of *fiction*?
    A. a story about a visit to an imaginary planet
    B. the biography of a famous sports star
    C. the true story of the deepest underwater dive
    D. an article about smog in Los Angeles

Writing Sample Write a story about an imaginary creature. Use conversation in your story. Write a good beginning, middle, and end.

Stop!

Unit 8: Posttest

1. Donna will introduce her cousin to her teacher. What is the best introduction?
   - **A.** Ramon, meet my teacher, Mr. Arcario.
   - **B.** Mr. Arcario, meet my cousin, Ramon. He is in second grade.
   - **C.** Mr. Arcario, meet my cousin.
   - **D.** Ramon, this is my teacher.

2. What important detail is missing from this telephone message?

   > Monday, 2:10 P.M.
   > To: Mr. Ortiz
   > Dr. Pollack called. Please call him back.

   - **A.** the name of the caller
   - **B.** the time and day the message was taken
   - **C.** whom the call is for
   - **D.** who wrote the message

3. What important detail is missing from this emergency message?

   > Hello? My name is Harvey Falk. I'd like to report an emergency. We need help at once at the town pool on May Road.

   - **A.** the name of the caller
   - **B.** the location of the emergency
   - **C.** what the emergency is
   - **D.** that there is an emergency

4. Dr. Sessler, who is a dentist, has come to talk to your class. Which would *not* be a good question to ask him?
   - **A.** How often should a person visit the dentist?
   - **B.** How much sleep does a ten-year-old need?
   - **C.** Can chewing sugarless gum harm my teeth?
   - **D.** How many times a day should I brush my teeth?

5. Herb Newkirk is filling out a form to join a baseball team. What should he write on the line that says GRADE?
   - **A.** Fourth
   - **B.** 10 years
   - **C.** January 28, 1971
   - **D.** Hillside School

6. Which of these statements is a fact?
   - **A.** Skating at Roller World is more fun.
   - **B.** Everyone will love skating at Roller World.
   - **C.** You'll see the best skaters at Roller World.
   - **D.** Roller World, the new place to skate, has opened.

7. Julie will introduce her friend to her aunt. What is the best introduction?
   - **A.** Aunt Clara, this is Lisa.
   - **B.** Lisa, I'd like you to meet my Aunt Clara.
   - **C.** Aunt Clara, meet Lisa. She plays the piano too.
   - **D.** Lisa, meet Aunt Clara.

Go on to the next page.

8. What important detail is missing from this telephone message?

> To: Josie   From: Mom
> Mrs. Lake called. The books you wanted are in the library.

- **A.** when the call was made
- **B.** the name of the caller
- **C.** who wrote the message
- **D.** whom the message is for

9. What important detail is missing from this emergency message?

> This is Charlotte Murphy. There is an emergency situation here. I see smoke coming from a second-floor window across the street. Come quickly.

- **A.** what the emergency is
- **B.** the name of the caller
- **C.** that the situation is an emergency
- **D.** the location of the emergency

10. The mayor is speaking at a town meeting. Which of these would *not* be a good question to ask the mayor?

- **A.** Do you think our town needs more police officers?
- **B.** Who would you consider is the best singer today?
- **C.** Are you going to run for mayor again next year?
- **D.** What is being done to clean up the town park?

11. Kelly Ruthers is filling out a form at school. What should she write on the line that says NAME OF TEACHER?

- **A.** 17B Canal Street
- **B.** Mr. M. Johnston
- **C.** Ruthers, Kelly
- **D.** Naponoch School

12. Which of these statements is a fact?

- **A.** People really enjoy Grapeade.
- **B.** Grapeade is the drink for everyone.
- **C.** Grapeade is a new fruit drink.
- **D.** You'll love the juicy flavor of Grapeade.

13. James will introduce his friend to his father. What is the best introduction?

- **A.** Dad, this is my friend, Carl. He plays on my team.
- **B.** Carl, say hi to my father.
- **C.** Carl, I'd like you to meet my father.
- **D.** Dad, meet Carl.

14. What important detail is missing from this telephone message?

> Pam called at 10:00 A.M. She wants you to return her call by 3:00 P.M.
>
> Diana

- **A.** whom the message is for
- **B.** the name of the caller
- **C.** what the message is
- **D.** who wrote the message

15. What important detail is missing from this emergency message?

> Hello. This is an emergency. I'm at the corner of Main St. and Kay Place. Someone has just been hit by a car.

- **A.** what the emergency is
- **B.** the location of the emergency
- **C.** that there is an emergency
- **D.** the name of the caller

Go on to the next page.

16. A famous baseball player is visiting your school baseball team. Which of these would *not* be a good question to ask him?

    A. How can I become a better ball player?

    B. Should fourth graders watch TV every day?

    C. Would you like to manage a baseball team?

    D. How many home runs have you hit?

17. Chris Presioso is filling out a form at the library. What should he write on the line that says STREET ADDRESS?

    A. (213) 971-8607

    B. California

    C. 3401 First Avenue

    D. Chris Presioso

18. Which of these statements is an opinion?

    A. You'll get more for your money at Stacey's Department Store.

    B. You can shop from 9:00 A.M. to 9:00 P.M. at Stacey's.

    C. Toys are sold at Stacey's Department Store.

    D. Stacey's Department Store is located on Pine Road.

Use this part of the Yellow Pages of a telephone directory to answer questions 19–22.

Florists — Retail
BRUCE'S FLOWERS
    21 Main Street 328-9109
CABBY'S FLORIST
    Milford Shopping Center 678-7911
FAIRFIELD FLOWERS INC
    83 George Ave 239-2183
HANSEN'S FLOWER SHOP
    21 Reef Rd 255-2309
KELLY'S FLORIST AND GREENHOUSE
    Waterside Rd 678-6609

19. What is the telephone number of Cabby's Florist?

    A. 678-7911   **B.** 239-2181

    C. 239-6606   **D.** 339-0025

20. Which florist has a greenhouse?

    A. Bruce's   **B.** Hansen's

    C. Fairfield   **D.** Kelly's

21. Which florist is on Reef Road?

    A. Bruce's   **B.** Fairfield

    C. Hansen's   **D.** Cabby's

22. What is the telephone number of the florist on George Avenue?

    A. 678-6609   **B.** 239-2183

    C. 328-9109   **D.** 678-3300

Use this map and legend to answer questions 23–26.

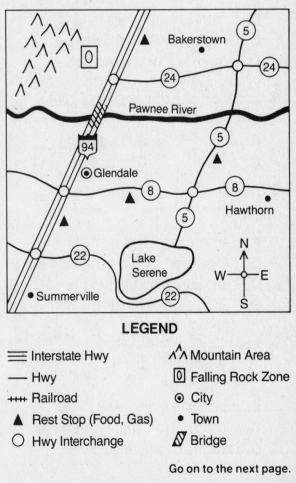

LEGEND

≡ Interstate Hwy   ʌʌ Mountain Area

— Hwy   ⓪ Falling Rock Zone

+++ Railroad   ⊙ City

▲ Rest Stop (Food, Gas)   • Town

○ Hwy Interchange   ◢ Bridge

Go on to the next page.

23. You are in Summerville. In which direction would you travel to reach Glendale?

    A. South **B.** North **C.** East **D.** West

24. How many rest stops are on the part of Interstate Highway 94 shown here?

    A. 4   **B.** 3   **C.** 2   **D.** 1

25. What is the symbol for Falling Rock Zone?

    A. ☐   **B.** ◉   **C.** ◯   **D.** ●

26. Along which route is the town of Hawthorn located?

    A. 24   **B.** 5   **C.** 94   **D.** 8

27. Which line of conversation is written correctly?

    A. "Where is Kim"? asked Lee.
    B. "Where is Kim? asked Lee."
    C. "Where is Kim?" asked Lee.
    D. Where is Kim? asked Lee.

28. In a story the *development* comes at the

    A. end   **B.** beginning
    C. middle   **D.** middle or end

29. Which line of conversation is written correctly?

    A. I answered "Here is my house,"
    B. I answered, "Here is my house."
    C. I answered, "here is my house."
    D. I answered, "Here is my house".

30. In a story the *conclusion* is

    A. a description of the main characters
    B. where the story takes place
    C. a problem the characters have
    D. how the characters solve a problem

31. Which line of conversation is written correctly?

    A. "I found your bat, Pat said."
    B. "I found your bat," Pat said.
    C. I found your bat", Pat said.
    D. "I found your bat" Pat said.

32. The *setting* of a story is usually described at the

    A. beginning   **B.** middle
    C. end   **D.** beginning or end

33. Which line of conversation is written correctly?

    A. George replied, He has a cold.
    B. George replied "He has a cold."
    C. George replied, "He has a cold."
    D. George replied, "he has a cold."

34. The *introduction* of a story usually tells about

    A. the author of the story
    B. a problem the characters have
    C. how the characters solve a problem
    D. the main characters

35. A story that an author has made up from his or her imagination is called

    A. fiction
    B. biography
    C. factual information
    D. poetry

Writing Sample Write a story about a trip to an imaginary place. Use conversation in your story. Write a good beginning, middle, and end.

                                                Stop!

End of Year Test

1. Which group of words is a sentence?
  A. Sounded like a train.
  B. A very loud noise.
  C. Is the bell ringing?
  D. Before the next class.

2. Which sentence is a declarative sentence?
  A. How quickly the boat is sinking!
  B. Why was Peggy late?
  C. Watch the baby, please.
  D. The magician waved a wand.

3. Which sentence is an imperative sentence?
  A. Turn off the television set.
  B. How bright the sun is!
  C. Where are the postcards?
  D. Our phone is broken.

4. What is the best answer to this question?
      Where is Egypt?
  A. Africa.
  B. In Africa.
  C. Egypt is in Africa.
  D. Egypt is a republic.

5. What is the complete subject of this sentence?
      The little chickens pecked at the seeds.
  A. pecked at the seeds
  B. The little chickens
  C. at the seeds
  D. chickens pecked

6. Which word in this sentence is a noun?
      The candle melted slowly.
  A. candle   B. the
  C. melted   D. slowly

7. Which word is the plural of *bus*?
  A. buss   B. bus
  C. buses   D. busies

8. Which word is the plural of *sheep*?
  A. sheeps   B. sheepes
  C. sheepies   D. sheep

9. Which word in this sentence is a common noun?
      Rosa stayed at a hotel in Iowa.
  A. stayed   B. Iowa
  C. Rosa   D. hotel

10. Complete this sentence correctly.
      Is ____ here today?
  A. Ms S L Brown
  B. Ms. S. L. Brown
  C. ms. s. l. Brown
  D. ms s l brown

11. Complete this sentence correctly.
      We visited the hot springs near ____ .
  A. denver, colorado
  B. denver, Colorado
  C. Denver, Colorado
  D. Denver, colorado

Go on to the next page.

12. Complete this sentence correctly.

Many _____ apartments were painted.

A. neighbors B. neighbors'
C. neighbor's D. neighbores

13. Which word in this sentence is a linking verb?

The two children were happy.

A. were B. children
C. happy D. two

14. Which word in this sentence is a helping verb?

Henry has missed his bus.

A. missed B. has
C. his D. bus

15. Which sentence has a verb in the past tense?

A. Molly bakes bread on Saturdays.
B. Who is knocking at the window?
C. Ned will know the answer.
D. The jet raced across the sky.

16. What is the contraction for *will not*?

A. wont B. willn't
C. won't D. will'nt

17. What is the past tense of the verb *rub*?

A. ruebed B. rubed
C. rubd D. rubbed

18. Complete this sentence correctly.

Who _____ Vicky a surprise party?

A. given B. give
C. gave D. gived

Read the paragraph and answer questions 19–21.

Most likely, the Tasmanian tiger is extinct. They were once plentiful in Tasmania, an island off Australia. These creatures were 4 feet long and striped. They carried their young in pouches, as kangaroos do. When Europeans settled in Tasmania, they drove the tigers out. No sign that this tiger still lives has been reported for over 45 years. A recent search did not turn up any. Some Tasmanians still claim that the tigers are alive in more distant parts of the island.

19. What is the main idea of the paragraph?

A. Tasmanian tigers are probably no longer living.
B. Tasmanian tigers are somewhat like kangaroos.
C. Although there are no signs of them, the tigers are still believed to exist.
D. Tasmanian tigers lived in Tasmania, an Australian island.

20. What is the topic sentence of the paragraph?

A. They carried their young in pouches, as kangaroos do.
B. These creatures were four feet long and striped.
C. Most likely, the Tasmanian tiger is extinct.
D. When Europeans settled in Tasmania, they drove the tigers out.

Go on to the next page.

21. Which sentence would add another detail that would also tell about the topic?
 A. The kangaroo's long, heavy tail gives it balance when it moves.
 B. Scientists would like to find a living Tasmanian tiger.
 C. Tasmania was discovered by Abel Tasman in 1642.
 D. There are plenty of kangaroos in Tasmania.

Read this paragraph and answer questions 22 and 23.

 Ms. Ray's fourth-graders made a school newspaper. The reporters interviewed teachers and students in the school. Then they wrote up their news stories. The editors read the stories and corrected them. First each student decided whether to be a reporter or an editor. Mr. French's class went on a field trip. Finally Ms. Ray typed up the paper and made copies.

22. Which sentence should be the *third* sentence in the paragraph?
 A. Finally Ms. Ray typed up the paper and made copies.
 B. Then they wrote up their news stories.
 C. First each student decided whether to be a reporter or an editor.
 D. The reporters interviewed teachers and students in the school.

23. Which sentence does *not* belong in the paragraph?
 A. Mr. French's class went on a field trip.
 B. Finally Ms. Ray typed up the paper and made copies.
 C. The reporters interviewed teachers and students in the school.
 D. The editors read the stories and corrected them

24. Which word in this sentence is an adjective?
 Today three letters arrived for Carl.
 A. three **B.** today
 C. for **D.** arrived

25. Complete this sentence correctly.
 Is this year's harvest the _____ ever?
 A. more larger **B.** larger
 C. largest **D.** most larger

26. Which word in this sentence is an article?
 The wind carried my balloons away.
 A. wind **B.** The
 C. my **D.** away

27. Which word in this sentence is an adverb?
 Sometimes John bakes oatmeal cookies.
 A. bakes **B.** Sometimes
 C. oatmeal **D.** cookies

Go on to the next page.

28. Which word in this sentence tells *how*?

　　Today we tiptoed quietly into class.

A. into 　　**B.** Today
C. tiptoed **D.** quietly

29. Complete this sentence correctly.

　　Jill read her report ____ .

A. well **B.** good
C. nice **D.** proud

30. Which word in this sentence is a pronoun?

　　Tell them Sherry went to the beach.

A. to 　　**B.** Sherry
C. them **D.** the

31. Which word can take the place of the underlined words in this sentence?

　　Our puppy rolled in the grass.

A. We **B.** They
C. Me **D.** It

32. Which word can take the place of the underlined word in this sentence?

　　Patty said, "Come to the store with Susie and Patty."

A. me 　**B.** her
C. them **D.** she

33. Which word can take the place of the underlined words in this sentence?

　　That red bike is my sister's.

A. ours **B.** hers
C. she 　**D.** my

34. Complete this sentence correctly.

　　Ray and ____ raced all the way home.

A. us **B.** me
C. I 　**D.** them

35. Complete this sentence correctly.

　　We all read quietly to ____ .

A. myself 　**B.** ourself
C. yourself **D.** ourselves

36. What is the simple subject of this sentence?

　　My favorite perfume is made from roses.

A. favorite **B.** perfume
C. My 　　**D.** roses

37. What is the simple predicate of this sentence?

　　Nina just painted the room purple.

A. painted
B. painted the room
C. just painted
D. Nina painted

38. Complete this sentence correctly.

　　Ben and Joe ____ to study for the test.

A. pretends **B.** has
C. wants 　**D.** promise

39. What is the best answer to the question?

　　Did a match start the fire?

A. Yes a match.
B. Yes.
C. Yes, a match started the fire.
D. Yes a match started it.

Go on to the next page.

40. Grant will introduce his friend Joyce to his band instructor. What is the best introduction?

    A. Mrs. Tulley, this is Joyce. She plays flute.

    B. Mrs. Tulley, meet Joyce.

    C. Mrs. Tulley, this is my friend.

    D. Joyce, this is our band instructor, Mrs. Tulley.

41. Which important detail is missing from this telephone message?

    Friday, 5:00 P.M. To: Mom
    Jenny will be late for dinner.

    A. when the call was made

    B. who wrote the message

    C. whom the message is for

    D. the name of the caller

42. Which important detail is missing from this emergency message?

    This is Claire Peters. This is an emergency. There has been a car accident. Please send help immediately.

    A. the name of the caller

    B. that there is an emergency

    C. what the emergency is

    D. the location of the emergency

43. Dr. Miller, who runs the city aquarium, has come to talk to your class. Which of these would *not* be a good question to ask her?

    A. How are seals trained?

    B. Do you have children?

    C. How many people visit the aquarium each year?

    D. Who collects fish for the aquarium?

44. Ralph Sharp is filling out a form to go to day camp. What should he write on the line that says CITY AND STATE?

    A. 43 Rosewater Rd.

    B. Sharp, Ralph

    C. Waterton, Minnesota

    D. (312) 555-1423

45. Which word in this sentence is an adjective?

    The little monkey holds out a cap.

    A. out   **B.** holds

    C. little   **D.** monkey

46. Complete this sentence correctly.

    A diamond is _____ than any other stone.

    A. most hard   **B.** more harder

    C. hardest   **D.** harder

47. Which word in this sentence is an article?

    Jeff left a package for Peter.

    A. a   **B.** for

    C. left   **D.** package

48. Which word in this sentence is an adverb?

    Our rabbit ate the lettuce hungrily.

    A. the   **B.** Our

    C. hungrily   **D.** ate

49. Which word in this sentence tells *when*?

    Does Sue always eat dinner quickly?

    A. quickly   **B.** always

    C. eat   **D.** Does

Go on to the next page.

50. Which word in this sentence is a pronoun?

       Did he blow out all the candles?

  A. the   **B.** all

  C. he   **D.** candles

51. Adele French is filling out a form at school. What should she write on the line that says TELEPHONE?

  A. 88 Summer Lane

  B. 9/18/85

  C. Topeka, Kansas

  D. (303) 622-7833

52. Which of these statements is a fact?

  A. Naturally you'll love *Naturally*.

  B. *Naturally* cereal is a perfect breakfast treat.

  C. *Naturally* cereal has raisins.

  D. Get smart. Get *Naturally* cereal.

53. Which of these statements is an opinion?

  A. You'll need four batteries for *Smarter*.

  B. *Smarter* is a computer game.

  C. Henry's Toy Store sells *Smarter* computers.

  D. *Smarter* is the best game you can buy.

54. In which section of the library would you look for a book about houses built by Native Americans?

  A. biography   **B.** fiction

  C. nonfiction   **D.** reference

55. You want to know if your school library has any books about whales. In which part of the card catalog should you look?

  A. subject cards

  B. author cards

  C. title cards

  D. magazine cards

Use this paragraph to answer questions 56-58.

    People have been making false teeth for more than 2,000 years. Many different materials have been used. Animal and human teeth were tried. Ivory and bones were carved into teeth. These all caused a problem with smell. Some rich people had teeth made from gold, silver, or precious stones. Finally porcelain was used successfully, and then plastic was tried. Later the problem of keeping the teeth in place was solved. Still no one enjoys wearing false teeth.

56. What is the main idea of this paragraph?

  A. Early teeth were made of ivory.

  B. Rich people have very valuable teeth.

  C. False teeth have been made from many materials.

  D. Porcelain and plastic are the best materials for false teeth.

Go on to the next page.

57. Which fact is *not* stated in the paragraph?

   A. Animal teeth were used for false teeth.

   B. George Washington wore false teeth.

   C. Keeping false teeth in place was a problem.

   D. Gold was used to make false teeth for rich people.

58. Which of these ideas from the paragraph is an opinion and not necessarily a fact?

   A. Ivory and bone caused a problem with smell.

   B. Animal and human teeth were tried.

   C. Finally porcelain was used successfully.

   D. No one enjoys wearing false teeth.

59. *Bugle* would come between which pair of guide words in the dictionary?

   A. buffalo–bulldoze

   B. bulldozer–bunk

   C. Bryant–buff

   D. brood–brute

Use this dictionary entry to answer question 60.

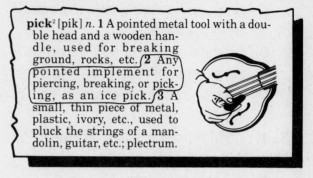

pick² [pik] *n.* **1** A pointed metal tool with a double head and a wooden handle, used for breaking ground, rocks, etc. **2** Any pointed implement for piercing, breaking, or picking, as an ice pick. **3** A small, thin piece of metal, plastic, ivory, etc., used to pluck the strings of a mandolin, guitar, etc.; plectrum.

60. The part of the dictionary entry that is circled tells you

   A. a definition of *pick*

   B. what part of speech *pick* is

   C. how to use *pick*

   D. how to pronounce *pick*

Look at the symbols in the pronunciation key from the dictionary. Use them to find the correct spelling for the word in question 61.

add, āce, câre, pälm; end, ēqual; it, īce; odd, ōpen, ôr-der; tŏŏk, pōōl; up, bûrn; ə = a in *above*, e in *sicken*, i in *possible*, o in *melon*, u in *circus*; yōō = u in *fuse*; oil; pout; check; ring; thin; this; zh in *vision*.

61. kot′ (ə)n

   A. cutting   **B.** kitten

   C. cotton   **D.** coating

Go on to the next page.

62. The table of contents of a book does *not* contain
    A. the page number on which each chapter begins
    B. the meanings of unfamiliar words
    C. the number of chapters in the book
    D. the names of each chapter

63. Which information is found in the index of a book?
    A. the author's name
    B. where to locate specific topics
    C. the number of pages in each chapter
    D. the copyright date

64. You would like to learn about the water and mineral resources of Vermont. In which volume of the encyclopedia would you look first?
    A. W   **B.** R
    C. M   **D.** V

Use this section from a dictionary to answer questions 65–66.

> **port**[1] [pôrt] *n.* A city or place where ships arrive and depart; harbor.
> **port**[2] [pôrt] *n.* A sweet, usually red wine.
> **port**[3] [pôrt] *n.* **1** A small opening in the side of a ship; porthole. **2** A covering for a porthole. **3** An opening, as in an engine, valve, etc., for the passage of air, gas, or a liquid.
> **port**[4] [pôrt] **1** *n.* The left side of a ship or boat, facing the bow. **2** *adj. use:* the *port* side; the *port* guns. **3** *v.* To turn to the left, as a ship.

65. Which entry for *port* goes with this sentence?
    Water leaked into our cabin through the *port*.
    A. 3   **B.** 1
    C. 2   **D.** 4

66. Which entry for *port* goes with the sentence?
    The best fish market is in the *port*.
    A. 2   **B.** 3
    C. 1   **D.** 4

67. Which pair of words are antonyms?
    A. gift–present
    B. rose–bud
    C. bad–worst
    D. calm–nervous

Use the information given below to answer questions 68 and 69.

> **happily**, adv., gladly, joyfully, joyously, delightedly, blissfully, cheerfully.
> *Antonyms*, sadly, gloomily, dismally, uncheerfully, cheerlessly, joylessly.

68. This kind of information would be found in
    A. the glossary of a book
    B. a thesaurus
    C. a dictionary
    D. the index of a book

69. What is a synonym for *happily*?
    A. gloomily   **B.** sadly
    C. blissfully   **D.** uncheerfully

70. Which topic is the best choice for a short report?
    A. The History of Bicycles
    B. Transportation
    C. Bicycle Racing Around the World
    D. Traffic Rules for Bicycle Riders

Go on to the next page.

71. You are taking notes for a report on jobs in television. Which of these ideas should go into your report?
- **A.** scientists design TV equipment
- **B.** film cameras lighter than TV cameras
- **C.** Emmy Awards given for best programs
- **D.** TV in most American homes in 1960's

Use this outline to answer questions 72–73.

The Pioneers

I. Heading west
   A. Wagon trains
   B. Dangers on the trail
   C. Crossing the Great Plains
II. Life in a frontier home
   A. Making furniture
   B. Spinning
   C. Food preparation
   D. Making candles
   E. _____

72. Which is a subtopic?
- **A.** Heading west
- **B.** The pioneers
- **C.** Dangers on the trail
- **D.** Life in a frontier home

73. Which would best fit in the blank next to II. E.?
- **A.** Making clothes
- **B.** Down the Ohio River
- **C.** The log schoolhouse
- **D.** City life

74. Which word has a *suffix*?
- **A.** away
- **B.** peaceful
- **C.** lamplight
- **D.** dollar

75. To which word would you add *im* to form a new word?
- **A.** common
- **B.** fresh
- **C.** place
- **D.** patient

76. Complete this sentence correctly.
   They want to go _____ .
- **A.** their
- **B.** too
- **C.** they're
- **D.** to

77. Which word is a compound word?
- **A.** forest
- **B.** thankful
- **C.** homesick
- **D.** doctor

Use this part of the Yellow Pages of a telephone directory to answer questions 78–79.

HARDWARE STORES
Bender's Hardware
  48 Washington Sq. 862-4105
Capital Hardware
  322 E. Lane Dr. 221-5115
Daniel's Hardware & Lumber
  8105 E. Belmore St. 862-7598
Dora's Supply Co.
  21 Lincoln Ave. 222-7545
East Community Hardware
  10 W. 7th St. 954-2996
Lawrence Hardware
  St. James Sq. 954-1111

78. What is the telephone number of East Community Hardware?
- **A.** 954-2996
- **B.** 954-1111
- **C.** 222-7545
- **D.** 862-4105

79. Which hardware store also sells lumber?
- **A.** Bender's
- **B.** Dora's
- **C.** Daniel's
- **D.** Lawrence

Go on to the next page.

Use this map of Cobb's Farm to answer questions 80 and 81.

LEGEND

⋀⋀⋀ Hills	Corn
═══ Country Road	Wheat
▭ Buildings	Soybeans
Livestock	Apple Orchards

80. What is the symbol for soybeans?

A. ☁ B. (livestock symbol)

C. (soybean symbol) D. ⋀⋀⋀

81. You are at the apple orchard. In which direction would you travel to reach Cobb's Pond?

A. north B. south
C. east D. west

82. What is the correct way to combine these sentences with *or*?

Wear your hat and coat.
You'll catch cold.

A. Wear your hat and coat, or, you'll catch cold.

B. Wear your hat and coat or you'll catch cold.

C. Wear your hat and coat, or you'll catch cold.

D. Wear your hat and coat Or you'll catch cold.

83. What must be done to correct the sentence?

Presents for Linda and Ann.

A. Add a subject.
B. Add punctuation at the end.
C. Capitalize the first letter.
D. Add a predicate.

84. What does the editing mark in this sentence tell the writer to do?

Call Mrs₀Lewis tonight.

A. Add a period.
B. Take out a word.
C. Add a word.
D. Make a capital letter.

85. What is the correct way to write this title of a book?

A. The Inn At Shell Cove
B. The inn at shell cove
C. The Inn at Shell Cove
D. the Inn at Shell Cove

86. What is the name for this letter part?

With love,

A. greeting B. closing
C. signature D. heading

Read these directions for planting lettuce.

A. Plant lettuce in early spring or late summer.
B. Spread seeds thinly in each row.
C. Cover the seeds with dirt.
D. Thin out small plants as they grow.

87. Where does this sentence belong?

Leave one foot between each plant to grow to full size.

A. after B B. after A
C. after D D. after C

Go on to the next page.

88. The word *last* has been added to this sentence from a direction paragraph. What does the editing mark on *paint* mean?

Last
∧Paint the completed model.

   A. Move the word to another place.
   B. Take the word out of the sentence.
   C. Spell the word correctly.
   D. Make the first letter lowercase.

89. What is the best way to combine these sentences?

   The boy was tall.
   The boy was thin.
   The boy was freckled.

   A. The boy was tall and thin and freckled.
   B. The boy was tall and thin, and freckled.
   C. The boy was tall, thin and freckled.
   D. The boy was tall, thin, and freckled.

90. What is the best way to combine the subjects of these two sentences?

   Suzy is at camp.
   My sister is at camp.

   A. Suzy and my sister is at camp.
   B. Suzy and my sister are at camp.
   C. Suzy is at camp and my sister is at camp.
   D. Suzy is and my sister is at camp.

91. Which sentence has a detail that tells *how*?

   A. At the concert Joe played the flute.
   B. All morning Joe played the flute.
   C. Joe played the flute with pleasure.
   D. Joe played the flute for the teacher.

92. What will this sentence look like after the editing changes are <u>made</u>?

At two o'clock we were ready.

   A. We at two o'clock were ready.
   B. We were ready at two o'clock.
   C. At two o'clock We were ready.
   D. We were ready. at two o'clock.

93. Which line of conversation is written correctly?

   A. "I need this book," Don said.
   B. "I need this book, Don said."
   C. "I need this book", Don said.
   D. "I need this book" Don said.

94. In a story, the problem faced by the main character(s) is presented in the

   A. introduction
   B. development
   C. conclusion
   D. introduction or conclusion

95. Which sentence contains a simile?

   A. I had a beet for a nose.
   B. My nose was dark red.
   C. My nose shone dark red.
   D. My nose was as red as a beet.

96. Which would *not* be a good place to look for factual information to use in reports?

   A. true adventure stories
   B. magazine articles
   C. tall tales
   D. biographies

Go on to the next page.

End-of-Year Test **87**

97. A fable is a
  A. kind of poem
  B. kind of true adventure story
  C. life story written by the person who lived it
  D. very short story that teaches a lesson

98. Which is an example of fiction?
  A. the life of the poet Elizabeth Barrett Browning
  B. the story of the building of the Sears Tower in Chicago
  C. a story about fairies in the forest
  D. a news article about a flood

99. Which line in this poem contains alliteration?
  (1) A polka-dotted clown
  (2) Beats a big bass drum.
  (3) Sha . . . boom! Ta . . . boom!
  (4) The circus has come!
  A. 2   **B.** 4
  C. 3   **D.** 1

100. What are the underlined words in this line from a play?
    Jim (*Running to the door*):
    Who's there?
  A. the name of a character
  B. scenery
  C. stage directions
  D. dialog

Writing Sample   Choose one of the writing assignments below. Complete the assignment on a separate sheet of paper.
• Write a descriptive paragraph about an imaginary palace. Use vivid words to describe the palace's appearance.
• Write a short story that includes a conversation between a wizard and the wizard's assistant. Make sure the setting of the story is appropriate.

                                          Stop!

ANSWER KEY FOR TESTS

Unit 1, Pretest and Posttest

1. C	2. D	3. A	4. C	5. B	6. A
7. C	8. D	9. D	10. B	11. C	12. B
13. A	14. B	15. D	16. A	17. C	18. D
19. A	20. C	21. D	22. B	23. D	24. C
25. A	26. B	27. B	28. D	29. B	30. C
31. C	32. D	33. A	34. B	35. A	

Unit 2, Pretest and Posttest

1. B	2. D	3. C	4. B	5. A	6. D
7. C	8. A	9. D	10. B	11. B	12. C
13. A	14. A	15. D	16. B	17. C	18. A
19. C	20. D	21. C	22. C	23. B	24. C
25. C	26. B	27. D	28. A	29. C	30. B
31. C	32. B	33. A	34. C	35. A	

Unit 3, Pretest and Posttest

1. D	2. C	3. C	4. B	5. D	6. B
7. A	8. C	9. D	10. A	11. B	12. D
13. D	14. B	15. A	16. D	17. C	18. A
19. C	20. D	21. B	22. B	23. D	24. C
25. C	26. D	27. C	28. A	29. A	30. D
31. D	32. B	33. B	34. C	35. A	

Unit 4, Pretest and Posttest

1. B	2. A	3. C	4. C	5. D	6. A
7. B	8. D	9. C	10. B	11. A	12. D
13. C	14. A	15. D	16. B	17. B	18. C
19. B	20. D	21. D	22. C	23. A	24. B
25. C	26. A	27. D	28. C	29. B	30. B
31. D	32. D	33. C	34. C	35. D	

Midyear Test

1. B	2. B	3. C	4. A	5. D	6. C
7. C	8. B	9. D	10. B	11. A	12. C
13. D	14. A	15. B	16. D	17. C	18. B
19. A	20. D	21. C	22. A	23. D	24. B
25. C	26. A	27. A	28. A	29. C	30. D
31. C	32. D	33. C	34. B	35. B	36. C
37. A	38. D	39. C	40. C	41. D	42. B
43. A	44. C	45. D	46. A	47. B	48. D
49. C	50. B	51. A	52. D	53. A	54. D
55. B	56. B	57. A	58. A	59. D	60. B

Unit 5, Pretest and Posttest

1. A	2. B	3. D	4. C	5. D	6. C
7. A	8. C	9. B	10. B	11. B	12. A
13. C	14. B	15. B	16. D	17. A	18. C
19. D	20. D	21. A	22. C	23. B	24. B
25. C	26. D	27. A	28. C	29. B	30. A
31. C	32. D	33. B	34. C	35. B	

Unit 6, Pretest and Posttest

1. C	2. D	3. A	4. B	5. D	6. C
7. B	8. A	9. D	10. C	11. A	12. D
13. B	14. B	15. C	16. A	17. A	18. D
19. C	20. A	21. B	22. C	23. A	24. D
25. C	26. B	27. B	28. C	29. A	30. D
31. C	32. B	33. D	34. C	35. A	

Unit 7, Pretest and Posttest

1. B	2. C	3. A	4. A	5. B	6. D
7. B	8. C	9. A	10. C	11. D	12. C
13. D	14. C	15. B	16. B	17. C	18. A
19. D	20. C	21. C	22. B	23. D	24. B
25. A	26. C	27. D	28. A	29. B	30. D
31. C	32. D	33. C	34. D	35. B	

Unit 8, Pretest and Posttest

1. B	2. D	3. C	4. B	5. A	6. D
7. C	8. A	9. D	10. B	11. B	12. C
13. A	14. A	15. D	16. B	17. C	18. A
19. A	20. D	21. C	22. B	23. B	24. C
25. A	26. D	27. C	28. C	29. B	30. D
31. B	32. A	33. C	34. D	35. A	

End-of-Year Test

1. C	2. D	3. A	4. C	5. B	6. A
7. C	8. D	9. D	10. B	11. C	12. B
13. A	14. B	15. D	16. C	17. D	18. C
19. A	20. C	21. B	22. D	23. A	24. A
25. C	26. B	27. B	28. D	29. A	30. C
31. D	32. A	33. B	34. C	35. D	36. B
37. A	38. D	39. C	40. A	41. B	42. D
43. B	44. C	45. C	46. D	47. A	48. C
49. B	50. C	51. D	52. C	53. D	54. C
55. A	56. C	57. B	58. D	59. A	60. A
61. C	62. B	63. B	64. D	65. A	66. C
67. D	68. B	69. C	70. D	71. A	72. C
73. A	74. B	75. D	76. B	77. C	78. A
79. C	80. B	81. B	82. C	83. D	84. A
85. C	86. B	87. C	88. D	89. D	90. B
91. C	92. B	93. A	94. B	95. D	96. C
97. D	98. C	99. A	100. C		

TEACHING AIDS

The Teaching Aids that accompany this level of *Language for Daily Use, Phoenix Edition* appear on the following pages. Included in the Teaching Aids are student response cards, a composition evaluation form, enrichment masters, parent letters, record-keeping forms, and test answer forms.

Student Response Cards: Cards illustrating punctuation marks and listing parts of speech and other terminology are provided for use with various lesson plans.

Composition Evaluation Form: A form for evaluating student composition is provided. A guide for using this form appears on page T26 of the Teacher's Edition for this level.

Enrichment Masters: Suggestions for creative activities that review and reinforce skills and unit concepts are provided.

Parent Letters: Letters that inform parents of the skills covered in each unit and suggest language arts activities they can do at home with their children are provided in English and Spanish.

Record-Keeping Forms: For your convenience, individual and class record forms are provided.

Test Answer Forms: Answer forms for pretests/posttests and midyear/end-of-year tests are provided.

Student Response Cards

.

?
.

!
.

,

" "

simple subject

simple predicate

contraction

Student Response Cards

I

me

common noun

proper noun

pronoun

antecedent

adjective

adverb

Student Response Cards

article

action verb

linking verb

helping verb

Student Response Cards

synonym

antonym

declarative

interrogative

Student Response Cards

imperative

exclamatory

complete
subject

complete
predicate

Composition Evaluation Form

Student's Name _____

Assignment _____

		Rating	Comments
1.	Handwriting	1 2 3 4 5	
2.	Spelling	1 2 3 4 5	
3.	Capitalization	1 2 3 4 5	
4.	Punctuation	1 2 3 4 5	
5.	Grammar/Usage	1 2 3 4 5	
6.	Sentence Structure	1 2 3 4 5	
7.	Paragraph Development	1 2 3 4 5	
8.	Organization of Ideas	1 2 3 4 5	
9.	Quality of Ideas	1 2 3 4 5	
10.	Word Choice/Style	1 2 3 4 5	

UNIT 1: Enrichment Master

1. Find a picture of an animal in a magazine. Cut it out. Paste it onto a piece of paper. Write sentences to tell about the picture. Tell something that is true about the animal, or make up a story.

2. Pretend you are an architect — a person who designs buildings. Draw a plan of a library. Put in the four main areas: fiction, nonfiction, biography, and reference. Be sure there is a space for the librarian's desk and the card catalog. Put in anything else you think the library needs.

3. Go to your school or public library. Look up *Poetry* in the subject catalog. Find a poetry book and look through it. Pick out a poem you like. Then write some sentences telling why you like the poem.

4. Find a poem you like in your school or public library. Copy the poem. Then read it to a classmate or to your teacher. Draw a picture illustrating the poem.

5. Pretend you are the author of a book. Think of a title for your book. Then make an author card to go in a card catalog. Include all necessary information. Use the author card on page 16 as a model.

6. Think of four jobs you might like to have. Then write one sentence about each job. Explain why you might like that job. Draw pictures of something you would use if you worked at each job. Have a friend guess the jobs.

7. Find a book in the library that is written for little children. Copy some of the short sentences from the book. Then combine some of the short sentences. Use the words *and*, *but*, and *or*.

8. Write a poem about traveling on a bus, train, car, or in an airplane. Use words such as *zoom*, *honk*, *roar*, *whoosh*, *clang*, *clank*, and other sound words in your poem.

9. If you were a library book, which kind of book would you like to be? Write five sentences about the kind of book you chose. If you chose a fiction book, tell about your characters. If you chose a nonfiction book, tell some information you might give.

10. Think of five questions about a topic that interests you. Find the answers to your questions in a library book. Write your questions and answers. Draw pictures to go with them.

UNIT 2: Enrichment Master

(1) Make up an imaginary town. Draw a map of the town. Label five houses with the names of people who live there and their street addresses.

(2) Choose a partner in class. Pick a book that both of you would read. After reading the book, you and your partner should each prepare your own oral report. Tell your oral book reports to each other. Write down how your reports are different and how they are alike. Discuss what you both thought about the book.

(3) Go to your school or public library. Find a book about a famous person. Read it. Pick one important or exciting thing that happens in the story. Draw a picture about it.

(4) Choose one of these items, which can be found in your classroom, to advertise.

pencil   book   desk   chalkboard
eraser   chalk   ruler   clock

Write a newspaper ad for the item. Use statements of fact and opinion in your ad.

(5) Find an ad in a magazine or newspaper. Underline statements of fact in the ad. Circle statements of opinion.

(6) Make a list of the names and titles of these people in your school.

your teacher   the nurse
a cafeteria helper   the librarian
the principal   your best
                      friend
the secretary   the bus driver

(7) Write the names of five items for each of these categories: animals, fruits, colors, sports, pets. Next to the name of each item, write the plural form of the word.

(8) Pretend you are a famous person. A biography has been written about you. Tell the title of the biography. Tell why you are famous. Draw a picture of the book cover of your biography.

(9) Choose a partner from your class. Have a contest to see who can think of the most proper nouns in five minutes. The proper nouns should have something to do with your life. For example, you might write the name of your school, your town, your sister, and so on.

(10) Think of a famous person who lived long ago. In your school or public library, find a book about that person. Read the book. Report to your class.

UNIT 3: Enrichment Master

(1) Think of five action verbs. Write them down. Then draw five pictures illustrating these verbs.

(2) Pick a partner from your class. Give your address to your partner. Write down your partner's address. Then write each other friendly letters. Address and stamp the envelopes. Send your letter to your partner's home. Have your partner send his or her letter to your home.

(3) What gift would you like more than anything else? Pretend that someone has given you that gift. Write a thank you note to the person who has given you the gift.

(4) Go to your school or public library to choose a play. Pick other students to play the characters. Pick a character for yourself to play. Practice the play, and put it on for your class.

(5) Ask several people to join you in a circle. Ask the first person who starts to begin with the letter *A*, using this as a model: "My name is Adam. I live on an ant farm. I sell apples." The second person must use the same model, but he or she should start with *B*. For instance, the second person could say, "My name is Betty. I live in Boston. I sell balloons." See if you can keep going until you get to the letter *Z*.

(6) Look in a dictionary for two unfamiliar words you read in your science or social studies book. Read the definitions. Use each word in a sentence.

(7) Pretend you are having a Halloween party. Take a piece of paper. Fold it in half to make a card. Write down all the information about your party on the card. Then draw a picture on your invitation.

(8) Choose a partner. Each person must write five action verbs, each on a separate piece of paper. Exchange papers, one at a time. Your partner picks an action verb to act out. Then you pick one from your partner.

(9) Write a letter to a friend, using a dictionary code. Think of some things to tell your friend. Look up each word you wish to write in a classroom dictionary. Instead of the word itself, write the respelling of the word. When you have finished, your letter will look as if it is written in a secret code. See if your friend can understand it.

(10) Think of a fairy tale that most people know. Rewrite the fairy tale in play form. Include stage directions and dialog. You may wish to work with a partner on this activity.

UNIT 4: Enrichment Master

(1) Pretend something very exciting happened to you on the way to school. Write a paragraph about it. Include a topic sentence and supporting details. Draw a picture of the exciting event.

(2) Choose a partner from your class. Each of you can choose a topic and write a paragraph about it. Then rewrite your paragraph, and have your partner rewrite his or hers. Put the sentences in a different order. Trade your rewritten paragraphs. Try to put the sentences in each other's paragraphs back in the right order.

(3) Write down directions on how to get from your house to a friend's house. Be sure your directions are complete and easy to follow. Make a map to go with your directions. Include street names, landmarks, and anything else that could help a stranger follow your directions. Draw an arrow to show the route.

(4) Make up an exciting event that might have happened to you. Tell about a problem or challenge. Then write an adventure story about the event. Tell what you did to solve the problem or meet the challenge.

(5) Pretend you have written a book on one of these subjects.

The Zoo	Games
Dinosaurs	Space Travel

Make up a table of contents for your book.

(6) Write a direction paragraph on one of these topics.

How to Fly a Kite
How to Plant a Seed
How to Build a Doghouse
How to Take a Picture

You may pick a topic of your own. Then make a picture to go with each step in the direction paragraph.

(7) Use your classroom or library encyclopedia. Look up one of these people.

Booker T. Washington	Margaret Mead
Orville Wright	Jane Addams

Read the article. Write down five interesting facts about the person.

(8) Draw a true adventure story showing something that happened to you. Your story may be like a comic strip with a different picture for each scene. Remember to show the challenge or problem you faced, and how you solved it.

UNIT 5: Enrichment Master

(1) Read this sentence, "It is an *amazing, beautiful, cold* day." Each of the adjectives starts with a different letter in alphabetical order. Think of adjectives that start with the other 23 letters of the alphabet. Put as many of them as possible in the sentence. Then read the whole sentence aloud.

(2) Pretend that you are describing a tree to someone who has never seen one. Write a description of a tree for the person. Use clear, descriptive adjectives. You may wish to select an object of your own choosing.

(3) Write a descriptive paragraph about a vacation you have taken or one you would like to take. Use adjectives, adverbs, and interesting verbs. Then draw a picture of your vacation.

(4) Write a short poem about some hobby you like. The poem does not have to rhyme. Use descriptive adjectives. Then using old magazines from home or from your classroom, cut out pictures of your hobby. Paste the pictures on colored paper to make a collage illustrating your poem. Copy your poem in your neatest handwriting. Paste the poem in the center of your collage.

(5) Choose a partner for this game. Think of an object. Describe your object, using only adjectives. Then ask your partner, "What am I?" For instance, if you were thinking of a frog, you would say, "I am small, green, live near ponds, and make a croaking sound. What am I?" When your partner guesses your object, let your partner take a turn choosing and describing your object.

(6) Select an object in your classroom. Ask a partner to close his or her eyes and feel the object. Then ask your partner to describe the object. Write down adjectives that describe the way the object feels to your partner.

(7) Find a poem you like in your school or public library. Pick out the adjectives in the poem. Then rewrite it, leaving out the adjectives. How does the poem change? Now rewrite it again. Use adjectives of your own in place of the adjectives you took out.

(8) Choose one of these people to be the main character of a tall tale.

> Zeke the Zookeeper
> Paula the Pilot
> Sara the Sailor
> Scott the Scientist

Write a tall tale about the character. Remember to use exaggeration.

UNIT 6: Enrichment Master

(1) Pretend you are writing a magazine article about your town. Think of as many facts as you can about your town. Write the article, and illustrate it with drawings of your town.

(2) Pretend you have discovered a new metal. Think of a name for it. Then write five questions you would want to find out about the metal.

(3) Pretend you are a writer for a travel magazine. Find information about a state in the United States. Write information that will make people want to visit that state.

(4) Choose a paragraph from a storybook. Copy it on a piece of paper. Then rewrite the paragraph. Use a pronoun to replace every noun.

(5) Pretend you are an astronaut. You have just landed on the planet Cetus. You see some strange creatures. Add subtopics to the outline that follows. Tell about the creatures. Make up a title for your outline.

    I. What the creatures look like
   II. What the creatures wear
  III. What the creatures eat

(6) Make up an imaginary animal. Write an article about your animal. Put in facts you have made up about the animal. Draw a picture of the animal to go with the article.

(7) Pick two partners in your class. You are going to make a magazine. Decide on the title and subject matter of your magazine. Each of you can research and write one article for the magazine. Illustrate your articles. Make a cover and a table of contents. Then staple the magazine together.

(8) Use all of these pronouns. Make a word-search puzzle. Then give your word-search puzzle to a friend to solve.

    I, we, he, she, they, you, it,
    me, us, him, her, them, my, our,
    his, your, their, its

(9) For each of the subjects below, think of five different topics that would be good for a two-paragraph report. Keep your list of topics. You may wish to refer to it when you have to write a report in class.

    Fish   Mexico   Jupiter

UNIT 7: Enrichment Master

① Pick a partner in your class. Each of you will write ten complete sentences. Now rewrite your sentences, mixing up the word order in each sentence. Trade sentences and try to write each other's sentences in their correct order.

② Read these groups of homophones.

sun/son   read/red
sale/sail   tail/tale

Write four sentences. Use one group of homophones in each sentence. You may suggest additional homophones for this activity.

③ Pick a partner. You and your partner will each write five sentences. In your sentences include words that tell *when, where, how,* or *why*. Then exchange your sentences. Label each sentence indicating which one tells *when, where, how,* or *why*.

④ Make a list of ten words with prefixes and suffixes that you studied in Unit 7. Then make a word-search or crossword puzzle using your words.

⑤ Pick two or three partners from your class. Each of you will think of a compound word. Divide the compound word into its two separate words. Take turns silently acting out each separate word in the compound word. Your partners will try to guess what the two words you are acting out are.

⑥ Make a compound-word rebus. Draw pictures illustrating words that form compounds. For example,

foot 🦶 + ball ⚾ = football 🏈

See if your classmates can guess your compound words.

⑦ Find a fable you like in your school or public library. Pick as many partners from your class as there are characters in the fable. Act out the fable for your class. Have the class try to guess the moral.

⑧ Find a fable you like in your school or classroom library. Draw pictures showing what happens in the fable. Then tell the fable to a friend.

UNIT 8: Enrichment Master

① Pretend you are writing a newspaper ad about skin diving. You must have three facts in your ad that will make people want to go skin diving. Look up skin diving in the encyclopedia. Then write an ad. You can put opinions into your ad too.

② Pick a partner from your class. Pretend you are calling him or her on the telephone. You are reporting an emergency. Have your partner write down the important information about the emergency.

③ Pick a partner from your class. Pretend your partner is the queen or king of an imaginary country. Make up a list of five questions that you would ask. Then interview your partner, asking questions about him or her and his or her imaginary country.

④ Pretend you met a giant. Write a story about it. Use conversation in your story.

⑤ Choose two partners from your class. Pick three famous people you and your partners can pretend to be. Each partner can introduce himself or herself as these famous people.

⑥ Look up one of these countries in an atlas.

   France   Morocco   India

Draw or trace the map of the country on a piece of paper. Use the atlas to find the capital city of the country. Label the capital on your drawing.

⑦ Pretend you own a business such as a garage, a laundry, a lawn service, and so on. Make up information for a Yellow Pages listing about your business. Include the name, address, and phone number. Remember your ad must interest people in your business or service.

⑧ Pretend you are starting a club. Make up a form for people who might want to join.

⑨ Write a conversation between any two of these people.

   a prince   a baseball player
   a reporter   a millionaire

Use quotation marks correctly.

⑩ Pretend you have just moved to a space colony on Mars. Draw a map of your colony.

Dear _____,

　　Your child has completed Unit 1 of *Language for Daily Use, Phoenix Edition*, a language arts program. In Unit 1 your child has studied how a sentence can express a statement, ask a question, give a command, or make an exclamation.

　　Examples:

　　Statement — The hamster is brown and white.

　　Question — Where is the new bike?

　　Command — Mow the lawn.

　　Exclamation — What a colorful parade!

Library and card-catalog organization have been studied to prepare your child to use the resources of a library. In addition, your child has learned to appreciate rhyme, rhythm, and some sound words used in poetry.

　　You may wish to help your child reinforce the skills studied in Unit 1. Here are some activities that may help your child.

- Ask your child to read aloud from a favorite fiction book. Using newspapers, magazines, and books, help your child locate examples of each of the four kinds of sentences.
- During a visit to the library, point out the librarian's desk and the card catalog. Help your child select books. Ask the librarian about special programs offered for your child's enjoyment and enrichment.
- Encourage your child to make greeting cards for special events in your family. Help your child to write a short greeting that rhymes or uses sound words.
- Select a poem that you and your child enjoy. Discuss the words that make the poem interesting and enjoyable.

If you have any questions, please feel free to contact me.

　　　　　　　　　　　　　　　　　　　Sincerely,

Dear _____ ,

Your child has just completed Unit 2 of *Language for Daily Use, Phoenix Edition*. In Unit 2 your child has identified singular and plural nouns as well as common and proper nouns.

Examples:
singular noun — *book*
plural noun — *books*
common noun — *city*
proper noun — *New York City*

The study skills of stating a main idea and finding supporting details were practiced. Both written and oral book reports were prepared. In addition, your child read a selection from a biography.

You may wish to help your child reinforce skills in the areas covered in Unit 2. Here are some activities that may help your child.

- Play a noun game with your child. Have your child identify common nouns from reading materials; then ask your child to name a proper noun for each common noun selected.
- Ask your child to read aloud from a social studies or science textbook. Have your child tell you what the selection is about in one sentence. This is the main idea of the selection. Then ask your child to tell the facts that add to or support the main idea.
- Listen to your child's account of a favorite book. Discuss the most exciting part and the main characters.
- Discuss the biography your child reads in class. Additional information on the person studied may be available in the library. Have your child write a biography of a family member. Provide details where necessary.

If you have any questions, please feel free to contact me.

Sincerely,

Dear _____,

Your child has completed Unit 3 of *Language for Daily Use, Phoenix Edition*. In Unit 3 your child has studied action verbs, linking verbs, and helping verbs.

Examples:

action verbs — *play, make, build*

linking verbs — *am, is, are, was, were*
(was raining, am singing)

helping verbs — *am, is, are, was, were, have, has, had, will (have walked, will sing)*

Your child's study skills have been expanded through practice in using a dictionary. Your child composed a friendly letter, a thank-you note, and an invitation. Your child also read a play.

You may wish to help your child reinforce some of the skills studied in this unit. The following activities may interest your child.

- Play a verb hunt game. Suggest that your child read aloud from a book, a magazine, or newspaper. Have your child be attentive to verbs during the reading. Then ask your child to identify a verb as an action verb, a linking verb, or a helping verb.
- Encourage your child to start a dictionary of new words. Each time an unknown word is heard or read, your child can record the word and its definition in a notebook. Have your child use these new words in sentences. Encourage their use in daily conversation.
- Encourage your child to write a friendly letter to a friend, a grandparent, or another relative.
- Ask your child to act out a scene from the play that was read in class. Discuss the kinds of costumes and scenery that would be appropriate for the play.

If you have any questions, please feel free to contact me.

Sincerely,

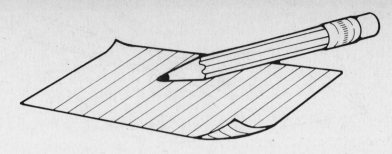

Dear _____ ,

    Your child has completed Unit 4 of *Language for Daily Use, Phoenix Edition*. In Unit 4 your child has learned to distinguish between the topic sentence of a paragraph and the sentences containing supporting details. In addition, your child has explored the variety of information to be found in the title page, the table of contents, the glossary, and the index of a book. The composition lessons stressed the writing of well-organized paragraphs that tell how to do something. In this unit your child also read an adventure story.

    The following activities may be helpful if you wish to assist your child in reinforcing the concepts and skills taught in Unit 4.

- Encourage your child to read aloud from a science or social studies textbook or other reading resources. Ask your child to identify the topic sentence in each paragraph. This is the sentence that tells what the paragraph is about.
- Let your child become familiar with the parts of a household reference book such as a cookbook. Ask your child to find favorite foods in your cookbook by using the table of contents and the index.
- Ask your child to write the directions from your home to the nearest fire alarm box or firehouse. Check the directions for accuracy.
- Listen to your child's retelling of the adventure story in this unit. The library has other adventure stories that your child may enjoy. Your child may wish to illustrate a favorite part of the adventure story. Encourage your child to share adventure stories that are a part of his or her daily experience.

If you have any questions, please feel free to contact me.

                         Sincerely,

Dear _____,

Your child has completed Unit 5 of *Language for Daily Use, Phoenix Edition*. In Unit 5 your child has identified adjectives and adverbs as describing words.

Examples: The mail carrier has a *huge* bag.
(adjective)
The bird sang *softly*.
(adverb)

Vocabulary-building skills were strengthened by studying words that mean the same thing as or the opposite of other words.

Examples: same as — *big, huge*
opposite — *big, small*

Your child wrote a descriptive paragraph containing both adjectives and adverbs. The reading experience in this unit included description in poems and in tall tales.

The following activities will offer you an opportunity to help your child reinforce the concepts and skills acquired in this unit.

- Listen as your child retells the tall tale in this unit. Ask your child to point out the adjectives and adverbs that show exaggeration. Encourage your child to read other tall tales that are available from the library.
- Encourage your child to create a tall tale using abundant exaggeration. Your child's tall tale can be used in a greeting card with an illustration added or it can be acted out with friends.
- Play a guessing game with your child. Take turns describing ordinary objects. Use adjectives and adverbs to describe how the object looks, sounds, feels, and moves. Guess each other's objects.

If you have any questions, please feel free to contact me.

Sincerely,

Dear _____,

    Your child has completed Unit 6 of *Language for Daily Use, Phoenix Edition*. In Unit 6 your child has identified pronouns as words used in place of nouns.

        Example: John bought three goldfish.

                He bought three goldfish.

The important study skills of taking notes and outlining have been practiced. In addition, your child studied the steps involved in preparing a research report. Your child read a factual magazine article.

    You may wish to help reinforce your child's skill in the areas studied in Unit 6. Here are suggestions for activities that may help your child.

- Play a *No Pronoun* game with your child. A player may keep talking on any subject until a pronoun is used. Then another player gets a turn. The player who talks the longest is the winner.

- Ask your child to divide a paper into four sections labeled vegetables, meat, dairy products, and fruits. Help your child record each type of food eaten in one day in the correct section. Point out that the finished list resembles an outline, explained in Unit 6. Your child may wish to plan a menu with you for a meal, using ideas from the four sections.

- During a visit to the library, look up material on a topic that interests your child. Help your child to make a list of books on the topic using the card catalog. Encourage your child to read one of the books listed.

- Have your child read a factual article from a magazine. Discuss the main ideas and details in the article.

    If you have any questions, please feel free to contact me.

                                 Sincerely,

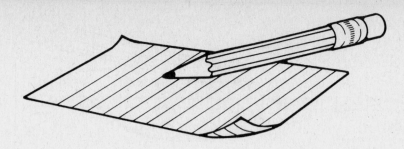

Dear _____,

    Your child has completed Unit 7 of *Language for Daily Use, Phoenix Edition*. In Unit 7 your child has identified the simple subject and simple predicate as the basic parts of a sentence. In addition, your child has learned to rearrange sentence parts to achieve variety in sentence structure. Vocabulary-building skills were strengthened by identification of root words with prefixes or suffixes, compound words, and words that sound the same but have different meanings. Your child's reading experience in this unit was with fables.

    If you wish to help your child reinforce concepts and skills acquired in Unit 7, the following activities may be helpful.

- Play a sentence jumble game with your child. Print a simple sentence. Then cut apart and mix up the words. Ask your child to arrange the words to form a meaningful sentence. Talk about different ways the words can be arranged to form sentences. Your child may wish to use sentences from newspapers and magazines for extra practice in this activity.
- Play a prefix game with your child. Select a common prefix such as *un* or *re*.

Examples: unfair   remake

Together, name as many words as possible that can be formed with these prefixes. Have your child make a list of the suggestions given.

- Play a suffix game with your child. Select a common suffix such as *ful* or *less*.

Examples: helpful   careless

Together, name as many words as possible that can be formed with these suffixes.

- During your next library visit, help your child locate a collection of Aesop's fables. Read and discuss some of the stories.

If you have any questions, please feel free to contact me.

                          Sincerely,

Dear _____,

   Your child has completed Unit 8 of *Language for Daily Use, Phoenix Edition*. In Unit 8 the skills needed to listen and speak well have been emphasized. The correct use of the telephone has been demonstrated, and the skill of following directions has been practiced. In addition, your child has observed the variety of information found in a telephone directory and in an atlas. A short story was read for enrichment and enjoyment.

   Here are some activities that you may use to help your child reinforce the concepts and skills acquired throughout the school year.

- With your child's help select a specific place where telephone messages can be recorded. Ask your child to help keep paper and pencils available for these messages.
- Help your child make a list of emergency phone numbers. If you have a list of emergency numbers, review them with your child.
- Help your child compile a phone directory with the names, addresses, and phone numbers of friends and relatives. If your child has a phone directory, help him or her update addresses and phone numbers.
- Encourage your child to share his or her pleasurable summer reading experiences with you by visiting the library often and discussing interesting stories.
- If you take a vacation away from your town or city, obtain maps of some of the places you plan to visit. Talk about the maps with your child. Help your child locate places of interest.
- Ask the librarian to point out the library section where collected short stories are located. Encourage your child to read a book of short stories.

Have a wonderful summer!

                                        Sincerely,

Estimado(a) (os) _____

    Su niño(a) ha terminado la Unidad 1 de lenguaje de *Language for Daily Use, Phoenix Edition.* En la Unidad 1 su niño(a) ha estudiado que una oración puede dar información (declarativa), puede hacer una pregunta (interrogativa), puede dar una orden (imperativa) puede hacer una pregunta exclamación (exclamativa).

    Ejemplos: declarativa—El conejo es de color café.

                interrogativa—¿Dónde está la bicicleta?

                imperativa—Cierra la puerta.

                exclamativa—¡Qué día tan bonito es hoy!

La organización de la biblioteca y el sistema del registro de tarjetas se han estudiado para preparar a su niño(a) para usar la biblioteca apropiadamente. Además su niño(a) ha aprendido a apreciar el ritmo, la rima y el tono de palabras en la poesía.

    Quizás usted desee repasar las destrezas que su niño(a) ha adquerido en esta unidad. Sugerimos las siguientes actividades que se pueden ejercer en español:

- Pídale a su niño(a) que lea en voz alta de su libro favorito de ficción. A través de periódicos, revistas y libros ayúdele a localizar ejemplos de los cuatro tipos de oraciones.
- Durante una visita a la biblioteca, indique dónde está el escritorio de su bibliotecario(a) y el registro de tarjetas. Ayúdele a seleccionar libros. Pregúntele a su bibliotecario(a) sobre los programas especiales que se ofrecen para la diversión y el enriquecimiento académico de su niño(a).
- Anime a su niño(a) que diseñe tarjetas para la familia de acontecimientos especiales. Ayúdele a escribir un breve mensaje que haga rima.
- Seleccionen un poema que sea del agrado suyo y de su niño(a). Discutan las palabras claves que hacen el poema interesante y agradable.

Si tiene preguntas, favor de comunicarse conmigo.

                        Atentamente,

Estimado(a) (os) ——————————————————————

   Su niño(a) ha terminado la Unidad 2 de lenguaje de *Language for Daily
Use, Phoenix Edition*. En la Unidad 2 su niño(a) ha identificado los
sustantivos singulares y plurales al igual que los nombres comunes y propios.
   Ejemplos: Sustantivo singular — libro
            Sustantivo plural — libros
            Nombre común — ciudad
            Nombre propio — Nueva York
   Se repasaron las destrezas necesarias para identificar los detalles
importantes y el tema central de un párrafo. También se leyó y se escribió
un resumen sobre un libro. Además, su niño(a) leyó parte de una biografía.
   Quizás usted desee repasar las destrezas que su niño(a) ha adquerido en
esta unidad. Sugerimos las siguientes actividades que se pueden ejercer en
español:

- A través de un juego, usted puede enseñarle el uso de los nombres.
  Seleccionen un libro de lectura. Pídale a su niño(a) que identifique los
  nombres comunes en el libro. Entonces pídale que para cada nombre
  común, que le dé un nombre propio.
- Pídale a su niño(a) que le lea en voz alta un párrafo de un libro de
  historia o de ciencias. Ahora pídale que le diga de qué trata el
  párrafo. La respuesta tiene que ser una sola oración, es el tema
  central del párrafo. Ahora, pídale que le dé los detalles que apoyan el
  tema central.
- Pídale a su niño(a) que le dé un resumen sobre su libro favorito.
  Discutan la parte más emocionante y los personajes principales.
- Discutan la biografía que su niño(a) leyó en la clase de lectura. Se
  puede encontrar más información sobre esta persona en la biblioteca.
  Pídale a su niño(a) que escriba una biografía de un miembro de la
  familia. Ayúdele con los detalles necesarios.

   Si tiene preguntas, favor de comunicarse conmigo.

                                        Atentamente,

Estimado(a) (os) _____

Su niño(a) ha terminado la Unidad 3 de lenguaje de *Language for Daily Use, Phoenix Edition.* En la Unidad 3 su niño(a) ha estudiado los verbos que demuestran acción, los verbos que conectan, y los verbos auxiliares.

Ejemplos: Verbos de acción—jugar, correr, hacer

Verbos que conectan—El *es* José.

Ella *es* alta.

(El verbo que conecta une el sustantivo únicamente con el predicado nominal y el predicado adjetival.)

Verbos auxiliares—*He* jugado béisbol.

Había jugado.

El artista *es* reconocido por todo el mundo.

(El Verbo auxiliar se emplea para conjugar ciertos tiempos.)

Su niño(a) ha ejercido el uso del diccionario. También escribió una carta informal, una carta de agradecimiento y una invitación. Su niño(a) también leyó un drama.

Quizás usted desee repasar las destrezas que su niño(a) ha adquerido en esta unidad. Sugerimos las siguientes actividades que se pueden ejercer en español.

- Anime a su niño(a) que componga un diccionario de palabras nuevas. Cada vez que oiga o lea una palabra que no reconozca, puede agregarla y escribir su significado. Pídale a su niño(a) que emplee estas palabras en oraciones y en sus conversaciones.
- Pídale a su niño(a) que dramatice una escena de la obra que leyó en la clase de lectura. Discutan el escenario y el vestuario teatral que sería apropiados para la obra.

Si tiene preguntas, favor de comunicarse conmigo.

Atentamente,

Estimado(a) (os) _____

    Su niño(a) ha terminado la Unidad 4 de lenguaje de *Language for Daily Use, Phoenix Edition.* En la Unidad 4 su niño(a) aprendió a distinguir entre la oración principal que lleva el tema central y las oraciones que contienen los detalles que apollan el tema. Además, ha investigado la variedad de información que se puede obtener en la portada, los índices y el glosario de un libro. Las lecciones de composición le enseñaron cómo organizar sus ideas en un párrafo con instrucciones sobre cómo hacer algo. En esta unidad su niño(a) también leyó un cuento de aventuras.

    Quizás usted desee repasar las destrezas que su hijo(a) ha adquerido en esta unidad. Sugerimos las siguientes actividades que se pueden ejercer en español:

- Anime a su niño(a) que lea en voz alta sus libros de ciencias, de historia, o de otros libros de información. Pídale que identifique la oración que comunica el tema central de cada párrafo. Ésta es la oración que indica de qué trata el párrafo.
- Ayúdele a su niño(a) a que se familiarice con libros de referenciá casera, como un libro de cocina. Pídale que encuentre su plato favorito en un libro de cocina buscándolo en las índices.
- Pídale a su niño(a) que escriba las instrucciones para ir desde la casa hasta la primera alarma de incendio o la estación de bomberos más cercana. Repase las instrucciones para asegurarse que son precisas.
- Escuche a su niño(a) mientras le relata el cuento de aventuras en esta unidad. En la biblioteca pueden encontrar otros cuentos de aventuras que quizás le gusten. También puede hacer un dibujo o una ilustración de su parte favorita del cuento. Anime a su niño(a) que comparta con usted las experiencias aventurosas que le sucedieron durante el día.

Si tiene preguntas, favor de comunicarse conmigo.

                              Atentamente,

Estimado(a) (os) _____

Su niño(a) ha terminado la Unidad 5 de lenguaje de *Language for Daily Use, Phoenix Edition.* En la Unidad 5 su niño(a) ha identificado los adjetivos y los adverbios como palabras que describen o modifican otras palabras en una oración.

Ejemplos: El cartero lleva un portacartas *grande.* (adjetivo)
El pájaro canta *suavemente.* (adverbio)

Para desarrollar el vocabulario se estudiaron los sinónimos y los antónimos.

Ejemplos: Sinónimos—grande, enorme (palabras semejantes)
Antónimos—grande, pequeño (palabras opuestas)

Su niño(a) también escribió un párrafo descriptivo con adjetivos y adverbios. La lectura en esta unidad incluyó las descripciones en poesías y en cuentos exagerados.

Quizás usted desee repasar las destrezas que su niño(a) ha adquerido en esta unidad. Sugerimos las siguientes actividades que se pueden ejercer en español:

- Permita a su niño(a) que le relate el cuento que se leyó en esta unidad. Pídale que le indique todos los adjetivos y adverbios que demuestran mucha exageración. Anime a su niño(a) que lea otros cuentos exagerados que encuentren en la biblioteca.
- Anime a su niño(a) que componga un cuento muy exagerado. Su niño(a) lo puede escribir en una tarjeta y hacer un dibujo. También puede dramatizarlo con sus amigos.
- A través de un juego de adivinanzas su niño(a) puede dominar el uso de los adjetivos y los adverbios. Describa un objeto común usando adjetivos y adverbios. Su niño(a) tiene que adivinar el nombre del objeto. En seguida, permita que su niño(a) describa algún objeto y usted lo adivina.

Si tiene preguntas, favor de comunicarse conmigo.

Atentamente,

Estimado(a) (os) _____

    Su niño(a) ha terminado la Unidad 6 de lenguaje de *Language for Daily Use, Phoenix Edition.* En la Unidad 6, su niño(a) ha identificado los pronombres como palabras que se usan en lugar de nombres.
    Ejemplo: Juan compró tres manzanas.
                El compró tres manzanas. (pronombre)
Su niño(a) aprendió a tomar apuntes y a componer un esquema. Además, su niño(a) estudió las etapas necesarias en la preparación de una investigación escrita. Su niño(a) leyó un artículo verídico de una revista.
    Quizás usted desee repasar las destrezas que su niño(a) ha adquerido en esta unidad. Sugerimos las siguientes actividades que se pueden ejercer en español:

- Participen en un juego donde no se puede usar ningún pronombre. El jugador puede hablar sobre un tema usando únicamente nombres. Al usar un pronombre pierde la oportunidad de seguir hablando. El siguiente jugador hace lo mismo. El jugador que dure más tiempo hablando es el que gana.
- Pídale a su niño(a) que divida una hoja de papel en cuatro secciones. Cada sección lleva uno de los siguientes títulos: (1) verduras (2) carnes (3) productos de leche (4) fruta. Ayúdele a recordar lo que ha comido en un día y escribir cada cosa en la sección correcta. Recuérdele que esta lista es semejante al esquema que se explicó en la Unidad 6. Su niño(a) le puede ayudar a decidir el menú para su siguiente comida a través de lo que ha escrito en las cuatro secciones.
- Cuando visiten la biblioteca, localicen materias sobre temas que sean interesantes para su niño(a). Ayúdele a componer una lista de libros sobre el tema usando el registro de tarjetas. Anime a su niño(a) que lea un libro de la lista.
- Haga que su niño(a) lea un artículo verídico de una revista. Discutan el tema y los detalles del artículo.

Si tiene preguntas, favor de comunicarse conmigo.

                          Atentamente,

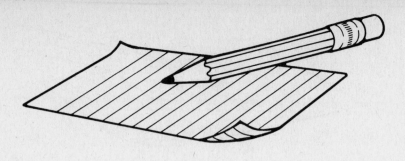

Estimado(a) (os) _____

    Su niño(a) ha terminado la Unidad 7 de lenguaje de *Language for Daily Use, Phoenix Edition.* En la Unidad 7 su niño(a) ha identificado el sustantivo sencillo y el predicado sencillo que son las partes principales de una oración. Además, su niño(a) ha aprendido a arreglar las diferentes partes de una oración en diferentes posiciones para tener variedad. El vocabulario de su niño(a) se ha enriquecido y fortalizado a través de la identificación de palabras raíces, con sus prefijos o sufijos, y palabras compuestas. También identificó palabras con sonidos semejantes pero que tienen significados diferentes (homónimos). En la lectura, su niño(a) ha leído unas fábulas.

    Quizás usted desee repasar las destrezas que su niño(a) ha adquerido en esta unidad. Sugerimos las siguientes actividades que se pueden ejercer en español:

- Escriba una oración sencilla. Recorte las palabras de la oración y mézclelas. Pídale a su niño(a) que componga una oración gramaticalmente correcta con estas mismas palabras. Discutan la variación de arreglos para formar una oración. Pueden seguir este juego utilizando oraciones de un periódico o de una revista.
- Usted puede enseñarle el uso del prefijo a través de un juego. Seleccione un prefijo común como *in* o *des*. Juntos traten de nombrar todos las palabras que se puedan formar con estos prefijos.
      Ejemplos: *In*correcto, *des*aparecer
                   *in*completo, *des*componer
- Juntos pueden hacer lo mismo con los sufijos. Seleccione un sufijo común como *able* o *mente*. Juntos traten de nombrar todas las palabras que se puedan formar con estos sufijos.
      Ejemplos: Agrad*able*   cariñosa*mente*
                  salud*able*   cuidadosa*mente*
- Durante la siguiente visita a la biblioteca, ayúdele a su niño(a) a encontrar *Las fábulas de Aesop* o un libro de fábulas en español. Lean y discutan la fábulas.

Si tiene preguntas, favor de comunicarse conmigo.

                                     Atentamente,

Estimado(a) (os) _____

   Su niño(a) ha terminado la Unidad 8 de lenguaje de *Language for Daily Use, Phoenix Edition*. En la Unidad 8 se le ha dado énfasis a las destrezas necesarias para escuchar y hablar con facilidad. Se ha demostrado la manera correcta para usar el teléfono. También ejerció su habilidad de seguir instrucciones. Además, su niño(a) descubrió la variedad de información que se puede encontrar en un directorio telefónico y un atlas. Se leyó un cuento para la diversion y el ènriquecimiento académico.

   Quizás usted desee repasar las destrezas que su niño(a) ha adquerido durante el año escolar. Sugerimos las siguientes actividades que se pueden ejercer en español:

- Con la ayuda de su niño(a), seleccione un lugar en particular donde se puedan escribir todos los mensajes de teléfono.
- Ayúdele a su niño(a) a hacer una lista de números de teléfonos necesarios en caso de emergencia.
- Ayúdele a su niño(a) a componer una guía de teléfono con los nombres, direcciones de residencia y números de teléfonos de todos sus amigos y parientes. Si su niño(a) ya tiene una guía personal de teléfonos, ayúdele a ponerla al día.
- Anime a su niño(a) que comparta con usted todas sus experiencias agradables de la lectura. Esto se puede llevar a cabo con visitas a la biblioteca y discutir los cuentos más interesantes.
- Si salen de vacaciones fuera de la ciudad, obtenga mapas de los lugares que visitarán. Hable sobre el mapa con su niño(a). Ayúdele a localizar los sitios de interés.
- Pídale a su bibliotecario(a) que le ayude en localizar la sección de cuentos cortos. Anime a su niño(a) que lea un libro de cuentos cortos.

Si tiene preguntas, favor de comunicarse conmigo.

Atentamente,

INDIVIDUAL RECORD FORM

Language for Daily Use / Phoenix Edition ■ Level Orange (4)

Student _____

School _____

Teacher _____

Grade _____

		Number Possible	Criterion	PRETEST Score / Date	PRETEST Diagnostic Category*	POSTTEST Score / Date	POSTTEST Diagnostic Category*	Comments
UNIT 1	Learning About Sentences, Using the Library, Writing Sentences, Reading Poetry	35	28					
UNIT 2	Learning About Nouns, Summarizing, Writing Book Reports, Reading a Biography	35	28					
UNIT 3	Learning About Verbs, Using the Dictionary, Writing Letters, Reading a Play	35	28					
UNIT 4	Learning About Paragraphs, Using Books, Writing Directions, Reading a Story	35	28					
Midyear	Evaluates mastery of skills and concepts in Units 1–4.	60	48					
UNIT 5	Learning About Adjectives and Adverbs, Building Vocabulary, Writing Paragraphs, Reading Poetry and Tall Tales	35	28					
UNIT 6	Learning About Pronouns, Organizing Information, Writing a Report, Reading a Factual Article	35	28					
UNIT 7	Building Sentences, Building Vocabulary, Writing Varied Sentences, Reading a Story	35	28					
UNIT 8	Listening and Speaking, Finding Information, Writing a Story, Reading a Story	35	28					
End-of-Year	Evaluates mastery of skills and concepts in Units 1–8.	100	80					

*Diagnostic Categories

M = Student has scored at or above the criterion level and should be able to move forward without additional practice in this skill.

R = Student has scored below the criterion level and probably needs more practice or instruction in this skill before moving forward.

CLASS RECORD FORM
Language for Daily Use / Phoenix Edition ■ Level Orange (4)

NAMES	UNIT 1		UNIT 2		UNIT 3		UNIT 4	
	Pretest	Posttest	Pretest	Posttest	Pretest	Posttest	Pretest	Posttest
Number Possible/Criterion	35/28	35/28	35/28	35/28	35/28	35/28	35/28	35/28

School _____

Grade _____

Teacher _____

Date Tested

| Midyear Test | UNIT 5 | | UNIT 6 | | UNIT 7 | | UNIT 8 | | | | | | End-of-Year Test |
	Pretest	Posttest	Pretest	Posttest	Pretest	Posttest	Pretest	Posttest					
60/48	35/28	35/28	35/28	35/28	35/28	35/28	35/28	35/28					100/80

Name _____

Class _____ Date _____

(Circle one) **Pretest** **Posttest**

(Circle one) Unit 1 2 3 4 5 6 7 8 9 10 11

1. Ⓐ Ⓑ Ⓒ Ⓓ   6. Ⓐ Ⓑ Ⓒ Ⓓ   11. Ⓐ Ⓑ Ⓒ Ⓓ   16. Ⓐ Ⓑ Ⓒ Ⓓ
2. Ⓐ Ⓑ Ⓒ Ⓓ   7. Ⓐ Ⓑ Ⓒ Ⓓ   12. Ⓐ Ⓑ Ⓒ Ⓓ   17. Ⓐ Ⓑ Ⓒ Ⓓ
3. Ⓐ Ⓑ Ⓒ Ⓓ   8. Ⓐ Ⓑ Ⓒ Ⓓ   13. Ⓐ Ⓑ Ⓒ Ⓓ   18. Ⓐ Ⓑ Ⓒ Ⓓ
4. Ⓐ Ⓑ Ⓒ Ⓓ   9. Ⓐ Ⓑ Ⓒ Ⓓ   14. Ⓐ Ⓑ Ⓒ Ⓓ   19. Ⓐ Ⓑ Ⓒ Ⓓ
5. Ⓐ Ⓑ Ⓒ Ⓓ   10. Ⓐ Ⓑ Ⓒ Ⓓ   15. Ⓐ Ⓑ Ⓒ Ⓓ   20. Ⓐ Ⓑ Ⓒ Ⓓ

21. Ⓐ Ⓑ Ⓒ Ⓓ   26. Ⓐ Ⓑ Ⓒ Ⓓ   31. Ⓐ Ⓑ Ⓒ Ⓓ
22. Ⓐ Ⓑ Ⓒ Ⓓ   27. Ⓐ Ⓑ Ⓒ Ⓓ   32. Ⓐ Ⓑ Ⓒ Ⓓ
23. Ⓐ Ⓑ Ⓒ Ⓓ   28. Ⓐ Ⓑ Ⓒ Ⓓ   33. Ⓐ Ⓑ Ⓒ Ⓓ
24. Ⓐ Ⓑ Ⓒ Ⓓ   29. Ⓐ Ⓑ Ⓒ Ⓓ   34. Ⓐ Ⓑ Ⓒ Ⓓ
25. Ⓐ Ⓑ Ⓒ Ⓓ   30. Ⓐ Ⓑ Ⓒ Ⓓ   35. Ⓐ Ⓑ Ⓒ Ⓓ

Midyear Test

1. Ⓐ Ⓑ Ⓒ Ⓓ   6. Ⓐ Ⓑ Ⓒ Ⓓ   11. Ⓐ Ⓑ Ⓒ Ⓓ   16. Ⓐ Ⓑ Ⓒ Ⓓ
2. Ⓐ Ⓑ Ⓒ Ⓓ   7. Ⓐ Ⓑ Ⓒ Ⓓ   12. Ⓐ Ⓑ Ⓒ Ⓓ   17. Ⓐ Ⓑ Ⓒ Ⓓ
3. Ⓐ Ⓑ Ⓒ Ⓓ   8. Ⓐ Ⓑ Ⓒ Ⓓ   13. Ⓐ Ⓑ Ⓒ Ⓓ   18. Ⓐ Ⓑ Ⓒ Ⓓ
4. Ⓐ Ⓑ Ⓒ Ⓓ   9. Ⓐ Ⓑ Ⓒ Ⓓ   14. Ⓐ Ⓑ Ⓒ Ⓓ   19. Ⓐ Ⓑ Ⓒ Ⓓ
5. Ⓐ Ⓑ Ⓒ Ⓓ   10. Ⓐ Ⓑ Ⓒ Ⓓ   15. Ⓐ Ⓑ Ⓒ Ⓓ   20. Ⓐ Ⓑ Ⓒ Ⓓ

21. Ⓐ Ⓑ Ⓒ Ⓓ   26. Ⓐ Ⓑ Ⓒ Ⓓ   31. Ⓐ Ⓑ Ⓒ Ⓓ   36. Ⓐ Ⓑ Ⓒ Ⓓ
22. Ⓐ Ⓑ Ⓒ Ⓓ   27. Ⓐ Ⓑ Ⓒ Ⓓ   32. Ⓐ Ⓑ Ⓒ Ⓓ   37. Ⓐ Ⓑ Ⓒ Ⓓ
23. Ⓐ Ⓑ Ⓒ Ⓓ   28. Ⓐ Ⓑ Ⓒ Ⓓ   33. Ⓐ Ⓑ Ⓒ Ⓓ   38. Ⓐ Ⓑ Ⓒ Ⓓ
24. Ⓐ Ⓑ Ⓒ Ⓓ   29. Ⓐ Ⓑ Ⓒ Ⓓ   34. Ⓐ Ⓑ Ⓒ Ⓓ   39. Ⓐ Ⓑ Ⓒ Ⓓ
25. Ⓐ Ⓑ Ⓒ Ⓓ   30. Ⓐ Ⓑ Ⓒ Ⓓ   35. Ⓐ Ⓑ Ⓒ Ⓓ   40. Ⓐ Ⓑ Ⓒ Ⓓ

41. Ⓐ Ⓑ Ⓒ Ⓓ   46. Ⓐ Ⓑ Ⓒ Ⓓ   51. Ⓐ Ⓑ Ⓒ Ⓓ   56. Ⓐ Ⓑ Ⓒ Ⓓ
42. Ⓐ Ⓑ Ⓒ Ⓓ   47. Ⓐ Ⓑ Ⓒ Ⓓ   52. Ⓐ Ⓑ Ⓒ Ⓓ   57. Ⓐ Ⓑ Ⓒ Ⓓ
43. Ⓐ Ⓑ Ⓒ Ⓓ   48. Ⓐ Ⓑ Ⓒ Ⓓ   53. Ⓐ Ⓑ Ⓒ Ⓓ   58. Ⓐ Ⓑ Ⓒ Ⓓ
44. Ⓐ Ⓑ Ⓒ Ⓓ   49. Ⓐ Ⓑ Ⓒ Ⓓ   54. Ⓐ Ⓑ Ⓒ Ⓓ   59. Ⓐ Ⓑ Ⓒ Ⓓ
45. Ⓐ Ⓑ Ⓒ Ⓓ   50. Ⓐ Ⓑ Ⓒ Ⓓ   55. Ⓐ Ⓑ Ⓒ Ⓓ   60. Ⓐ Ⓑ Ⓒ Ⓓ

Name _____

Class _____ Date _____

End-of-Year Test

1. Ⓐ Ⓑ Ⓒ Ⓓ	6. Ⓐ Ⓑ Ⓒ Ⓓ	11. Ⓐ Ⓑ Ⓒ Ⓓ	16. Ⓐ Ⓑ Ⓒ Ⓓ
2. Ⓐ Ⓑ Ⓒ Ⓓ	7. Ⓐ Ⓑ Ⓒ Ⓓ	12. Ⓐ Ⓑ Ⓒ Ⓓ	17. Ⓐ Ⓑ Ⓒ Ⓓ
3. Ⓐ Ⓑ Ⓒ Ⓓ	8. Ⓐ Ⓑ Ⓒ Ⓓ	13. Ⓐ Ⓑ Ⓒ Ⓓ	18. Ⓐ Ⓑ Ⓒ Ⓓ
4. Ⓐ Ⓑ Ⓒ Ⓓ	9. Ⓐ Ⓑ Ⓒ Ⓓ	14. Ⓐ Ⓑ Ⓒ Ⓓ	19. Ⓐ Ⓑ Ⓒ Ⓓ
5. Ⓐ Ⓑ Ⓒ Ⓓ	10. Ⓐ Ⓑ Ⓒ Ⓓ	15. Ⓐ Ⓑ Ⓒ Ⓓ	20. Ⓐ Ⓑ Ⓒ Ⓓ
21. Ⓐ Ⓑ Ⓒ Ⓓ	26. Ⓐ Ⓑ Ⓒ Ⓓ	31. Ⓐ Ⓑ Ⓒ Ⓓ	36. Ⓐ Ⓑ Ⓒ Ⓓ
22. Ⓐ Ⓑ Ⓒ Ⓓ	27. Ⓐ Ⓑ Ⓒ Ⓓ	32. Ⓐ Ⓑ Ⓒ Ⓓ	37. Ⓐ Ⓑ Ⓒ Ⓓ
23. Ⓐ Ⓑ Ⓒ Ⓓ	28. Ⓐ Ⓑ Ⓒ Ⓓ	33. Ⓐ Ⓑ Ⓒ Ⓓ	38. Ⓐ Ⓑ Ⓒ Ⓓ
24. Ⓐ Ⓑ Ⓒ Ⓓ	29. Ⓐ Ⓑ Ⓒ Ⓓ	34. Ⓐ Ⓑ Ⓒ Ⓓ	39. Ⓐ Ⓑ Ⓒ Ⓓ
25. Ⓐ Ⓑ Ⓒ Ⓓ	30. Ⓐ Ⓑ Ⓒ Ⓓ	35. Ⓐ Ⓑ Ⓒ Ⓓ	40. Ⓐ Ⓑ Ⓒ Ⓓ
41. Ⓐ Ⓑ Ⓒ Ⓓ	46. Ⓐ Ⓑ Ⓒ Ⓓ	51. Ⓐ Ⓑ Ⓒ Ⓓ	56. Ⓐ Ⓑ Ⓒ Ⓓ
42. Ⓐ Ⓑ Ⓒ Ⓓ	47. Ⓐ Ⓑ Ⓒ Ⓓ	52. Ⓐ Ⓑ Ⓒ Ⓓ	57. Ⓐ Ⓑ Ⓒ Ⓓ
43. Ⓐ Ⓑ Ⓒ Ⓓ	48. Ⓐ Ⓑ Ⓒ Ⓓ	53. Ⓐ Ⓑ Ⓒ Ⓓ	58. Ⓐ Ⓑ Ⓒ Ⓓ
44. Ⓐ Ⓑ Ⓒ Ⓓ	49. Ⓐ Ⓑ Ⓒ Ⓓ	54. Ⓐ Ⓑ Ⓒ Ⓓ	59. Ⓐ Ⓑ Ⓒ Ⓓ
45. Ⓐ Ⓑ Ⓒ Ⓓ	50. Ⓐ Ⓑ Ⓒ Ⓓ	55. Ⓐ Ⓑ Ⓒ Ⓓ	60. Ⓐ Ⓑ Ⓒ Ⓓ
61. Ⓐ Ⓑ Ⓒ Ⓓ	66. Ⓐ Ⓑ Ⓒ Ⓓ	71. Ⓐ Ⓑ Ⓒ Ⓓ	76. Ⓐ Ⓑ Ⓒ Ⓓ
62. Ⓐ Ⓑ Ⓒ Ⓓ	67. Ⓐ Ⓑ Ⓒ Ⓓ	72. Ⓐ Ⓑ Ⓒ Ⓓ	77. Ⓐ Ⓑ Ⓒ Ⓓ
63. Ⓐ Ⓑ Ⓒ Ⓓ	68. Ⓐ Ⓑ Ⓒ Ⓓ	73. Ⓐ Ⓑ Ⓒ Ⓓ	78. Ⓐ Ⓑ Ⓒ Ⓓ
64. Ⓐ Ⓑ Ⓒ Ⓓ	69. Ⓐ Ⓑ Ⓒ Ⓓ	74. Ⓐ Ⓑ Ⓒ Ⓓ	79. Ⓐ Ⓑ Ⓒ Ⓓ
65. Ⓐ Ⓑ Ⓒ Ⓓ	70. Ⓐ Ⓑ Ⓒ Ⓓ	75. Ⓐ Ⓑ Ⓒ Ⓓ	80. Ⓐ Ⓑ Ⓒ Ⓓ
81. Ⓐ Ⓑ Ⓒ Ⓓ	86. Ⓐ Ⓑ Ⓒ Ⓓ	91. Ⓐ Ⓑ Ⓒ Ⓓ	96. Ⓐ Ⓑ Ⓒ Ⓓ
82. Ⓐ Ⓑ Ⓒ Ⓓ	87. Ⓐ Ⓑ Ⓒ Ⓓ	92. Ⓐ Ⓑ Ⓒ Ⓓ	97. Ⓐ Ⓑ Ⓒ Ⓓ
83. Ⓐ Ⓑ Ⓒ Ⓓ	88. Ⓐ Ⓑ Ⓒ Ⓓ	93. Ⓐ Ⓑ Ⓒ Ⓓ	98. Ⓐ Ⓑ Ⓒ Ⓓ
84. Ⓐ Ⓑ Ⓒ Ⓓ	89. Ⓐ Ⓑ Ⓒ Ⓓ	94. Ⓐ Ⓑ Ⓒ Ⓓ	99. Ⓐ Ⓑ Ⓒ Ⓓ
85. Ⓐ Ⓑ Ⓒ Ⓓ	90. Ⓐ Ⓑ Ⓒ Ⓓ	95. Ⓐ Ⓑ Ⓒ Ⓓ	100. Ⓐ Ⓑ Ⓒ Ⓓ